Healthcare Informatics

Improving Efficiency
and Productivity

Healthcare Informatics

Improving Efficiency and Productivity

Edited by Stephan P. Kudyba

CRC Press
Taylor & Francis Group
Boca Raton   London   New York

CRC Press is an imprint of the
Taylor & Francis Group, an **Informa** business
AN AUERBACH BOOK

CRC Press
Taylor & Francis Group
6000 Broken Sound Parkway NW, Suite 300
Boca Raton, FL 33487-2742

Library of Congress Cataloging-in-Publication Data

Healthcare informatics : improving efficiency and productivity / editor, Stephen Kudyba.
    p. ; cm.
   Includes bibliographical references and index.
   ISBN 978-1-4398-0978-5 (alk. paper)
   1. Medical informatics. 2. Organizational effectiveness. I. Kudyba, Stephan, 1963-
   [DNLM: 1. Medical Informatics. 2. Efficiency, Organizational. W 26.5 H43451 2010]

R858.H383 2010
610.285--dc22
                                                    2009048608

Visit the Taylor & Francis Web site at
http://www.taylorandfrancis.com

and the CRC Press Web site at
http://www.crcpress.com

Dedication

To my family for their unending support over the years,
especially to my wife, Cherryl, whose unyielding passion to care for patients
provided an essential inspiration to produce this work.

Contents

Foreword

James H. Goodnight, PhD, CEO of SAS

To anyone who works in the information technology industry, the contrast is quite stark: How is it possible that one of the largest economic forces and ethical priorities on the planet—healthcare—is not a leading example of using information technology? On the one hand, we have sequenced the human genome—an unparalleled achievement that would not have been possible without leading-edge technology. And yet, on the other hand, when you go to your doctor for a simple physical examination, chances are that your critical health information is recorded on paper and put on a shelf, inaccessible to you, your other care providers, or researchers trying to find better treatments.

So it may be with some trepidation that you pick up a book about health informatics. It seems almost impossible that an industry so mired in paper can use something as computer oriented as analytical software. Where can you even start?

The first step is recognizing a truth that exists in every modern organization. There is not a lack of information; rather, there is a lack of usability of already existing information. In 2008, the analyst firm IDC released a document called *The Diverse and Exploding Digital Universe*. The report, which focused on the ever-growing volumes of electronic information around the world, drew the following comparison:

> The number of digital 'atoms' (1s and 0s) in the digital universe is already bigger than the number of stars in the universe. And, because the digital universe is expanding by a factor of 10 every five years, in 15 years it will surpass Avogadro's number (6.022×10^{23}).

By any measure, those are large numbers. And despite the lack of progress in adopting electronic medical records, the data mountain in healthcare is large and growing. Every new drug brought to market in the United States is supported by years of research stored in databases. Every major health institution has repositories of patient data waiting to be analyzed. Every care provider and payer has financial and operational data sitting inside its enterprise. We are limited only in our creativity and commitment to find needed improvements.

Barriers to technology adoption—accessibility, usability, data standards, computer fluency, physical distance among stakeholders, data privacy, and others—have had a long-standing impact on healthcare. But over the past 10 years, many of these perceived and actual barriers have slowly collapsed. The "consumerization" of technology brought about through home computers, portable music players, digital photography, cell phones, and many other innovations has produced an industry of healthcare practitioners with a much greater technology comfort level, and much higher expectations of "the world of the possible." As computer processor and network bandwidth capacities have grown exponentially, the opportunity to bring powerful, user-friendly software to the practice of medicine has been unlocked. And concerns over patient safety and the escalating costs of care have produced clear demands from consumers and regulators: find smarter ways of working and produce better health outcomes for patients.

Unfortunately, even with a new generation of systems and devices collecting healthcare data, there is only a small correlation between data, information, and knowledge. Our efforts to use modern, web-based technologies to collect better information faster serve the need of adding to our data mountains, but do little to increase human knowledge of health and disease. The key to crossing that knowledge chasm is analytics. To build better treatments, we need to analyze the factors that affect treatment efficacy. To lower administrative costs, we need to identify where and why we are incurring unnecessary costs and how we should focus our improvements. To prevent medical errors, we need a deeper understanding of the causes and proven interventions. Healthcare not only has a plethora of problems that can be solved with analytics, but the most important questions we currently face in healthcare can only be addressed with analytics.

Other industries have already found ways to use the power of analytics to dramatically improve their businesses. For example, if you have ever received a phone call from your credit card company asking about charges to your credit card that you know you did not make, you have seen one of the many applications of advanced analytics. In a fraction of a second, credit card analytical systems are able to assess the probability of a given transaction being fraudulent and take corrective measures to prevent the payment from actually occurring in the first place. This approach saves millions in fraudulent claims as well as their subsequent recovery costs. Could we be doing the same with healthcare claims?

Another area where other industries are reaping the rewards of advanced analytics is customer intelligence. Retail organizations are using advanced analytics to better understand their customers—who they are, what they do, what they like, and how best to interact with them. Retailers want to know more than just the name, address, and phone number of the people they serve. They want to know how to be a better provider of goods and services to each individual consumer—creating compelling offers for things that are most likely to resonate with each individual consumer, delivered in a way that each specific consumer prefers, and avoiding inundating them with things that do not really matter to them as individuals. Campaign management, marketing optimization, and similar analytical solutions give these companies the ability to grow their relationships with their customers. Could we use a similar approach to proactively build better doctor-patient relationships?

There are still plenty of challenges in our health technology evolution. But there has never been a more important time to look to analytics. We owe it to ourselves and future generations to do all we can to make our healthcare systems work smarter, be more effective, and reach more people. The power to know is at our fingertips; we need only embrace it.

Preface

Healthcare informatics, increasing productivity and efficiency, addresses the critical issue regarding the ongoing debate over rising costs in the healthcare industry, namely: Can the incorporation of information technologies drive efficiencies to help reduce costs and enhance the quality of care for patients? The answer is a resounding yes. Technologies that facilitate the input, storage, access, analysis, and communication of data and information for practitioners, administrators, researchers, and regulators can help identify inefficiencies in procedures across the spectrum of healthcare services. The application of knowledge generated from the availability of information should ultimately result in enhanced resource allocations, reduce costs, and promote the pipeline for new innovations.

This book is comprised of two major sections that address these concepts. The first part of the work provides an introduction and background to the state of affairs in our current healthcare system and describes the theoretical underpinnings, such as information and knowledge management, project management, and strategic initiatives essential to achieving successful informatics-based implementations within healthcare organizations. Some example project implementations are included in the early chapters as well. The latter half of the book focuses on actual applications that have been incorporated by various healthcare organizations along with corresponding strategic management issues that were involved for successful project rollouts. These applications include e-commerce, the creation of digital data, business intelligence, and high-end analytics initiatives.

Section 1: An Introduction to Informatics, the State of Our Current Healthcare System, and Critical Strategic Initiatives to Consider in Achieving Effective Informatics-Based Projects

Chapter 1 provides an introduction to the complexities involved in managing resources in our current healthcare system and how management theory and informatics applications can increase efficiencies in the various functional areas in healthcare services. Chapter 2 extends the description of problematic areas in healthcare and provides extensive background on current initiatives that are under way in the promotion and investment in informatics in the industry. It then provides strategic concepts that are critical to achieving successful healthcare information technology (HIT) and electronic health record (EHR) applications.

Chapter 3 provides a robust description of project management issues that are essential in the implementation process of various informatics projects, and Chapter 4 adds a complementary focus of best practices in informatics implementations and includes a detailed description of a successful computer physician order entry (CPOE) system project at Mission Hospital in Asheville, North Carolina. Chapter 5 addresses the area of project management in informatics and stresses the importance of involving the skills of nursing staff to achieve successful technology rollouts. A brief case study describing this concept is included. The final chapter in this first section of the book stresses the importance of knowledge management and provides strategic insights in achieving knowledge transfer among healthcare service personnel in the dissemination of information made available from various informatics platforms such as EHRs and clinical decision support systems (CDSSs). Effective knowledge transfer should ultimately enhance the quality of care for patients.

Section 2: Information Management and Increased Healthcare Efficiency through E-commerce, Business Intelligence, and Advanced Analytic Applications

Chapter 7 begins this section describing an e-commerce self-service patient check-in application at New Jersey's Newark Beth Israel Hospital. The steps to achieving the successful implementation along with the productivity-improving results are included as well. Chapter 8 provides an introductory section addressing the realm of informatics analytics and the significant impact areas such as business intelligence and quantitative-based methods of data mining can have on improving efficiencies in a variety of healthcare applications.

Chapter 9 describes a successful informatics project that focuses on the creation of digital assets from paper-based resources at New Jersey's Saint Clare's Health System. It then includes an introduction to business intelligence, describing how this concept can drive efficiencies regarding regulatory issues, hospital workflow activities, and others. Chapter 10 describes three different successful informatics projects at Trinity Health. The first illustrates how informatics helped reduce excesses in length of stay (LOS); the second involves a web-based clinical indicator system that improved patient safety; and the third involves efficiency gains resulting from an ADE alert system. ADE systems refer to computerized adverse drug event initiatives.

Chapter 11 delves into the realm of advanced analytics and describes how various data mining methods can be used to drive efficiencies across a variety of healthcare applications. Chapter 12 extends the discussion on data mining and illustrates how these quantitative-based methods enhance decision support activities in the area of colorectal cancer. Finally, the book ends with Chapter 13, which provides insights on the utilization of data mining to identify problem areas in healthcare billing and financial activities. It also illustrates how advanced algorithms can help identify patient populations at risk for hepatitis.

About the Editor

Stephan Kudyba (MBA, PhD) is a faculty member in the management department at NJIT, where he teaches courses in the graduate and executive MBA curriculum addressing the utilization of information technologies, business intelligence, and information and knowledge management to enhance organizational efficiency. He has published numerous books, journal articles, and magazine articles on strategic utilization of data, information, and technologies to enhance organizational and macro productivity. Dr. Kudyba has been interviewed by prominent magazines and speaks at university symposiums, academic conferences, and corporate events. He has over twenty years of private sector experience in the United States and Europe, having held management and executive positions at prominent companies, and maintains consulting relations with organizations across industry sectors with his company Null Sigma, Inc. He holds an MBA from Lehigh University and a PhD in economics with a focus on the information economy from Rensselaer Polytechnic Institute.

Contributors

Billie Anderson
SAS Institute
Carey, North Carolina

Peter Basch
MedStar Health
Washington, D.C.

Mary Beattie
Health First
Rockledge, Florida

Jason Burke
SAS Institute
Carey, North Carolina

Paul Conlon
Trinity Health
Novi, Michigan

Cali M. Davis
University of Alabama
Tuscaloosa, Alabama

Jeffrey W. Erdley
Health Research Insights, Inc.
Franklin, Tennessee

Johnny E. Gore
Health Research Insights, Inc.
Franklin, Tennessee

Tomas Gregorio
Newark Beth Israel Medical Center
Newark, New Jersey

J. Michael Hardin
University of Alabama
Tuscaloosa, Alabama

D. Arlo Jennings
Mission Health System
Asheville, North Carolina

James F. Keel III
Mission Health System
Asheville, North Carolina

Rajiv Kohli
William and Mary College
Williamsburg, Virginia

Stephan P. Kudyba
New Jersey Institute of Technology
Newark, New Jersey

Jeremy D. Lowery
Health Research Insights, Inc.
Franklin, Tennessee

Ann McKibbon
McMaster University
Hamilton, Ontario, Canada

Thomas Miner
Trinity Health
Novi, Michigan

Terry Moore
Hackensack University Medical Center
Hackensack, New Jersey

Theodore L. Perry
Health Research Insights, Inc.
Franklin, Tennessee

Frank Piontek
Trinity Health
South Bend, Indiana

Marc Rader
AristaCare Health Services
South Plainfield, New Jersey

Wullianallur Raghupathi
Fordham University
New York, New York

Christi Rushnell
Health First
Rockledge, Florida

Larry Sellers
Mercy Medical Center
Sioux City, Iowa

Richard Temple
AristaCare Health Services
South Plainfield, New Jersey

Michael H. Zaroukian
Michigan State University/Sparrow
   Health System
Lansing, Michigan

Chapter 1

An Introduction to the U.S. Healthcare Industry, Information Technology, and Informatics

Stephan Kudyba and Richard Temple

Contents

Healthcare is probably one of the most complex business models in American industry given the uniqueness of the marketplace in which it operates. It is perhaps the only industry where the consumer does not necessarily pay for the service he or she receives, but rather third parties (in this case, insurance companies) negotiate arrangements with service providers to determine payment rates and types of service that are to be paid on the consumer's behalf. The nature of the services required corresponds to a variety of ailments that are attributed to vast numbers of patients—factors that add to the mix of issues to manage. Complexities for healthcare organizations are heightened when considering the numerous data exchanges that are involved with services provided to patients. Data exchanges can be plagued by myriad formats, captured, and stored in a variety of repositories. These exchanges introduce further complexities in the form of "vocabularies," or in other words, the coding languages that are required to identify types of services that vary considerably from payer to payer, state to state, and service type to service type. Also, data in general come from a multitude of different "niche" systems and are presented in many different ways (e.g., text reports, spreadsheets, ANSI X12 formats, etc.) and need to be integrated and presented to a caregiver or analyst in a consistent and coherent manner. It is the combination of all these factors that begins to describe the underpinnings of the spectrum of healthcare informatics.

Data provide the building blocks to information, a vital resource to administrators, practitioners, and decision makers in healthcare organizations. The process of transforming data into information is a daunting task, and given the complexities described above, the task is particularly challenging in this unique industry. This challenge must be managed, as healthcare is one segment of American industry where incorrect decisions or errors can cost lives or put innocent people in significant danger. The need to understand what patterns of treatment for a variety of different conditions will produce the best outcomes is profound. Adding to the challenge are the financial burdens healthcare providers are experiencing, as reimbursements are being cut and more and more conditions are being mandated in order to pay for services rendered. Healthcare organizations invariably lose money on certain classes of patients, and it is critical to understand where those areas are and how to address them.

Information Technology, Informatics, and Healthcare Productivity

One way to better manage the complex nature of this industry is through the incorporation of information technologies. Web platforms, data storage, analytic software, telecom and wireless communications systems, etc., can help provide critical information and speed information dissemination to those who require it, when they require it.

Table 1.1   Growth in Investment in Information Technologies

Year	Investment in Information Technology as a Proportion of Industrial Equipment and Software (%)
1980	30.7
1990	41.1
1999	47.2

Source: Economic Report of the President 2001, Table B-18, p. 296.

During the mid-1990s organizations across industry sectors retooled their information technology infrastructures in response to dramatic innovations in storage, processing, analytics, and bandwidth (see Table 1.1). The enhanced capabilities facilitated by these technologies offered organizations opportunities to increase productivity in a variety of ways. Factors such as the dissemination of critical information to decision makers regarding process performance; the ability to communicate within organizations, across industry sectors, and on the global spectrum; and simplifying procedures, to name a few, enabled organizations to better manage available resources in providing a good or service to the ultimate consumer.

The significant investment in information technologies was initially questioned by many as to the payoff or gains from these dollar outlays for hardware, software, telecom platforms, etc. This debate sparked myriad research from the academic and private sector arenas to investigate the potential gains to IT. Resulting studies illustrated positive returns to investment in information technologies by firms operating across industry sectors.[1-3] On a macro economic perspective, U.S. productivity grew dramatically from levels achieved over the previous decade (see Figure 1.1).

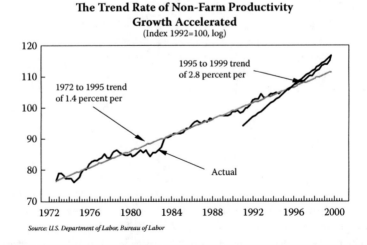

The Trend Rate of Non-Farm Productivity Growth Accelerated
(Index 1992=100, log)

Source: U.S. Department of Labor, Bureau of Labor

Figure 1.1

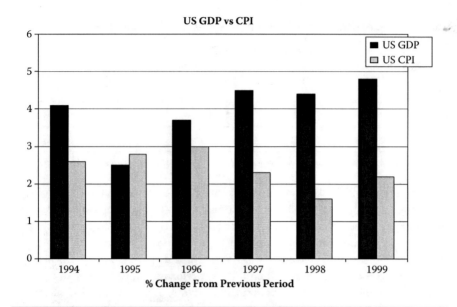

Figure 1.2   U.S. GDP data: U.S. Commerce Department Bureau of Economic Analysis; U.S. Consumer Price Index: U.S. Department of Labor, Bureau of Labor Statistics.

This jump in productivity enabled the U.S. economy to grow at a robust pace without experiencing a noteworthy acceleration to price inflation as gains in efficiency helped reduce costs throughout the economic system (see Figure 1.2). These productivity gains have been maintained into current times as companies continue to invest in and apply information technologies in a variety of process-enhancing ways.

One industry, however, lagged behind the strong pulse in leveraging information technology, and this involved healthcare organizations. The fragmented nature of the industry is often cited as a reason for the lag in technological implementations along with the adherence to traditional paper-based procedural modes of operations. The structure of the industry involving numerous individual hospitals, and health-related entities created a dichotomous environment that involved diverse naming procedures and formatting standards of and breakdowns in the ability to share critical data resources. Paper-based methods of operations (e.g., charting by physicians and nurses) limited the creation of vital data resources that describe critical treatment activities of patients.

These factors reduced gains in efficiency that otherwise could be achieved based on network effects of information sharing. In other words, the lack of data resources and the existence of disparate data resources involving diverse naming conventions existing in a variety of storage devices corresponding to separate providers of health services (e.g., hospitals, clinics, private practices) deter the ability of healthcare organizations to create robust information resources from available data. With only pieces of the puzzle (e.g., data existing in isolated systems, information in paper-based form) healthcare providers are limited in the amount of information available to them when attempting to enhance their knowledge regarding service effectiveness and efficiency.

To further clarify this point, we need to turn to the evolution of the Internet. Forms of the Internet were actually in existence well before the information boom of the 1990s (e.g., the government ARPANET was in existence in the 1970s). However, the true gains in efficiency resulting from utilization of the Internet for consumers and businesses alike were not achieved until network effects took hold. This refers to the fact that the network of users who had access to the Internet needed to reach critical mass.[4] As more and more consumers and businesses had access to the Internet, it became a viable mechanism to communicate and conduct commerce. In comparison, as data resources in the healthcare industry become more standardized and integrated within health organizations and across systems of corresponding service providers, the ability to extract information from and generate knowledge regarding better allocating resources to enhance process efficiencies in financial, clinical, and administrative activities should increase dramatically. The result should be less wasted resources, enhanced process performance, and a lower-cost operating environment.[5]

Given recent consolidation of individual providers into systems of providers (e.g., healthcare systems); advancements in hardware, software, telecom, and Internet-based technologies; the ability of treatment and diagnosis-based technologies to help enhance data capture; the creation of digital data resources from paper-based procedures; and enhanced data input and communication of information, healthcare providers are on the cusp of experiencing increased operational efficiencies that will enable them to manage their cost structure while providing the best care possible to patients. The incorporation of billing and financial-related technologies, decision support systems, data management, and analytic capabilities enables healthcare providers to enhance their ability to identify misallocations of resources and increase the effectiveness and speed of processes in administrative, financial, and clinical activities.

Enhanced efficiencies made possible by investment in information technologies could result in significant cost savings to healthcare providers. These gains are critical in addressing the ongoing growth in healthcare expenditures in the United States, which now account for roughly 17% of GDP. If productivity gains from investment in information technologies experienced in other industries are achieved in the healthcare sector, savings in the form of reduced expenditures could exceed $300 billion.[6] Investment in technologies that seek to promote a more automated delivery system through worklflow and medical records systems, evidenced-based decision support systems, integration of information between healthcare providers, and streamlining the current claims-based transactions billing system to an all-electronic payment at point of service system can yield substantial savings to healthcare providers and ultimately the consumer/patient.[7]

Productivity, Efficiency, and the Uniqueness of Healthcare

Despite the fact that the healthcare industry possesses unique characteristics from those of other sectors (e.g., doctor-patient relationships and the ultimate objective of providing the best quality of care to patients that can override established business profit optimization goals), healthcare still entails procedures and processes that can be made more efficient.

Technologies can help providers discover more effective treatment tactics that may reduce ineffective, redundant, and unnecessary tests and procedures that inconvenience the patient and the provider and increase costs. They can reduce bottlenecks in administrative processes that can alleviate waiting times for patients and direct them to the most appropriate areas to address their problems. They can alleviate complexities in billing activities that can result in overbilling recipients. Technologies can help enhance preemptive treatment to mitigate illnesses from developing into fully developed chronic diseases.

Some critics of applying management and business concepts in the healthcare sector argue that treating patients should not be considered a business. They argue that these initiatives could adversely affect patient treatment and care as the quest for achieving enhanced operational performance may dictate procedures. The answer to this critique lies in monitoring the overall activities of health providers, and this process includes enhancing the patient experience. The bottom line to all these capabilities is helping allocate the correct resources to the demand for those resources. Accomplishing this helps preserve the essence of healthcare organizations and those individuals involved in providing treatment for patients. With the aid of accurate and timely information, and the ability to communicate and apply that information, physicians, nurses, technicians, and administrators can improve the process of caring for those in need in a more efficient, less costly manner. Techniques and methodologies that create, disseminate, and analyze data comprise the realm of informatics. Two basic definitions of informatics are provided to clarify what is meant by this concept.

> **Informatics:** The sciences concerned with gathering, manipulating, storing, retrieving, and classifying recorded information.
>
> **Source: wordnetweb.princeton.edu/perl/webwn**

Health informatics or medical informatics is the intersection of information science, computer science, and health care. It deals with the resources, devices, and methods required to optimize the acquisition, storage, retrieval, and use of information in health and biomedicine. Health informatics tools include not only computers but also clinical guidelines, formal medical terminologies, and information and communication systems.

Source: Wikipedia

Effective Informatics through Management Theory

Pure investment in information technologies is not the final solution to enabling providers to operate more productively. Applications in management theory are essential to ensure effective implementation and utilization of these technologies to best leverage their capabilities to increase labor and process productivity. Management theory that must be considered includes strategic management, management information systems, project management, knowledge management and organizational behavioral, quantitative techniques, and decision support theory, to name a few. These management concepts focus on the acquisition of technologies that provide the correct functionality to facilitate a particular process and proper implementation of the technology to ensure its proper utilization (this includes creating a receptive culture within the organization by users to adopt the platform as an essential tool to enhance their daily routines). Theoretical concepts also address analyzing, communicating, and best utilization of the results and outputs of systems that are used.

Project and Knowledge Management

Project management addresses methods that support successful implementations of information technologies. It addresses the incorporation of correct tactics to acquire the most appropriate technology platform to facilitate an organizational need in the most seamless way possible. For example, when a healthcare provider wants to implement a new database system that facilitates the conversion of paper-based routines into digital assets for clinical and treatment activities, the organization must consider which technology best offers the most feasible functionality corresponding to the operational structure of the organization. This includes the cost of the technology, scalability, ability to integrate with existing systems, and user friendliness. Once the technology is chosen, factors to promote the most seamless integration into the work environment must be considered. This includes timing schedules, training for users, and eventual complete rollout to the workforce. Knowledge management (KM) theory overlaps project management to some extent when considering the implementation stages of new technologies. It addresses the additional critical factors of ensuring the system's adoption by users with the ultimate goal that it becomes a key component to the everyday activities of its users and stakeholders. Knowledge management also addresses those factors that support leveraging the output produced by users working with systems and the dissemination and collaboration of corresponding information among individuals connected to processes and procedures. In other works, KM theory promotes the active utilization of information and creation of knowledge within an organization, concepts that drive best practices, and innovation.[8,9]

Other management-related concepts also must be considered in attempting to best leverage information technologies, and these involve such strategic initiatives as Six Sigma, Total Quality Management, supply chain management, and workflow optimization, and advanced analytics such as data mining. The process of treating a patient incorporates a network of activities that are complementary and interdependent in nature, where breakdowns in aspects of one operational entity can cause disruptions to the overall process of patient care. The patient treatment process can include diagnosis, prescription of medications, radiology and lab tests, administration of treatment procedures, monitoring of results and outcomes, etc. These activities include input from numerous personnel in corresponding operational departments in the healthcare organization. Workflow analytic methodologies must be considered to better understand the efficiencies of the entire treatment process. The overall process can be compared to managing a supply chain or supply network of activities that are complementary and interdependent with the ultimate objective of achieving the best allocation of available resources to provide the best care to corresponding patients. These management methodologies can be augmented with the incorporation of statistical and quantitative-based analytics such as the Six Sigma approach.

Six Sigma and Data Mining

Six Sigma is an analytic method that leverages available data resources and incorporates statistical applications and visual capabilities to monitor process variance and efficiencies. By analyzing data resources corresponding to various operational processes with the utilization of statistical techniques, analysts can better determine which types of practices result in unacceptable variances in performance metrics.[10] For example, are there bottlenecks in the network of activities in the radiology department that produce high time delay variances in getting x-ray results back to an attending physician? More robust and sophisticated techniques to analyze data involve the utilization of quantitative methods to process data and statistical testing to determine patterns and trends that may exist in particular service activities. Traditional regression methods and data mining methodologies enable analysts to better identify reoccurring trends in the various activities of healthcare services. Resulting models can determine whether particular treatment procedures result in enhanced health outcomes according to patient populations, whether particular procedural activities result in unacceptable outcome measures, etc.

Business Intelligence and Decision Support Systems

Other methods of data analysis that can help increase the knowledge of healthcare practitioners involves the more simple creation and presentation of reports and graphics through online analytic processing and dashboards. The advantage of these methods is that they focus on presenting data in a timely and understandable manner, where decision makers can quickly view these analytic platforms to identify factors impacting operational performances.

These various data-driven software technologies and initiatives comprise the realm of decision support systems and business intelligence. The functionalities of the components, including report generation, trend and pattern detection, quantitative and statistical-based analytics, complemented with graphical interfaces provide users/decision makers in various functional areas of healthcare organizations with timely, actionable information to enhance strategizing. Informatics to improve efficiencies includes optimizing resource allocations corresponding to a variety of activities and procedures. The utilization of decision support systems and business intelligence that leverage essential data resources can ultimately help reduce lag times in patients waiting for treatment, adjust treatment procedures to enhance outcomes, reduce inefficiencies in billing, reduce lag times in lab and radiology exam completion and reporting times, etc. The ultimate result is better management of healthcare operations and costs and care effectiveness and outcomes for patients.

Four Areas of Focus for Healthcare Efficiencies

With all of the turbulence existing in the healthcare landscape, it is little wonder that healthcare organizations are embracing the potential of leveraging information technologies and informatics and their ability to enhance efficiencies. Informatics applications and capabilities within the healthcare spectrum can be categorized into four discrete areas:

- Financial: Tracking activity-based costing, ensuring that services rendered are properly billed and compensated and that expenses stay within acceptable budgetary parameters.
- Clinical compliance: Ensuring that the appropriate procedures are applied to the right patient at the right time, making sure that staffing patterns and other reportable parameters are within acceptable mandated bounds, and alerting as quickly as possible when they are not.

■ Quality improvement: Analyzing clinical data to see which treatment protocols provide the best outcomes in an economically sustainable way.
■ Patient satisfaction/marketing: What aspects of a patient's stay were problematic—How are those measured, identified, and remedied for the future?

The following sections will take a quick look at each of these areas to give a broader sense of just how informatics can be so important in managing the critical factors that healthcare leadership needs to better understand in order to properly manage their respective organizations.

Financial Activities

Hospitals and many other healthcare providers have undergone a drastic transformation during the last fifteen to twenty years. This transformation is characterized by the change in environment, as is evidenced by organizations who saw their role almost as benevolent charities whose mission it was to provide care to all without particular regard to reimbursement (the guiding assumption was "if you bill it, they will pay"), to rough-and-tumble competitive businesses who needed to track all aspects of financial performance to satisfy their boards, shareholders, and other organizational stakeholders. Over this period of time, large public companies or large organizations have invested significant sums and acquired many healthcare organizations with the expectation of receiving an aggressive return on their investments. Also, during this time, regulations on healthcare payers were loosened, which helped spark the managed care (HMO) and "capitated payment" (fixed monthly payment to providers not directly tied to specific visits) movements. As more players entered the healthcare space with specific bottom-line interests, reimbursement schemas became increasingly more complex; more entities needed to be measured (e.g., are we getting more in monthly capitated payments than we are paying out in actual patient encounters?). With all this going on, one can only imagine how critical it became to understand in great detail what one's reimbursement and cost foundation was, where timeliness and accuracy of information describing these activities were critical to determine potential trends over time. Modeling capabilities needed to be generated to analyze corresponding data, and alert mechanisms needed to be incorporated to highlight what key indicators breached certain predetermined levels.

Computerized financial systems have been in existence in healthcare for decades. Their ability to generate data and report-driven balance sheets, profit-and-loss statements, and other relevant accounting reports points to an acute need for informatics. For instance, many hospitals, especially not-for-profit systems, finance growth and other capital initiatives through the use of fixed income securities (e.g., bonds), many of which may be guaranteed by a governmental or quasi-governmental authority. There are conditions attached to many of these securities that if certain key financial indicators breach agreed-upon values, sanctions may be invoked that may include deeming these bonds as in "technical default." This can have far-reaching implications for organizations in terms of ongoing financial viability, future access to credit, and changes in administrative personnel or on board membership in impacted organizations. It is critical for an organization to be able to, at the very least, access vital information that would indicate whether variances in financial metrics exceeded preestablished thresholds of acceptance and, also, to know *in advance* that trends among various other key indicators may be leading the organization to this precipice.

There are also financial metrics that are unique to healthcare that speak to how efficiently the organization is being run and, indirectly, what the quality of care is likely to be based on important factors such as staffing patterns. Some of the metrics that are typically tracked include "FTEs (full-time equivalent employees) per occupied bed" (e.g., is the organization staffing its units commensurate with the patient volume on those units?), "net revenue" versus "net cash collected" (is the organization getting properly reimbursed for what it thinks it is rightfully owed for the services it renders?), and productive hours and agency hours (e.g., is the organization having to rely on expensive and less predictable agency nursing to fulfill its regulated staffing requirements), to name a few.

With the advent of managed care and capitated contracts with payers, a whole new realm of tracking becomes critical. These types of contracts have become increasingly more complicated over the years, and it can be a challenge for an organization to have an accurate sense of the correct monetary allocation for particular types of services. Issues such as what services may not be reimbursable, what services may qualify as "outliers," and under what circumstances "extraordinary" services would entitle the organization to reimbursement over and above the agreed upon base rate from the payer may need to be considered. Contract management systems surfaced during the 1990s to address this new paradigm and have, over the years, become a much more important part of a healthcare organization's informatics tool kit. Combining information from contract management systems, such as gauging receipts for particular services by particular payers with financial decision support systems, becomes strategic for healthcare providers. Tracking both revenue as a whole and costs per different types of services (e.g., activity-based costing) and disseminating profitability information of different aspects of managed care contracts to decision makers provide the strategic information to implementing more effective initiatives.

Compliance Issues

The next area in which informatics could yield significant efficiencies involves the realm of clinical compliance. There are important regulations that can impact an institution's accreditation status if procedures are not strictly adhered to.

Organizations such as the Joint Commission or the Department of Health have very stringent and detailed regulations as to the exact protocols that need to be followed under different care circumstances. Also, governmental entities are reporting on websites accessible to the public the different levels of compliance of organizations to protocol standards. This can translate into lost revenue, lost market share, or diminished stature for those who underperform their competitors by registering subpar results of relevant indicators. For instance, at a relatively basic level, any patient who enters a facility exhibiting signs of respiratory problems is supposed to be given smoking cessation counseling. Another example is that any patient presenting at a hospital with signs of a cardiac event is to be given an aspirin right away. These are basic care guidelines that are universally recognized as being important in ensuring that a patient has a desired health outcome. The challenge, however, arises when considering how an entity can capture this type of data and disseminate reports that indicate whether rules are complied with or not. With this information, organizations can take strategic initiatives to mitigate any undesirable performance variances.

There are also important factors to consider regarding time and allocation of resources to minimize the risk of complications to certain classes of patients. For instance, certain patients can be identified as having an elevated risk of skin integrity issues (pressure ulcers, etc.) based on a test that yields what is referred to as a Braden score. Patients with a Braden score in excess of a certain threshold must have their caregivers turn them in their beds once every two hours in order to avoid negative health outcomes resulting from staying in one position for too long. Best-of-class healthcare providers are going to want to know: (1) Did they properly identify all patients who were at risk for pressure ulcers, and (2) did they administer the correct procedure to those patients once identified as an at-risk population candidate?

Another commonly tracked factor in a patient population is individuals that are classified in the "falls risk" category. In other words, based on one or two different scales used by providers, patients can be identified as having a greater risk of falling, which means more risk of complications, longer (unreimbursed) lengths of stay, broken limbs, and ultimately perhaps, increased legal liability exposure for the organization. Informatics, at an operational level, identifies falls risk patients and facilitates analysis of other aspects of electronic medical records (EMRs) to ensure that proper protocols are in place to mitigate the negative ramifications of falls risk.

Individuals often think of informatics as management reporting—something that is reported after the fact and is based on a particular retrospective point of view. While this aspect of informatics is necessary, its real incremental power is to provide timely information to individuals who can proactively implement initiatives to mitigate negative outcomes. For example, a charge nurse on a given unit can have access to data quickly showing that three hours (instead of two) have elapsed since a patient with skin integrity issues was turned. He or she can then address the situation right away, before complications set in. This most certainly saves lives, improves outcomes, and enhances financial controls.

Regulatory mandates govern areas such as medication reconciliation and pain assessments as well, where, once again, informatics enables organizations to better identify breakdowns in processes and procedures that cause subpar performance results, so appropriate steps can be taken to adjust resource allocations such as staffing to mitigate negative outcomes. When addressing the issue of optimizing staffing resources within the organization, there exist a number of complicated factors to consider. The notion of "acuity tracking," or matching the severity of the conditions in a particular hospital unit with staffing allocations, should be considered. Also, since staffing schedules tend to be projected a number of weeks into the future, census trends need to be analyzed. Factors such as day of week or time of year (e.g., winter months involving snow and ice could result in increased injuries and demand for healthcare services) must be considered. Proper staffing in light of these various factors can contribute to improved and more comprehensive care, which in turn will contribute to better outcomes, fewer complications, fewer medical errors, etc. However, as noted, because staffing decisions are made based on best estimates of what may happen in the future, it becomes all the more important to have the best data available to ideally model what these needs will be. Informatics can synthesize data from myriad different systems, such as EMRs, financial systems, and even external web-based systems that can provide information on factors outside the hospital walls, such as temperature or perhaps the severity of the flu season in the area, and can enhance the understanding of potential demand for staffing resources.

Quality Improvement in Clinical and Operational Activities

Another area that is rapidly maturing in the healthcare provider arena involves the growing utilization of devices that can interface directly with an EMR system and, ultimately, an informatics system. Ventilators, "smart" pumps, IVs, vital sign tracking monitors, and other devices like these can "talk" to EMRs and populate data directly into an EMR. Some EMRs, facilitated by information technologies, offer a capability to page a clinician or otherwise provide a real-time alert if a certain clinical value is outside accepted medical bounds. These technologies also add to existing data elements to enhance the overall data resources for more advanced analytics.

Statistically based analytics such as correlations can help providers identify the best possible order sets to use for a given condition (in conjunction with evidence-based medicine protocols). Informatics incorporating statistical correlations and causation can identify that individuals who receive a certain type of specialized therapy have much shorter lengths of stay and lower rates of readmission than those who do not. Analytics can also allow for comparing different clinical regimens to factors such as "patient satisfaction survey" scores. It can identify whether certain high-priced medications or medical devices may provide a less desirable outcome than lower-priced medications, and can identify which doctors have a predisposition to order those medications or devices. Looking at physician comparisons, informatics will enable hospitals and other organizations to compare physician ordering patterns with desired outcomes such as reduced length of stay, lower readmissions, fewer complications or comorbidities, and revenue generation metrics. This provides a key level of accountability for all involved in the interdisciplinary plan of care of a patient to ensure that the right people are doing the right things at the right time.

Many factors affiliated with clinical compliance apply to our third area of focus: quality improvement programs. At the end of the day, all healthcare providers certainly strive to provide the highest quality of care possible at all times. However, attempting to define what constitutes quality can be elusive. Recently, regulatory agencies and payers have offered their own parameters as to what constitutes quality care. So-called "pay for performance" programs and "never event" prohibitions have helped crystallize much of what providers need to measure in order to demonstrate to appropriate agencies or payers that they are adopting the correct procedures for their patients. Pay-for-performance programs specify that there will be either incentives or penalties based on a provider's demonstrated compliance with a certain set of quality protocols. If the provider complies effectively, incentive payments are provided. If not, differing levels of reduction of payment come into play. Never events are significant medical errors that can cause grave patient harm, and Medicare and other payers have made it a policy that they will not reimburse providers for costs incurred from provider events that should *never* happen—hence the name never events. Not only does pay-for-performance and never event tracking impact the long-term financial viability of healthcare organizations, but these types of statistics now are among those that typically are compiled by governmental agencies, benchmarked, and posted on websites, where consumers (potential customers) can view them and compare them with those of a provider's competition.

Other indicators that are being tracked and reported via the web include hospital-acquired infection rates, readmissions, and average waits to see a doctor in an emergency department. It becomes imperative that healthcare organizations develop the wherewithal to track these types of metrics accurately, and in ways that allow for interceding proactively to address procedural issues to manage negative outcomes in the pipeline. Benchmarking, or comparing an organization against its peers and against what is considered to be acceptable performance, is becoming increasingly common and increasingly visible to larger sections of the public. For a provider, knowing where its performance *should* be early in the game allows for more aggressive programs to be designed and deployed to ensure that the organization is applying the most optimal procedures.

The concept of quality improvement can also be articulated in a somewhat different but extremely important way as well. While, as noted above, there are a multitude of clinical metrics that often can and should be shared both internally and externally, quality improvement can also be construed as using data to improve business processes in general and enforce accountability for appropriate and acceptable performance. Informatics can be used, for instance, to compare the length of time it takes physicians in an emergency room to see a patient. This can be a significant motivating factor to enhance performance by comparing individuals to their peers. In general, informatics enables healthcare providers to aggregate and analyze data in constructive and actionable ways, the results of which are continuous improvement in various procedures throughout the organization.

Customer Relationship Management in Healthcare

Our final aspect of healthcare operations that can benefit immensely from informatics is the realm of patient satisfaction. As noted earlier, healthcare institutions increasingly have to view themselves as businesses, and part of maintaining a viable business is producing positive experiences for your customers. In the healthcare industry customers can take on a number of forms, ranging from patients to patients' families to doctors. Providing an exceptional experience for customers remains a significant goal for healthcare organizations, as it promotes repeat visits from individuals in need of services. Happy customers also provide good word-of-mouth recommendations of their experiences that helps rein in new customers, which maintains positive demand and, hopefully, increased revenue. Much of this is intuitive, certainly, but what is not so intuitive is how a healthcare institution gauges satisfaction rates of its customers.

Measuring patient satisfaction in a healthcare setting can take on two separate forms. One form, and perhaps the most common, involves the process of having an unbiased, objective third-party organization send out a survey to patients soon after they have left the facility. This third-party organization (Press-Ganey and Healthstream are two such noteworthy players) sends out a survey with a standard set of questions to recently discharged patients from all of its facilities. Some percentage of the patients respond, and the responses are tabulated and trended over time and broken out by parameters that the organizations generally make available. An added bonus of working through these third-party organizations is that participating healthcare institutions get an extra benefit of being able to benchmark how their responses fare against those of a wide array of similar peer organizations. These kind of data can point to areas where an organization needs to fine-tune certain operational processes that are resulting in patient dissatisfaction. These surveys offer the patient the opportunity to add comments to his or her response, where proactive healthcare organizations can build systems to automatically route these comments to the appropriate decision makers in the organization and track the timeliness of issue resolution. Medicare regulations spell out a formal procedure for what are called grievances, which have mandates attached to them about how facilities need to address them. Clearly tracking these to ensure the responses to these grievances stay within the bounds of the regulations is most important for the organization in order for it to avoid falling out of Medicare compliance parameters, which may lead to financial or other, perhaps more severe, sanctions.

The second type of patient satisfaction issues can be gleaned from surveys that are administered directly to the patient while he or she remains in the facility. These surveys allow for an organization to receive more timely feedback of issues as they are occurring and take steps to address them and, if necessary, initiate a formal "service recovery" procedure for particular types of unfortunate customer service situations. The general process for how this type of survey works involves interviewing patients (assuming they are fit to be interviewed) at certain time intervals and asking them questions regarding issues, such as their perception of the food they received, the demeanor of nurses, etc. Responses can be entered into a database and tracked and trended over time through the utilization of informatics methods, which can also drilldown to identify if particular areas are problematic. Furthermore, certain types of responses and comments can be routed automatically to key individuals, and processes can be built to track the timeliness and completeness of responses to these issues. The main advantage about this type of survey is the rapid response capability it offers. The organization can find out right away if something is wrong and can react and correspond directly with the individual to ensure that the remedy to the problem was effective. This can transform a dissatisfied customer to a satisfied one.

More and more, informatics can and does provide value in a multitude of different care settings and in a number of different operational processes. Organizations invariably will derive significant benefits from having a mechanism to generate an accurate read of data on all fronts and being able to turn that data into actionable information. This information enhances the knowledge of service providers who can implement appropriate strategic initiatives to enhance efficiencies throughout the organization.

Closing Comments on the Issue of Data Privacy

A critical element that needs to be maintained, preserved, and perhaps strengthened refers to the privacy safeguards of healthcare-related data of individuals. The integration of data resources from various healthcare providers and databases no doubt enhances efficiencies from analytics capabilities and information generation. As the process of developing more robust data resources enhances efficiencies, it also introduces the requirement for well-defined and strictly enforced standards to protect the privacy rights of individuals regarding health-related data. New privacy policies (mentioned below) need to be designed to address any changes that transpire within the realm of data access and exchanges in the evolving healthcare system. The U.S. Department of Health and Human Services issued a privacy rule to implement the requirement for the Health Insurance Portability and Accountability Act of 1996 (HIPAA), which addresses the use and disclosure of individuals' health information. A major goal of the privacy rule is to ensure that individuals' health information is properly protected while allowing the flow of health information needed to provide and promote high-quality healthcare and to protect the public's health and well-being. The rule strikes a balance that permits important uses of information while protecting the privacy of people who seek care and healing.[11] New initiatives are currently addressing privacy requirements in this evolving data-intensive environment. The American Recovery and Reinvestment Act of 2009 (ARRA) incorporates improvements to existing law, covered entities, business associates, and other entities that will soon be subject to more rigorous standards when it comes to protected health information.[12] As data resources become more comprehensive, so too should policies that safeguard individual privacy rights.

References

1. Lehr, W., and Lichtenberg, F. 1998. Computer use and productivity growth in US federal government agencies, 1987–1992. *Journal of Industrial Economics* 46(2):257–279.
2. Brynjolfsson, E., and Hitt, L. 2000. Beyond computation: Information technology, organizational transformation, and business performance. *Journal of Economic Perspectives* 14(4).
3. Kudyba, S., and Diwan, R. 2002. Increasing returns to information technology. *Information Systems Research*, March 104–111.
4. Shaprio, C., and Varian, H. 1998. *Information rules: A strategic guide to the network economy.* Boston: Harvard Business Press.
5. Kudyba, S., and Diwan, R. 2002. *Information technology, corporate productivity and the new economy.* Westport, CT: Greenwood Publishing.
6. Hillestad, R., Bigelow, J., Bower, A., Girosi, F., Meili, R., Scoville, R., and Taylor, R. 2005. Can electronic medical record systems transform health care? Potential health benefits, savings, and costs. *Health Affairs* (Millwood) 24 (5) September–October: 1103–1117.
7. Patterson, N. 2009. *The ABCs of systemic healthcare reform: A plan for driving $500 billion in annual savings out of the US healthcare system.* Healthcare Industry Brief. Cerner Corporation. www.cerner.com/ABCs.
8. Davenport, T., and Prusak, L. 2000. *Working knowledge.* Boston: Harvard Business Press.
9. Davenport, T., Harris, J., DeLong, D., and Jacobson, A. 2001. Data to knowledge to results: Building an analytic capability. *California Management Review* 43:117–38.

10. Pande, P., Neuman, R., and Cavanagh, R. 2000. *The Six Sigma way: How GE, Motorola, and other top companies are honing their performance.* New York: McGraw-Hill.
11. U.S. Department of Health and Human Services. Summary of the HIPAA privacy rule. http://www.hhs.gov/ocr/privacy/hipaa/understanding/summary/privacysummary.pdf.
12. American Recovery and Reinvestment Act of 2009. http://frwebgate.access.gpo.gov/cgi-bin/getdoc.cgi?dbname=111_cong_bills&docid=f:h1enr.pdf.

Chapter 2

Quality Time in Healthcare
Strategies for Achieving National Goals for Meaningful Use of Health Information Technology

Michael H. Zaroukian and Peter Basch

Contents

To foster healthcare quality and satisfaction, the time health professionals and patients spend interacting with each other should be quality time—important, informative, productive, meaningful, and interpersonally connected. High-quality care is supported when providers, patients, and family members can interact in a mutually convenient and productive manner, with the right information available at the right time and in the right format to effectively and efficiently support the best possible care decisions and actions. Unfortunately, continued overreliance on paper-based care processes and clinical information flow contributes to the enormous waste and waiting that characterizes much of the current U.S. healthcare delivery system, taking time, energy, and resources away from activities that can improve the value of healthcare. However, clinical information systems that are poorly designed, inadequately implemented, not meaningfully used, or not optimized to transform care also represent barriers to clinical quality and workforce productivity goals. In this chapter, two practicing physicians and clinical informatics leaders share their experiences with leading organizational change, healthcare process redesign, electronic health record implementation, and information management improvement strategies to provide a perspective and recommendations for achieving national goals for meaningful use of health information technology to capture and share data, advance clinical care processes, and improve health outcomes.

Introduction: The State of Our Current Healthcare System

When it comes to delivering healthcare in the United States today, the fable *Our Iceberg Is Melting*[1] is a fitting metaphor for the disastrous health and economic consequences our country and people will ultimately face if leaders fail to act quickly enough to transform care in a manner that dramatically improves quality and value. In the iceberg fable, noted change leadership expert John Kotter and colleagues illustrate the plight of a colony of penguins coming to the sudden, if not unanimous, realization that their iceberg—the basic foundation of their lives on which they all depend—was at great risk of collapse. Despite the implacable nay-saying of a vocal penguin in the leadership group who argued that change was both unnecessary and dangerous, the influential majority of penguin leaders soon recognized that the survival, health, and happiness of the colony they serve and protect required quickly achieving a shared sense that the status quo was unacceptable and that effective action was urgently needed. The leaders also realized they must come together as a guiding coalition, create a shared vision of a better future, communicate it widely and repeatedly, remove barriers to effective action, gain visible and meaningful short-term successes, reinforce and build on each success, and anchor the improvements in the culture. Finally, the authors provide a framework strategy for survival and success that builds on Kotter's previous work[2] and is relevant to transforming quality in healthcare organizations of any size, from solo physician practices to large healthcare delivery networks.

Along the way, the iceberg fable provides abundant examples of the challenges we in healthcare face in seeing system problems clearly, changing longstanding habits, overcoming barriers to organizational culture change, engaging stakeholders, and consistently aligning their behaviors toward a shared vision of improved quality and value. Indeed, while this chapter focuses on how health information technology (HIT) can be used as a powerful tool to support quality at the point of care, such efforts will fall far short of their full potential unless they are paired with a reformed payment policy that rewards thoughtful health information management and quality outcomes.[3]

In his compelling novel *Why Hospitals Should Fly*,[4] John Nance takes many of the important lessons described in John Kotter's work to the next level, as well as adding several of his own from the aviation industry to show just how important cultural change is to our ability to make the transformational changes needed to improve healthcare quality and safety. This compelling book is necessarily a fiction because it describes a hospital (St. Michael's Memorial) that does not yet exist, one that has gotten everything working right and everyone working together with an intense focus on patient safety, service quality, interpersonal collegiality, barrier-free communication, and support for front-line caregivers. However, St. Michael's seems both real and possible because it represents a combination of best practices and effective leadership that can be found in other industries as well as in real-world healthcare settings today. St. Michael's chose to harvest the lessons learned and best practices developed in aviation and leading healthcare institutions and put them to work to dramatically improve safety, collegiality, communication, workforce vitality, process standardization, information technology support, and other elements of organizational care transformation. St. Michael's and the professionals who work there provide a clear and detailed view of how an ideal healthcare environment would look and feel to those giving and receiving care. Like the novel's protagonist, Dr. Will Jenkins, readers of *Why Hospitals Should Fly*[4] may initially be discouraged at the gap between what is possible and what exists in our healthcare delivery system today. However, they can also find comfort and inspiration in the many examples of strategies St. Michael's leaders used to transform the organization and overcome barriers to needed change.

For those less than convinced of the urgent need to transform the U.S. healthcare delivery system, a few statistics and a review of recent events may be instructive. For example, World Health Organization statistics from 2007 showed U.S. per capita healthcare costs to be the highest in the world and more than 50% higher than the next highest nation.[5] U.S. healthcare expenses consumed 16% of the nation's gross domestic product in 2007, with total health spending projected to grow from $2 trillion in 2005 to $4 trillion in 2015. While these much higher expenditures might be justifiable if the vast majority of dollars yielded consistently high value care, such appears to be far from the case. Indeed, it has been estimated that up to 30 to 50% of healthcare spending in the United States is "pure waste."[6,7] A 2008 PricewaterhouseCoopers report[8] examined the issue of healthcare spending waste in detail, estimating that slightly more than half of the $2.2 trillion spent on healthcare in the United States was wasteful. Major contributors included practicing defensive medicine (redundant, inappropriate, or unnecessary tests and procedures), excessive healthcare administrative costs, and the cost of conditions that are considered preventable through lifestyle changes (obesity, tobacco consumption). The authors of the report correctly recommended addressing these three major cost drivers by facilitating healthier individual behaviors, attacking the clinical problems of overuse, underuse, and misuse of tests and treatments, and eliminating those administrative or other business processes that add costs without creating value.

Not only have higher expenditures on healthcare in the United States failed to translate into higher overall quality, but key quality and system performance indicators showed that the United States is actually lagging behind other developed nations.[9] This is due in no small part to limited access to primary care services, with nearly 46 million individuals representing 16% of the U.S. population living without health insurance in 2005, a number that has not substantially improved in the years since. Unfortunately, this problem is only likely to worsen as underpayments for primary care, preventive care, chronic disease management, and care coordination have combined with high medical school debt and perceptions of primary care practice burdens to create a shortage of primary care physicians. Recent trends consistently show that U.S. medical school graduates increasingly eschew primary care[10] for specialties in which their care duties are more focused and payments for care and procedures are higher.

The unsustainable nature of the growth in healthcare expenses is further reinforced by data showing progressively increasing numbers of Medicare beneficiaries accumulating at the same time that the number of workers paying into the Medicare system is declining.[11] Among the contributing factors to healthcare expenses that have prompted calls for government action is the wide variation in use of tests and treatments without evidence that higher expenditures are associated with higher quality,[12,13] and even some evidence of an inverse correlation.[14,15] The impact of the primary care provider shortage on costs and quality[16] and the urgency of taking action to address the problem are underscored by the evidence that primary care is generally associated with better preventive care,[17,18] lower preventable mortality,[19] and similar quality with lower resource consumptions than specialty care for certain conditions, such as back pain,[20] diabetes, and hypertension.[21]

Unfortunately, the public debate regarding the preferred approaches for moving toward meaningful, beneficial, and enduring health reform has degenerated into partisan political rancor fueled by powerful special interest groups with vested interests in the status quo. This has the effect of obscuring, distorting, distracting, and delaying discussion of the real and substantive issues that need to be worked out. In the meantime, our healthcare iceberg is still melting. Surveys such as those conducted by the Commonwealth Fund[22] have made it clear that the public wants change to address healthcare quality, access, and costs. Desired changes included organizing care systems to ensure timely access, better care coordination, and improved information flow among doctors and with patients. Respondents also wanted health insurance administrative simplification and wider use of health information systems. Since there is compelling evidence that the status quo is not sustainable, it is important to look at potential drivers of change that will help us redesign care so that quality is a system property supported by appropriate and meaningful use of HIT.

Drivers of Change to Promote a More Productive Industry

While this chapter focuses on strategies for combining change leadership, practice assessment, process redesign, and HIT to assist practitioners in optimizing care quality and value, it is important to cite a few additional writings and events that highlight problems with the existing healthcare delivery system, underscore the urgency of healthcare system redesign, and serve as powerful drivers of change that have also informed our suggested approaches. For example, the Institute of Medicine (IOM) has commissioned several books describing a number of pervasive and critically important defects in the U.S. healthcare delivery system and recommended strategies for addressing them. Two of the most important of these books, *To Err Is Human: Building a Safer Health System*[23] and *Crossing the Quality Chasm: A New Health System for the 21st Century*,[24] shone a bright light on the defects in the current system and how such defects compromise the nation's ability to ensure the consistent delivery of high-quality care to all. Such defects result in care that is far too often fragmented, ineffective, error-prone, unsafe, inefficient, expensive, inaccessible, delayed, disparate, or insensitive to patient needs and preferences. The IOM also emphasized the reality that humans cannot be error-free, and indicated that the healthcare delivery system must be fundamentally redesigned, not just repaired, if meaningful gains in quality are to be achieved.

Much has also been written in recent years about the essential role of HIT in repairing some of the pervasive and critically important defects in the U.S. healthcare delivery system. Here again, the IOM did pioneering work, publishing and subsequently revising a book on computer-based patient records,[25] describing what would afterwards be more commonly referred to as electronic medical records (EMRs) and electronic health records (EHRs) as essential to both private and public sector objectives to transform healthcare delivery, enhance health, reduce costs, and strengthen the nation's productivity. However, the IOM also correctly identified many barriers to widespread implementation of EHR systems and predicted the need for a "major coordinated national effort with federal funding and strong advisory support from the private sector"[24] to accelerate needed change.

Some have estimated that approximately $80 billion in annual savings can be expected out of an estimated $2 trillion total (4%) from widespread implementation, optimization, and appropriate use of HIT,[26,27] although a 2008 Congressional Budget Office (CBO) report[28] underscored the degree to which this number may be sensitive to a number of assumptions and factors. The report also highlighted the current perverse incentives built into healthcare financing and delivery in which "the payment methods of both private and public health insurers in many cases do not reward providers for reducing some types of costs—and may even penalize them for doing so."[28] On the other end of the savings prediction spectrum, it has been estimated that if healthcare could produce productivity gains similar to those in telecommunications, retail, or wholesale industries, average annual spending on what is currently considered waste in healthcare could be decreased by $346 billion to $813 billion.[26] It is this combination of the potential for significantly lowering wasteful spending, the evidence that the right combination of HIT and institutional culture can lead to important gains in quality and value,[29] and the urgency of needed change that has prompted healthcare organizations and federal government officials to "bet on EHRs"[30] by making funding available to physicians and hospitals to improve quality through HIT.

The "Game Changers"

The federal government placed its "bet" by introducing a new and powerful driver for HIT adoption and appropriate use on February 17, 2009, when President Obama signed the Health Information Technology for Economic and Clinical Health (HITECH) Act, a large component ($31.2 billion gross investment, $19.2 billion net of expected savings) of the much larger ($787 billion) economic stimulus package known as the American Recovery and Reinvestment Act (ARRA) of 2009.[31] The HITECH Act made the IOM recommendation for a major coordinated national effort with federal funding a reality, with $29.2 billion ($17.2 billion net) available starting in 2011 for use as incentive payments to Medicare- and Medicaid-participating physicians and hospitals that use certified EHR systems in a "meaningful" way.

ARRA also provided for the creation of two advisory committees under the Federal Advisory Committee Act (FACA) that would be charged with making recommendations to the national coordinator for health information technology (HIT). Both of these advisory committees have since been formed and are constituted in a way that is consistent with the IOM's recommendations for involvement of experts from the private sector. The HIT Policy Committee has been given the responsibility of "making recommendations on a policy framework for the development and adoption of a nationwide health information infrastructure, including standards for the exchange of patient medical information,"[32] while the HIT Standards Committee has been charged with making recommendations "on standards, implementation specifications, and certification criteria for the electronic exchange and use of health information,"[32] with an initial focus on the policies developed by the HIT Policy Committee.

With codification into law of the national coordinator for HIT, improved funding for the Office of the National Coordinator (ONC), the passage of ARRA and the HITECH Act into law, and the appointment of the HIT Policy Committee and the HIT Standards Committee, early energy has turned to defining the goals, objectives, measures, and criteria by which physicians and hospitals will qualify for payments for meaningful use of HIT, along with the standards needed to support the goals for meaningful use. ARRA authorizes the Centers for Medicare and Medicaid Services (CMS) to reimburse physician and hospital providers who are meaningful users of EHR systems by providing incentive payments starting in 2011 and gradually phasing down over four years. Meanwhile, physicians and hospitals not actively using an EHR in compliance with the meaningful use definition by 2015 will be subject to financial penalties under Medicare.

It is important to emphasize that meaningful use does not mean simply having an EHR system in place and in use. Meaningful use will require that physicians and hospitals progress through a series of increasingly demanding sets of behaviors, proceeding from EHR use to capture and exchange data, then to improve care processes, and finally to achieve improved patient health outcomes. While the final criteria for meaningful use were not yet published at the time of this writing, it is almost certain that payment for meaningful use starting in 2011 will require providers to use electronic data capture to demonstrate attention to five healthcare priority areas:

- Improving quality, safety, efficacy
- Engaging patients and families
- Improving care coordination
- Improving population and public health
- Ensuring adequate privacy and security protections for patients

By 2013, physicians and hospitals will need to demonstrate use of advanced care processes with decision support to qualify for additional reimbursement for meaningful use. By 2015, payment for meaningful use will depend on achievement of improved clinical outcomes for selected conditions and a minimum level of performance on measures of efficiency and safety.

Conditions that are common, important, preventable, costly, and highly amenable to treatment have been targeted for early emphasis in meaningful use goals, objectives, and measures. Examples include diabetes mellitus, hypertension, hypercholesterolemia, smoking, obesity, preventive care services, safer medication prescribing in the elderly, and prevention of venous thromboembolism in surgical patients.[33] Efficiency and safety measures will likely include avoidance of preventable emergency department visits and hospitalizations, decreasing inappropriate use of imaging studies, computerized provider order entry, use of evidence-based order sets, advanced electronic prescribing, barcode medication administration, device interoperability, multimedia support, advanced clinical decision support use, and external data reporting on quality, safety, and efficiency.

Developing a Plan

While the financial incentives available from the HITECH Act may be sufficient to help providers and systems justify the capital expenditures required to implement and make meaningful use of EHR systems, without long-term payment reform that creates a sustainable business case for managing information and improving outcomes, we are concerned that providers will not continue to meaningfully use their EHRs after the HITECH incentives cease in 2016, even in the face of possible financial penalties. Fortunately, payment reform has also been prominent in recent healthcare discussions.[34–37] Implementing and using EHR systems in a meaningful way is likely to have a net cost over the next several years, especially for those who do not yet have robust EHR systems in place and in regular use. With losses in physician efficiency that are nearly universal in the early stages of EHR implementations, other short-term benefits that make striving "worth it" to physicians and staff will be required or adopted, and meaningful use is likely to be limited at best.

In addition to the necessary prerequisite of appropriate payment policy, we recommend that providers focus squarely on improving patient care quality, something that all health professionals resonate with and are individually committed to. Physicians should be frequently reminded that they have a shared responsibility for quality,[38] that their participation in EHR system configuration and meaningful use is essential to achieving the organization's quality goals, and that having HIT alone is insufficient unless it is used in a meaningful way in an organizational culture strongly committed to quality, safety, and collegiality. By quality we mean the six elements described by the IOM in its *Quality Chasm* report:[24] care that is consistently patient centered, effective, safe, timely, efficient, and equitable. This emphasis on quality (especially safety), collegiality, and support for those at the front lines of care is what enabled John Nance's fictional St. Michael's Memorial Hospital to make its transformational journey to quality in *Why Hospitals Should Fly,*[4] and it provides a road map for how each of us can use EHR systems and dollars to reward meaningful use to accelerate the transformation of our own hospitals and office practices in alignment with our main rationale for doing so, namely, ensuring that high-quality care is consistently available for all.

While hospital executives, practice leaders, and front-line providers are increasingly mindful of the importance and urgency of acting on their responsibilities and opportunities for improving care quality while containing costs, they may also be currently using HIT systems and support structures beset with some of the same defects as the healthcare system they were intended to support. Such legacy systems may have been designed and implemented without adequate clinician input, making them a poor fit for health professionals at the point of care. The systems may also not "talk to each other," either through product integration or interfaces, requiring redundant data entry and risking introduction of errors of commission or omission that threaten patient safety, care effectiveness, workflow efficiency, or service timeliness. Physicians also quickly learn to ignore systems that do not respond quickly or reliably enough for their needs, and develop paper-based workarounds that enable them to justify ignoring HIT systems and training opportunities even when they are available and encouraged.

Engaging physicians and convincing them of the importance of HIT to achieving shared organizational quality goals is a crucial early step that will increase the likelihood that they will be "willing to strive"[39] to achieve meaningful EHR use. Assessing organizational HIT readiness[40] is also important, as is ensuring that HIT systems are designed, built, validated, tested, and implemented with clinician input. We encourage design strategies that improve usability by decreasing the reading, writing, navigating, and thinking load[41] to the minimum necessary to improve the user experience and help clinicians make and execute optimal care decisions.

To speed care transformation and create a high-reliability organization that inspires the trust and satisfaction of patients and providers, HIT strategists should create, prioritize, and execute plans reflecting awareness of and responsiveness to the critical success factors and potential failure paths of major IT system implementations,[42–48] incorporate approaches that encourage adoption and regular use of EHR systems,[39] and manage the activities required by busy health professionals, taking into consideration the ongoing stressful care transformation process. Boiled down to its bare essentials, a successful journey to qualifying for meaningful EHR use requires building a successful three-tier care transformation framework (Figure 2.1) and then assessing and assisting users in moving from basic to advanced EHR use (Figure 2.2).

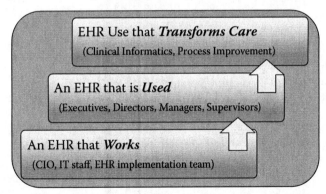

Figure 2.1   Electronic Health record system-enabled care transformation framework: Stepwise goals and change leaders.

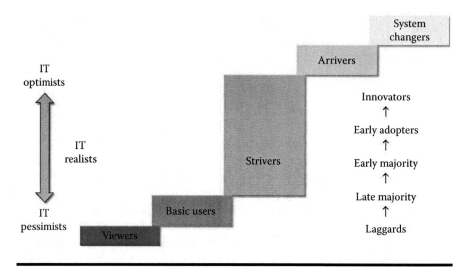

Figure 2.2 Attitudes regarding use of information technology and stages[48] of EHR use.

The foundational requirement in an EHR system-enabled care transformation framework (Figure 2.1) is an EHR system that works. This means that the IT staff and EHR implementation team combine to complete the IT technical infrastructure and build tasks required to deliver an EHR system that functions according to agreed upon user requirements and is dependable and responsive. The second requirement is an EHR system that is used. This outcome is fundamentally dependent on the leadership and culture of the organization. Responsibility for physician engagement and alignment around a shared quality agenda,[38] accountability all the way to the board of directors, and elimination of "normalization of deviance"[4] from important policies and procedures regarding EHR training and use in patient care are all critical to quality and meaningful use. All of these depend on the combination of formal organizational leadership and the building of a culture in which coworkers support each other in meaningful use and correct themselves and each other when deviance from standards for appropriate use are observed. The third requirement is an EHR system that transforms care, which requires the clinical informatics leadership, expertise, and resources to formulate and execute the principles and strategies for use of HIT and EHR systems to accelerate continuous process improvement and care transformation.

At the individual EHR user level, it is important to recognize the differences between people with regard to their attitudes about change and the adoption of new technology, as well as factors (incentives and inducements) that affect their willingness to strive to progress from simple data viewing and basic EHR use to become highly competent users and even system changers (Figure 2.2).[49] Those with an EHR system that is already in place have most likely already identified the 15% or so of those IT optimistic individuals in their organization who are best characterized on the Rogers' technology adoption curve[50] as innovators or early adopters of IT. Supported by appropriate payment policy but otherwise with minimal encouragement, these individuals can be counted on to strive to become highly competent EHR users and will spontaneously help build enthusiasm for EHR adoption and meaningful use by others as well. With appropriate training and support, some of these folks will become EHR champions or super-users that can be relied on to help other users make progress, try out enhanced EHR features and functionalities, or serve on EHR advisory committees.

Roughly two-thirds of the individuals in an organization can be expected to use the EHR early on only if it is communicated by leadership as a clear expectation with monitoring and accountability. The early majority represents about half of this group and is more accepting of change than the more skeptical late majority. Understandably, executives can generally only get behind expectation setting with accountability when it is clear to them that the organization has installed an EHR that works, making it reasonable to hold people accountable for EHR training and regular, appropriate use.

However, inevitably the organization will be left with approximately 15% of its people lagging behind. These so-called laggards[50] often simply prefer the old way of doing things. They tend to be suspicious and critical of new approaches. In some cases they not only prefer the status quo but may inadvertently disrupt the change process or even deliberately "poison the well" for others trying to lead or implement sorely needed organizational change. Without the input of considerable energy from others, laggards are unlikely to use the EHR or to use it appropriately until it has become the way almost everyone else is doing their work. For some, they will only use the EHR when the old way (e.g., paper, transcription, verbal orders) is no longer provided as an option. Rarely, some would rather leave an organization than adopt the new technology. Informatics experts and clinical leaders commonly struggle to decide how best to deal with these individuals. At one end of the spectrum, they may either accept or manage the clinician's unwillingness to adopt and use an EHR by allowing full exemption from EHR use (paper documentation with postencounter document scanning and indexing), accepting "EHR lite" use (dictation and transcription, viewing and signing results), or providing EHR-competent scribes. At the other end of the spectrum, employed laggards may face financial penalties or termination from employment if they are persistently unwilling or unable to become regular and meaningful users of the EHR system, while nonemployed laggards may face suspension or revocation of admitting or consulting privileges.

There are many trade-offs in any approach to resolving the problems associated with laggard noncompliance with EHR training or use expectations. Our advice is to set reasonable expectations and accountability for EHR use in advance and then measure, monitor, and enforce the expectations consistently. This should be done independent of rank, experience, or extent of push back about the adequacy of the system for use, particularly if other physicians and staff are consistently able to use the same EHR system to safely and effectively deliver similar care for similar patients using reasonable workflows. Failure to do so will simply teach others that foot dragging or negative behaviors are acceptable and effective ways of resisting needed change, while decreasing the morale of those who have exhibited the professionalism and dedication to strive to become competent and meaningful EHR users.

Assessing and Redesigning Your Practice

"Every system is perfectly designed to get the results it gets."[51] While this is a sobering comment in light of the defects in the U.S. healthcare delivery system described above, it also suggests the path to improved quality in healthcare—by carefully redesigning care, we can expect better results. The challenge is to identify resources and implement strategies that allow us to regularly deliver to our patients what Berwick and colleagues have termed the "triple aim"[52] of better experience of care (patient centered, effective, safe, timely, efficient, and equitable), better health for the population, and lower total per capita costs. While front-line clinicians may feel they have limited ability to influence healthcare redesign at a macro level, each local care team working closely and regularly with each other to provide care to a specific group of patients constitutes a clinical microsystem that, through a process of practice assessment and redesign,[53-55] can expand access,[56] improve effectiveness, advance safety, enhance patient and staff satisfaction, decrease waste and waiting, and leverage HIT to automate otherwise cumbersome manual processes. The Dartmouth Institute for Health Policy and Clinical Practice maintains a comprehensive and useful set of clinical microsystem resources on its website,[57] including *Clinical Microsystem Assessment Tool*[58] and *Clinical Microsystem Action Guide.*[59]

Another rich source of useful information and tools for assessing practices and improving care delivery systems is the Institute for Healthcare Improvement (IHI) website.[60] Particularly relevant and helpful resources include improvement methods,[61] presentation handouts from previous annual international summits on redesigning the clinical office practice,[62] and white papers,[63] including topics such as going lean in healthcare,[64] engaging physicians in a shared quality agenda,[38] transforming care at the bedside,[65] and improving the reliability of healthcare.[66]

Finally, there are numerous resources available from a number of professional organizations and societies to assist in developing strategies and plans for selection, implementation, and use of HIT and EHR systems to improve quality and achieve meaningful use. For example, the Health Information Management and Systems Society (HIMSS) offers useful conferences, educational programs, information, and resources in a wide variety of areas spanning the spectrum of healthcare reform, EHR systems, clinical informatics, IT privacy and security, interoperability, IT standards, ambulatory information systems, and financial systems.[67] Likewise, the American Medical Informatics Association (AMIA)[68] provides programs and resources to support the effectiveness of healthcare industry professionals in using information and IT to support patient care, public health, teaching, research, administration, and related policy. Specialty societies have also made useful resources for EHR selection, implementation, and meaningful use available, such as the Center for Practice Improvement and Innovation at the American College of Physicians[69] and the Center for Health IT at the American Academy of Family Physicians.[70]

Information Technology Strategies for Achieving Meaningful Use

Once the hospital or office practice leadership has shaped its culture and systems so that physicians and staff can be counted on to use clinical information systems regularly and appropriately, the next issue is to determine the HIT and EHR features and functionalities that are necessary or desirable. Qualifying for CMS payments for meaningful use means having the HIT and EHR tools in place and in use to meet the goals, objectives, and measures listed in the meaningful use matrix[71] developed by the Health Information Technology Policy Committee as part of the ARRA and HITECH Act. In this section, we outline specific IT strategies for achieving these meaningful use goals, objectives, and reporting requirements. Rather than detailing the differences between provider and hospital objectives and measures, we will emphasize the system features and functionalities that need to be in place and used to qualify for meaningful use.

Policy Priority 1: Improve Quality, Safety, Efficiency, and Reduce Health Disparities

The care goals for this health outcomes policy priority are to (1) provide the patient's care team with access to comprehensive patient health data, (2) use evidence-based orders sets and computerized provider order entry (CPOE), (3) apply clinical decision support (CDS) at the point of care, (4) generate lists of patients who need care and use the lists to reach out to patients, and (5) report to patient registries for quality improvement and public reporting. The 2011 objectives include expectations for electronically capturing in coded format information to allow tracking and reporting on key clinical conditions. To that end and for each patient, qualifying providers and hospitals will be expected to:

- Use CPOE (with providers entering orders directly)
- Implement drug–drug, drug-allergy, and drug-formulary checks
- Maintain a current problem list based on ICD-9 or SNOMED (Systemized nomenclature of medicine), a collection of medical terminology
- Use electronic prescribing for permissible prescriptions
- Maintain an active medication list
- Maintain an active medication allergy list
- Record demographics (race, ethnicity, gender, insurance type, primary language)
- Record advance directives
- Record vital signs (height, weight, blood pressure)
- Calculate and display body mass index (BMI)
- Record smoking status
- Incorporate laboratory/test results into EHR as structured data
- Generate lists of patients by specific conditions
- Report quality measures to CMS
- Send patients reminders per patient preference for preventive/follow-up care
- Implement one clinical decision rule relevant to specialty or high clinical priority
- Document progress note for each office encounter
- Check insurance eligibility electronically from public and private payers, where possible
- Submit claims electronically to public and private payers

Electronically capturing these data in a structured format is critical to ensuring that the EHR database contains the necessary information for reporting quality measures to CMS, which for 2011 include the percentage of:

- Diabetics with A1c under control
- Hypertensive patients with blood pressure under control
- Patients with LDL under control
- Smokers offered smoking cessation counseling
- Patients with a recorded BMI
- Orders entered directly by physicians through CPOE
- Patients receiving high-risk medications
- Patients over fifty with annual colorectal cancer screening
- Female patients over fifty receiving annual mammogram
- Patients at high risk for cardiac event on aspirin prophylaxis
- Patients receiving flu vaccine
- Percent of lab results incorporated into EHR in coded format
- Medications entered into EHR as generic when generic options exist in the relevant drug class

■ Orders for high-cost imaging services with specific structured indications recorded
■ Claims admitted electronically to all payers
■ Patient encounters with insurance eligibility confirmed

To meet the 2011 objectives and electronically report the measures, we recommend the following EHR functionalities (supported by a practice management system or third-party vendor solutions where relevant) be installed and operational:

■ Structured data entry mechanisms acceptable to users for entering patient demographics, advance directives, orders, problems, medications, allergies, vital signs, relevant history (e.g., smoking status), and interventions (e.g., smoking cessation counseling)
■ Functioning interfaces from the laboratory and radiology information systems to the EHR for receiving results
■ E-prescribing capability that includes drug–drug, drug-allergy, and drug-formulary checks
■ Clinical decision support functionality (calculating and displaying BMI, creating clinical decision rules)
■ Registry functionality with actionable views and communication tools (secure messaging for reminders)
■ Electronic insurance eligibility checking and claims submission capability
■ EHR data mining and reporting tools

Policy Priority 2: Engage Patients and Families

The care goal for this health outcomes policy priority is to provide patients and families with timely access to data, knowledge, and tools to make informed decisions and to manage their health. To demonstrate meaningful use, providers and hospitals will be expected to:

■ Provide patients with an electronic copy of, or electronic access to, their health information (including lab results, problem list, medication list, allergies, discharge summary, procedures)
■ Provide access to patient-specific educational resources
■ Provide clinical summaries for patients for each encounter

Assessing the degree of patient and family engagement will entail reporting the following measures to CMS, which for 2011 include the percentage of:

■ Patients with electronic access to personal health information
■ Patients with access to patient-specific educational resources
■ Encounters where a clinical summary was provided

To meet the 2011 patient and family engagement objectives and electronically report the measures, we recommend the following functionalities be installed and operational:

- EHR-supported workflows that result in capture of relevant information to populate the clinical encounter
- The ability at the point of care to electronically transmit educational materials to the patient from within usual EHR workflows (e.g., electronically send rather than print handouts)
- A secure, EHR-linked patient web portal with the capability to support selective EHR chart views (e.g., problem list, medication list, allergies, lab results), messaging, condition-specific educational resources, encounter summaries, and an option for the patient to have a personal health record (PHR).

Policy Priority 3: Improve Care Coordination

The care goal for this health outcomes policy priority is to exchange meaningful clinical information among professional healthcare teams. The 2011 objectives for care coordination are to:

- Exchange key clinical information among providers of care and patient-authorized entities electronically
- Perform medication reconciliation at relevant encounters and each transition of care

The care coordination reporting requirements for 2011 are:

- Thirty-day readmission rate
- Percent of encounters where medication reconciliation was performed
- Implemented ability to exchange health information with external clinical entities (labs, medication lists, care summaries)
- Percent of care transitions where summary care record is shared (any modality)

To meet the 2011 care coordination objectives and electronically report the measures, we recommend the following functionalities be installed and operational:

- An EHR-integrated secure clinical messaging solution that allows secure sending and receipt of summary data (e.g., continuity of care document (CCD)), messages, and electronic chart documents to other patient-authorized entities, whether or not the external entity has an EHR system in place
- An audit system to record and report instances of exchange of health information, including summary care records shared, as well as the context in which they occur (e.g., admission, discharge, transfer, referral)

■ Medication reconciliation functionality that allows for recording of medication changes between visits and at transitions of care, as well as incorporating evidence of fill history to capture medications prescribed but not filled and medications added or changed by other providers

Policy Priority 4: Improve Population and Public Health

The goal of this health outcomes policy priority is communication with public health agencies. The 2011 objectives for improving population and public health are to:

■ Submit electronic data to immunization registries where required and accepted
■ Submit electronic syndrome surveillance data to public health agencies according to applicable law and practice

The population and public health reporting requirements for 2011 are:

■ Report up-to-date status of childhood immunizations
■ Percent of reportable laboratory results submitted electronically

To meet the 2011 population and public health objectives and electronically report the measures to CMS, we recommend the following EHR functionalities be installed and operational:

■ Immunization recording tools that capture all relevant immunization data in a structured manner to support reporting to state immunization registries and CMS
■ An interface from the EHR to the external immunization registry in regions where actual submission of immunization information is required and can be accepted
■ Auditing tools for reporting on all structured data (e.g., lab results) submitted electronically to public health entities

Policy Priority 5: Ensure Adequate Privacy and Security Protections for Personal Health Information

This health outcomes policy priority seeks to ensure privacy and security protections for confidential information through operating policies, procedures, and technologies and compliance with applicable law. It also works toward the goal of providing transparency of data sharing to patients. The 2011 objectives for privacy and security protections are:

■ Compliance with HIPAA privacy and security rules
■ Compliance with fair data sharing practices set forth in the national privacy and security framework[72]

The privacy and security protections reporting requirements for 2011 are to:

■ Demonstrate full compliance with the HIPAA privacy and security rule[73]
■ Conduct or update a security risk assessment and implement security updates as necessary

To meet the 2011 privacy and security protection objectives and electronically report the measures to CMS, we recommend the usual organizational IT technical approaches for safeguarding patient information (e.g., firewalls, virtual private networks, intranets, data encryption, prevention of local device storage, strong authentication) and strong organizational policies and procedures for identity proofing, user authentication, and authorization, as well as for preventing, detecting, and taking action on instances of suspected breaches in patient data privacy, confidentiality, and security. In addition, we recommend the following EHR functionalities be installed and operational:

■ EHR system configuration to support strong user authentication and role-based privileges
■ Use of EHR functionalities to "hide" information that a particular user is not authorized to view under any circumstances (e.g., highly confidential documents, sensitive charts)
■ Activation of "break the glass" tools (where appropriate) to warn users in advance of potentially unauthorized chart or information access, with options to record a reason for seeking access (e.g., emergency), enhanced auditing of those who proceed, and additional scrutiny of those who do not
■ Activation of auditing tools to enable tracking of all relevant details of EHR system access, chart access, patient data and document viewing, modification, deletion, storage, printing, and transmission
■ Ability to facilitate delivery and electronically record delivery of privacy practices notices to individual patients
■ Creation of automated reports using filters that have a high signal-to-noise ratio, creating a short list of individuals that are highly likely to have accessed patient data inappropriately, rather than a long list of individuals, most of whom accessed charts appropriately

Meaningful Use: The Road Ahead

At the time of this writing, the objectives and measures for meaningful use in 2013, 2015, and beyond were less well defined, so they will be described in less detail and with less certainty here. Having said that, it is reasonable to expect that the criteria for meaningful use will become progressively more challenging and will move from an emphasis in 2011 on data capture and sharing to an emphasis in 2013 on advanced clinical processes and in 2015 on improved patient outcomes. In 2013, providers and hospitals seeking payments for meaningful use will be expected to expand their use of CPOE and evidence-based order sets, do their hospital clinical documentation in an EHR, e-prescribe discharge medications, manage chronic conditions using patient lists and decision support, utilize more CDS at the point of care, have specialists report data to external registries, and implement closed-loop medication management, including electronic medication administration records and computer-assisted medication administration.

Patient-facing objectives for 2013 are expected to include providing access for all patients to a personal health record or patient web portal populated with health data in real time, offering secure patient–provider messaging capability, providing patient-specific educational resources in common primary languages, recording patient preferences, documenting family medical history, and uploading data from home monitoring devices. Care coordination requirements for 2013 will likely require retrieving and acting on electronic prescription fill data, production and sharing of an electronic summary care record for every transition of care, and medication reconciliation at each transition of care from one health setting to another.

By 2013, population and public health objectives are expected to include receiving immunization histories and recommendations from immunization registries, receiving health alerts from public health agencies, and providing sufficiently anonymized electronic syndrome surveillance data to public health agencies with the capacity to link to personal identifiers. Privacy and security protection objectives will include the use of summarized or de-identified data when reporting data for population health purposes so that information is available with minimal privacy risk.

Meaningful use objectives for 2015 will include achieving minimal levels of performance on quality, safety, and efficiency measures. Providers and hospitals will be expected to have implemented CDS for national high-priority conditions, interoperable medical devices, and multimedia support for imaging technology. By 2015, patients should have access to online self-management tools and be able to report electronically on their experiences of care. Health information exchanges of various types should facilitate access to comprehensive patient data from all available and appropriate sources, enable use of epidemiologic data in clinical decision making, and allow for automated real-time surveillance for adverse events, near misses, disease outbreaks, and bioterrorism. Clinical dashboards and dynamic and *ad hoc* quality reports should also be routinely available. Privacy and security goals for 2015 include providing patients with an accounting of treatment, payment, and healthcare operations disclosures on request, as well as minimizing the reluctance of patients to seek care because of privacy concerns.

The requirements for meaningful use described above are strenuous but achievable, and those who have traveled significantly down the path of EHR implementation and optimization have already done much of the "heavy lifting" required to qualify for early meaningful use payments. However, even these organizations will need to press forward with deliberate speed to keep up with the meaningful use requirements over time. On the other hand, hospitals and practices that are still at the "starting line" with regard to EHR adoption and meaningful use by virtue of not yet having started in earnest to plan for, select, implement, and optimize an EHR system will find it challenging to implement and achieve meaningful use of EHRs according to the current published time frames. We are hopeful that the ARRA-planned and -funded health information technology regional extension centers[74] (HITRECs; also known as regional health information technology extension centers, or RHITECs) will help many physicians and health systems to meet that challenge.

We also expect that use of a buddy system for EHR implementation and optimization will be important to the prospects for success in this effort. In the EHR buddy system approach, a hospital or physician practice that has yet to implement an EHR system chooses to accept considerable assistance from, or even tags on to, an organization with a well-established EHR system and knowledgeable, experienced implementation teams and clinical informatics leadership. Such a decision significantly decreases the risks and costs of EHR implementation and meaningful use in exchange for a willingness to be a part of an existing governance structure and participate according to its rules, potentially including a shared chart model on a common database.

Whether the buddy system approach to extending EHR systems and expertise will be offered by enough of those qualified to provide EHR implementation assistance is unknown, particularly in the absence of specific incentives for such organizations to catalyze meaningful use for others. It is also unclear whether such assistance will be seen as attractive to large numbers of hospitals and physician office practices considering whether and how they will strive to meet the criteria for meaningful EHR use.

In closing, we are reminded once again that our healthcare iceberg is melting. For all the risks associated with change, failing to adopt and meaningfully utilize EHR systems will only further risk leaving our patients behind, while the healthcare system they depend on crumbles under the weight of inconsistent quality, excessive waste, and unsustainable cost increases. Though far from perfect, we see ARRA and the HITECH Act, along with the HITRECs and the various federal agencies promoting use of HIT, as powerful catalysts to drive change. We also see provider payment reform as necessary for durable change, by transitioning a significant fraction of payment away from volume and procedures and instead rewarding HIT-powered improvements in quality and outcomes. While EHR systems are also far from where they need to be to optimally support effectiveness, efficiency, interoperability, safety, and health information exchange, many are good enough to make striving to implement and use them reasonable and worth rewarding. It's "quality time"—time to get moving and transform care.

References

1. Kotter J, Rathgeber H. 2006. *Our iceberg is melting: Changing and succeeding under any conditions.* New York: St. Martin's Press.
2. Kotter J. 1996. *Leading change.* Boston: Harvard Business School Press.
3. Park T, Basch P. 2009. *Wedding health information technology to care delivery innovation and provider payment reform.* Washington, DC. Full information about this reference is at: http://www.americanprogress.org/issues/2009/05/health_it.html
4. Nance J. 2008. *Why hospitals should fly—The ultimate flight plan to patient safety and quality care.* Bozeman, MT: Second River Healthcare Press.
5. World Health Organization. 2007. *World health statistics 2007.* Geneva: World Health Organization.
6. O'Neill PH. 2006. Testimony in hearings before the Senate Committee on Commerce. Senate Committee on Commerce. 109th Congress, 2nd session. Washington, DC.
7. Milstein A. 2004. Testimony in hearings before the Senate Committee on Health, Education, Labor, and Pension. Senate Committee on Health, Education, Labor, and Pension. 108th congress, 2nd session. Washington, DC.
8. PricewaterhouseCoopers Health Research Institute. 2008. *The price of excess: Identifying waste in healthcare spending.* Dallas, TX: PricewaterhouseCoopers.
9. Ginsburg JA, Doherty RB, Ralston JF Jr., Senkeeto N, Cooke M, Cutler C, et al. 2008. Achieving a high-performance health care system with universal access: What the United States can learn from other countries. *Ann Intern Med* 148:55–75.
10. Brotherton SE, Etzel SI. 2008. Graduate medical education, 2007–2008. *JAMA* 300:1228–43.
11. Kaiser Family Foundation. 2009. *Medicare beneficiaries and the number of workers per beneficiary.* Menlo Park, CA: Henry J. Kaiser Family Foundation.
12. Fisher ES, Wennberg DE, Stukel TA, Gottlieb DJ, Lucas FL, Pinder EL. 2003. The implications of regional variations in Medicare spending. Part 2. Health outcomes and satisfaction with care. *Ann Intern Med* 138:288–98.
13. Fisher ES, Wennberg DE, Stukel TA, Gottlieb DJ, Lucas FL, Pinder EL. 2003. The implications of regional variations in Medicare spending. Part 1. The content, quality, and accessibility of care. *Ann Intern Med* 138:273–87.
14. Baicker K, Chandra A. 2004. Medicare spending, the physician workforce, and beneficiaries' quality of care. *Health Aff* (Millwood) *Suppl Web Exclusives* W184–97.
15. Gawande A. 2009. The cost conundrum. *The New Yorker*, June 1.
16. Zerehi MR. 2008. How is the shortage of primary care physicians affecting the quality and cost of medical care? Philadelphia, PA: American College of Physicians. White Paper.
17. O'Malley AS, Forrest CB. 2006. Immunization disparities in older Americans: Determinants and future research needs. *Am J Prev Med* 31:150–58.
18. Lewis CE, Clancy C, Leake B, Schwartz JS. 1991. The counseling practices of internists. *Ann Intern Med* 114:54–58.
19. Macinko J, Starfield B, Shi L. 2003. The contribution of primary care systems to health outcomes within Organization for Economic Cooperation and Development (OECD) countries, 1970–1998. *Health Serv Res* 38:831–65.

20. Carey TS, Garrett J, Jackman A, McLaughlin C, Fryer J, Smucker DR. 1995. The outcomes and costs of care for acute low back pain among patients seen by primary care practitioners, chiropractors, and orthopedic surgeons. The North Carolina Back Pain Project. *N Engl J Med* 333:913–17.

21. Greenfield S, Rogers W, Mangotich M, Carney MF, Tarlov AR. 1995. Outcomes of patients with hypertension and non-insulin dependent diabetes mellitus treated by different systems and specialties. Results from the medical outcomes study. *JAMA* 274:1436–44.

22. How SKH, Shih A, Lau J, Schoen C. 2008. *Public views on U.S. health system organization: A call for new directions*, The Commonwealth Fund, 11:1–15.

23. Kohn L, Corrigan, J, Donaldson, MS, eds. 2000. *To err is human: Building a safer health system*. Washington, DC: National Academy Press.

24. Committee on Quality Health Care in America IOM. 2001. *Crossing the quality chasm: A new health system for the 21st century*. Washington, DC: National Academy Press.

25. Dick RS, Steen EB, Detmer DE, eds. 1997. *The computer-based patient record: An essential technology for health care*. Rev. ed. Washington, DC: National Academy Press.

26. Hillestad R, Bigelow J, Bower A, Girosi F, Meili R, Scoville R, et al. 2005. Can electronic medical record systems transform health care? Potential health benefits, savings, and costs. *Health Aff* (Millwood) 24:1103–17.

27. Walker J, Pan E, Johnston D, Adler-Milstein J, Bates DW, Middleton B. 2005. The value of health care information exchange and interoperability. *Health Aff* (Millwood).

28. Girosi F, Meili R, Scoville R. 2005. *Extrapolating evidence of health information technology savings and costs*. Santa Monica, CA: Rand Corporation.

29. Chaudhry B, Wang J, Wu S, Maglione M, Mojica W, Roth E, et al. 2006. Systematic review: Impact of health information technology on quality, efficiency, and costs of medical care. *Ann Intern Med* 144:742–52.

30. Halamka JD. 2006. Health information technology: Shall we wait for the evidence? *Ann Intern Med* 144:775–76.

31. American Recovery and Reinvestment Act of 2009. In: 111 ed. USA, p. 407. http://healthit.hhs.gov/portal/server.pt?open=512&objID=1325&parentname=CommunityPage&parentid=1&mode=2

32. Health Information Technology Federal Advisory Committees. 2009. Washington, DC: U.S. Department of Health and Human Services.

33. Meaningful use. 2009. Washington, DC: U.S. Department of Health and Human Services. http://healthit.hhs.gov/portal/server.pt?open=512&objID=1325&parentname=CommunityPage&parentid=1&mode=2

34. Basch P. 2009. Consensus from contradiction: An emerging case for healthcare payment reform plus health IT. In: *iHealthBeat*. Washington, DC: Advisory Board Company.

35. Mechanic RE, Altman SH. 2009. Payment reform options: Episode payment is a good place to start. *Health Aff* (Millwood) 28:w262–71.

36. Rother J. 2009. A consumer perspective on physician payment reform. *Health Aff* (Millwood) 28:w235–37.

37. Kahn CN 3rd. 2009. Payment reform alone will not transform health care delivery. *Health Aff* (Millwood) 28:w216–18.

38. Reinertsen JL, Gosfield AG, Rupp W, Whittington JW. 2007. *Engaging physicians in a shared quality agenda*. IHI Innovation Series white paper. Cambridge, MA: Institute for Healthcare Improvement.

39. Zaroukian MH, Sierra A. 2006. Benefiting from ambulatory EHR implementation: Solidarity, Six Sigma, and willingness to strive. *J Healthcare Inf Manag* 20:53–60.
40. Health information technology donations: A guide for physicians. 2008. Chicago.
41. Rucker DW, Steele AW, Douglas IS, Coudere CA, Hardel GG. 2006. Design and use of a joint order vocabulary knowledge representation tier in a multi-tier CPOE architecture. *AMIA Annu Symp Proc* 2006:669–73.
42. Ash JS, Berg M, Coiera E. 2004. Some unintended consequences of information technology in health care: The nature of patient care information system-related errors. *J Am Med Inform Assoc* 11:104–12.
43. Ash JS, Sittig DF, Poon EG, Guappone K, Campbell E, Dykstra RH. 2007. The extent and importance of unintended consequences related to computerized provider order entry. *J Am Med Inform Assoc.* 14(4):415–423.
44. Koppel R, Wetterneck T, Telles JL, Karsh BT. 2008. Workarounds to barcode medication administration systems: Their occurrences, causes, and threats to patient safety. *J Am Med Inform Assoc* 15:408–23.
45. Koppel R, Leonard CE, Localio AR, Cohen A, Auten R, Strom BL. 2008. Identifying and quantifying medication errors: Evaluation of rapidly discontinued medication orders submitted to a computerized physician order entry system. *J Am Med Inform Assoc* 15:461–65.
46. Harrison MI, Koppel R, Bar-Lev S. 2007. Unintended consequences of information technologies in health care—An interactive sociotechnical analysis. *J Am Med Inform Assoc* 14:542–49.
47. Koppel R, Metlay JP, Cohen A, Abaluck B, Localio AR, Kimmel SE, et al. 2005. Role of computerized physician order entry systems in facilitating medication errors. *JAMA* 293:1197–203.
48. Koppel R. 2005. What do we know about medication errors made via a CPOE system versus those made via handwritten orders? *Crit Care* 9:427–28.
49. Miller RH, Sim I, Newman J. 2004. Electronic medical records in solo/small groups: A qualitative study of physician user types. *Medinfo* 2004:658–62.
50. Rogers EM. 2003. *Diffusion of innovations.* 5th ed. New York: Free Press.
51. Batalden P. 1984. *Every system is perfectly designed to get the results it gets.* www.dartmouth.edu/~cecs/hcild/hcild.html
52. Berwick DM, Nolan TW, Whittington J. 2008. The triple aim: Care, health, and cost. *Health Aff* (Millwood) 27:759–69.
53. Godfrey MM, Nelson EC, Batalden PB. 2004. Assessing your practice: The green book. Dartmouth College, Institute for Healthcare Improvement.
54. Godfrey MM, Nelson EC, Batalden PB. 2005. Assessing, diagnosing and treating your inpatient unit. In: *Clinical microsystems greenbooks.* 2nd ed. Hanover, NH: Dartmouth College.
55. Godfrey MM, Nelson EC, Batalden PB. 2005. Assessing, diagnosing and treating your outpatient specialty care practice. In: *Clinical microsystems greenbooks.* 2nd ed. Hanover, NH: Dartmouth College.
56. Murray M, Tantau C, eds. 2002. *Improving patient access to care—Primary care.* 2nd ed. Lebanon, NH: Trustees of Dartmouth College.
57. *Clinical microsystems.* Hanover, NH: Dartmouth College.
58. Johnson JK. 2003. *Clinical microsystem assessment tool.* 2nd ed. Lebanon, NH: Dartmouth College. http://dms.dartmouth.edu/cms

59. Godfrey MM, Nelson EC, Batalden PB, Wasson JH, Mohr JJ, Huber T, et al. 2004. *Clinical microsystem action guide.* 2nd ed. Hanover, NH: Dartmouth College.

60. IHI.org. A resource from the Institute for Healthcare Improvement. Cambridge, MA: Institute for Healthcare Improvement.

61. IHI.org. Improvement methods. Cambridge, MA: Institute for Healthcare Improvement.

62. 10th Annual International Summit on Redesigning the Clinical Office Practice. 2009. Cambridge, MA: Institute for Healthcare Improvement.

63. IHI.org. White papers. Cambridge, MA: Institute for Healthcare Improvement.

64. Institute for Healthcare Improvement. 2005. *Going lean in health care.* Cambridge, MA: Institute for Healthcare Improvement.

65. Rutherford P, Lee B, Greiner A. 2004. *Transforming Care at the Bedside.* IHI Innovation Series White Paper. Boston: Institute for Healthcare Improvement.

66. Nolan T, Resar RCH, Griffin FA. 2004. *Improving the Reliability of Health Care.* IHI Innovation Series White Paper. Boston: Institute for Healthcare Improvement.

67. Health Information Management and Systems Society. *HIMSS topics and tools.* Chicago: Health Information Management and Systems Society.

68. American Medical Informatics Association. Bethesda: American Medical Informatics Association. www.amia.org (accessed Jan. 20, 2010).

69. Center for Practice Improvement and Innovation. 2009. *Electronic health record systems.* Philadelphia: American College of Physicians.

70. Center for Health IT at the AAFP. 2009. Leawood, KS: American Academy of Family Physicians.

71. *Meaningful use matrix.* 2009. Washington, DC: U.S. Department of Health and Human Services.

72. Office of the National Coordinator for Health Information Technology. 2008. *The nationwide privacy and security framework for electronic exchange of individually identifiable health information.* Washington, DC: Office of the National Coordinator for Health Information Technology.

73. Office for Civil Rights. 2003. *OCR privacy brief: Summary of the HIPAA privacy rule.* Washington, DC: U.S. Department of Health and Human Services.

74. Department of Health and Human Services. Friedman C. 2009. *Health Information Technology Extension Program.* Washington, DC: Department of Health and Human Services.

Chapter 3

A Project Management Framework of Healthcare Informatics Initiatives

Christi Rushnell and Mary Beattie

Contents

No one would debate that healthcare organizations are under increased pressure to perform. Healthcare costs continue to skyrocket out of control. Information technology systems are seen as one way to streamline processes and take costs out of a healthcare organization. However, healthcare information systems, specifically clinical information systems, are some of the most complex systems to install. Couple that with the changes in processes necessary to realize the potential savings in expenses and improved quality and safety, and you have one of the toughest projects in any industry to manage.

Solid project management methodologies exist, and if incorporated into the installation process for healthcare information systems, the result should be a more successful launch of an application and greater probability for a successful use of the application integrated into the clinical or business process workflow.

This chapter will examine a methodology for project management in a healthcare setting focusing on the life cycle of a project as well as methodologies for incorporating process improvement techniques into a project to receive the most value from an implementation.

Project Management for Healthcare

Project Management Definition

Project management is a formal management discipline, dating as far back as the 1950s. The discipline consists of planning, organizing, and managing resources to reach the successful completion of specific goals and objectives.[1] Although the formal adoption of methodologies started in the 1950s, the use of project management dates back much further. Engineers and architects managed their projects without the formal Gantt charts and PERT diagrams that today's practitioners are so used to. Although there are a variety of definitions, the most common is to look at a project as a temporary endeavor, *one that has a distinct beginning and end,* undertaken to create a unique product, service, or result. Projects and operations differ primarily in that operations are ongoing and repetitive, while projects are temporary and unique.

Healthcare Project Environment

The discipline of project management is utilized by all types of industries. The construction and software industries, specifically, have adapted many of the formal methodologies to meet their particular needs. Healthcare, by contrast, has been slow to adapt to the formal methodologies available. However, if any industry needs formal methodologies for managing temporary endeavors, it is the healthcare industry; the fast pace of healthcare change calls for a more streamlined project management approach.[2] In the healthcare informatics arena alone there are so many projects to complete, and the informatics projects are competing with patient-care-focused projects, aging building improvement projects, and new revenue-producing service lines. Not unlike other industries, healthcare organizations have long-term risk and financial consequences for project delays, making the successful management of all projects an absolute necessity.

Healthcare is a highly regulated industry, and managing this regulation takes a concerted effort. Managing healthcare information technology projects assists an organization to meet its operational and financial goals. For most project managers, the typical triangle of constraints of time, finances, and resources is enough of a challenge. In healthcare information technology, a fourth constraint comes into play: regulations, whether they come from the state level or national level, must be considered in every project. Adding in the fourth area of focus changes the traditional triangle to a rectangle; however, including regulation as a formal constraint allows a project team to focus on all four areas equally (Diagram 3.1).

Formal project management skills allow an organization utilizing proven standards on practice to receive proven results. A project's success is not always guaranteed if project management principles are utilized; however, without those standards, failure is almost certain.

Project Methodology

Completing project work can be accomplished in a variety of ways, so much so that not having a common, agreed to methodology can often lead to confusion for the project team as well as operational leadership expecting to see results. Adopting a common framework and educating all departments to that methodology streamlines the work effort and ensures everyone working on a specific project is following the same script. It serves as a guide to the organization as it selects its projects, project teams as they plan the work, management as they supply the required oversight, and sponsors and customers as they collaborate in the design and delivery of new business and change. A commonly utilized methodology is outlined in

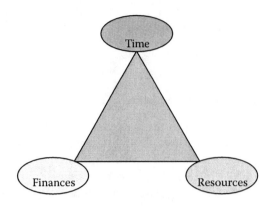

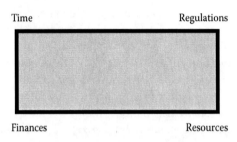

Diagram 3.1　Triangle of constraints is above. Adding a fourth constraint such as regulations elongates the traditional triad to a rectangle.

the Project Management Institute's (PMI®) *A Guide to Project Management Body of Knowledge (PMBOK® Guide)*. It should apply equally well to and meet the requirements of projects large and small. The remainder of this chapter addresses project management methodologies, utilizing PMBOK as a baseline approach.

This chapter describes the process a project manager should use during the five established phases of every project: initiating, planning, execution, managing and controlling, and closeout. As the reader goes through this chapter, a description of each phase, tasks, and deliverables will be suggested. Following this methodology will provide consistency and repeatable processes to help ensure successful project management.

In defining this methodology, we hope to reach the following goals:

■ Establish common points of reference vocabulary for talking and writing about the practice of project management
■ Increase the awareness and professionalism of good project management by those responsible

■ Establish a common collaborative environment where everyone engaged in project work recognizes and understands what is required and the importance of key factors for improving project results

Project Management Office

Before going much further, a good project manager must understand the role a project management office can play in his or her success. Although not a mandatory office, and in healthcare, often not a formal department, a project management office (PMO) is a valuable resource to a project manager. A PMO will have a structure in place to organize projects and manage the project pipeline to reduce the amount of time spent analyzing projects that should not be considered or do not align with strategic objectives. They will keep a complete project portfolio reducing the number of redundant projects undertaken by various business units. Doing so gives the organization a better understanding of true project resource commitments. Better prediction of the impact of projects on ongoing future operations will help managers avoid making commitments that could jeopardize future results. Understanding the true cost of projects is a first step toward managing that cost. Alignment with other organizational oversight committees will allow for proper alignment with financial and quality functions. Benefits management and postproject benefits assessment will lead to processes that ensure that predicted benefits are actually realized. Using standard, repeatable, reliable project practices allows better communication and more important, better control and predictability of project outcomes. Project failures will be reduced; cost and schedule overruns will be reduced. Projects must employ standards that bring them to completion with quality and efficient use of resources; these standards should be tested and modified continuously to ensure that they contribute positively toward that end. For many larger healthcare organizations, projects are a constant where a strong PMO is a way to ensure productivity gains, not losses, are the norm.

Project Life Cycle Phases

Each project phase section of the document is organized as follows:

■ Overview
■ Tasks (table)
■ Deliverables

Phase I: Project Initiation

Overview

Generally, healthcare organizations are comprised of people highly creative and full of energy. These people deal with everyday issues that range from the insignificant to saving patient lives, so they can be quite creative in conceiving solutions to the problems they face. Hopefully, they present these solutions to the PMO as potential projects.

Projects come about for a variety of reasons and can present themselves at any time. Projects may differ in the degree of benefit that they can bring to the organization, and cost can vary from the very small to the very expensive. Management generally recognizes that great care must be taken in considering which projects to embrace and which to defer. Therefore, most organizations eventually discover that they need a process that will allow them to choose among the project candidates.

The section process occurs during the very first stage of the project life cycle: initiation. The initiation phase is that time in the life cycle of a project when the project idea is defined, evaluated, and then approved by an executive committee or other review group. The project management profession has learned that this process works best when the strategic mission, justification for the project, its significant deliverables, risks, and estimated costs, resource requirements, and other significant information about the project are documented and reviewed in a formal manner. This process provides the executive review group, the project sponsor, and other stakeholders an opportunity to validate the project's potential benefits and costs. In a project management office environment, these project requests are generally reviewed against the project portfolio for further discussion of the right fit with other project initiatives.

The initiation phase provides benefits that include:

■ Serving as a guide for the project team as they determine and articulate key aspects of a proposed project that will help in the decision process.
■ Development of a business case that helps ensure that the organization chooses the best projects that meet its needs and that chosen technology projects will be a successful fit for the organizational needs.
■ Development of a charter that promotes an early collaboration between the project sponsor, the customer(s), and the project team. Early establishment of a good relationship among these key project contributors can help ensure healthy collaboration later in the project.
■ A well-written business case to clearly establish and communicate what is being proposed, expected benefits, the technical approach to be taken, and how project deliverables fit into ongoing operations.

The initiation phase is a success when it leads the organization to select the most pressing business issues for resolution and to choose effective technology to resolve them, and ensures that the organization makes a good investment that is consistent with its long-term strategies.

Activities

The following is a list of key activities necessary for successful development of a business case and initiation of a project:

1. Establish a project sponsor/leader. Every aspect of a project requires someone to guide it, and the initiation phase is no exception. The project sponsor, who may ultimately be different than the project owner or manager, is responsible for defining the purpose of the project and its goals and objectives, gathering strategic and background information, determining high-level planning, and estimating budgets, schedules, and high-level resource requirements for the life of the project. The project owner will coordinate resources and activities to develop and complete the business case and any other materials required for project approval. Since it generally takes more than one person to fully develop a business case, a team of individuals may be required to research, create estimates, and perform other work necessary for the business case document. This team may not actually carry out the project once approved.

Task: Establish a Project Sponsor/Leader	
	Select a project sponsor or leader
	Select team members to assist with initiation phase activities

2. Identify sponsor role and responsibilities. The project sponsor is the single individual, generally at an executive level, who is responsible for the strategic direction and financial support of a project. The project sponsor must have the authority to define project goals, secure resources, from a both financial and a human resource level, and resolve organizational and priority conflicts. Lack of project sponsorship can be a major contributor to project failure, so this role is a key factor in the success of every project.

    Project sponsor responsibilities include:

    – Champion the project from initiation to completion
    – Guide the development and articulation of the project business case
    – Present the overall vision and business objectives for the project
    – Secure final funding and resourcing for the project
    – Serve as executive liaison to key stakeholders (e.g., senior management, business owners, and stakeholders)
    – Support the project team

Task: Identify a Sponsor	
	Identify sponsor roles and responsibilities
	Obtain acceptance of project accountability from project sponsor
	Sponsor understands his or her role and is engaged

3. Define the business need or opportunity. The statement of need or identified opportunity should explain, in business terms, how the proposed project will address specific needs or opportunities within the organization. This statement cannot be general but instead must be specific as to the issue being addressed.

This information allows an organization to determine how much of its resources (including dollars required as well as people's time) to put into the project. This allows the business decision to be made based on how well the project is expected to meet the business need identified or take advantage of the opportunity.

Task: Define the Business Need or Opportunity	
	Identify the business need or opportunity
	Determine the resource requirements of the business need or opportunity
	Determine how the business need or opportunity will address the problem
	Determine what would happen if no change is made
	Document the business need or opportunity and its detail in the business case

4. Identify business objectives and benefits. Every project has a requirement for an investment of time, money, or both. Business objectives define the results that must be achieved for a proposed solution to effectively address the business need or opportunity. Business objectives should be written so they are clearly identified as the immediate reason for investing in the project. Objectives are quantifiable success factors against which the organization can measure how well the proposed solution addresses the business need or opportunity.

Task: Identify Business Objectives and Benefits	
	Determine business objectives to ensure they support the business need or opportunity
	Identify process improvement opportunities
	Identify benefits of meeting business objectives
	Use SMART (specific, measurable, achievable, realistic, and time-sensitive) business objectives
	Determine financial cost savings and quality of service improvements
	Document the business objectives and benefits in the business case

5. Ensure alignment with strategic mission and vision. Every project that an organization commits to must be aligned with its mission and vision to effectively support its business strategy. Many organizations have made use of project portfolio management as a key process in project selection and oversight, which provides for each project to be reviewed for alignment with strategic business goals, selecting only those projects that are best fit for the organization. This works best when HIT (for technology projects) and business end users partner as part of the process.

Task: Ensure Alignment with Strategic Mission and Vision	
	Review the organization's strategic business plan
	Review information technology's strategic business plan
	Review business owner or department business plan
	Review current business and technical environment to avoid duplication and ensure fit
	Review project business need and objects to ensure alignment with strategic business plans
	Document how the project is aligned with organization, department, and information technology strategic vision in the business case

6. Identify and engage key stakeholders. Stakeholders are defined as individuals and organizations that have a vested interest in the success or failure of the project. During the initiation phase, stakeholders often provide assistance to the project team to define, drive, change, and contribute to the definition of scope. Stakeholders can be key to the success of the project through their buy-in and participation.

To ensure project success, the project team must identify key stakeholders early in the project. As "customers," their needs and expectations must be clearly defined and managed throughout the life cycle of the project. Stakeholders who are not supportive of project goals must be either made into supporters or, at the very least, brought to a place of passive agreement to the project.

Task: Identify Key Stakeholders	
	Identify internal stakeholders (internal to the organization)
	Identify external stakeholders (external to the organization)
	Determine stakeholder needs and expectations

	Document key stakeholders in the business case
	Establish a plan to manage key stakeholder expectations throughout the project life cycle

7. Determine cost-benefit and schedule estimates. Projects are often part of a larger product life cycle. For example, when a new financial or clinical system is put into place, it is understood that the system will require maintenance and occasional upgrades over its lifetime, will involve operational or support costs, and at some point will be replaced with yet another system. Therefore, the true cost of the overall product must include both the implementation and ongoing operational and maintenance costs.

During the initiation phase, it is important to compare alternative approaches, including full product life cycle costs rather than just project implementation costs. This provides the organization with a true picture of the cost of ownership and demonstrates how the solution provides the greatest value over its lifetime.

Cost-benefit: For the business case, estimate all one-time costs, such as development, acquisition, or purchase of hardware, software, middleware, licenses, leases, implementation costs, including project implementation, professional services, or other resource costs, and then total the costs so that they can be monitored throughout the course of the project life cycle and beyond into operations. Examples of these costs may be:

- Maintenance
- Required enhancements
- Upgrades
- Ongoing operation expenses

Calculating the anticipated benefits of the project includes considering tangible and intangible operational benefits, cost savings, cost avoidance, and other benefits that may be identified. These estimates of cost and benefit will determine the anticipated cost savings, revenue gain, and other benefits that are expected to result from the project.

Next, determine how the project will be funded. The project sponsor will play a key role in helping to secure appropriate funds and resources for the project. While this process varies from one organization to the next, it is common for an organization to have a financial budget that may include projected projects, or those previously identified as critical to the organization's strategic vision, as well as a pool of funds that may be discretionary. In some organizations, projects may be funded by the phase of the project so that each phase is evaluated independently and future funding is driven by the success of the project in meeting its anticipated objectives. Projects may be funded from a variety of sources, including internal and external sources, so be sure to indicate the amount of funds required, their primary source, and any special caveats or requirements of each contributor.

It is also recommended that the operational funding resources, those resources that will continue to fund the operational expenses once the project is complete, be identified along with the details of the costs. It is important that all financial considerations, for both implementation and ongoing support of the project, be clearly identified.

Schedule: The initiation phase of most projects does not generally include specific scheduling or schedule planning. While there should be general agreement on the scope of the project, specifics regarding implementation are not generally available in this phase. For this reason, it is usually not expected that anything more than a high-level schedule be provided. This should be made clear in the business case.

The high-level schedule information should include critical tasks, their expected duration, major decision points such as go/no-go decisions, and milestones. Milestones are major events that are identified as completed or not completed on a specified due date. Larger projects, those of lengthy duration or having multiple parts, are done in phases (e.g., evaluation, configuration, activation, etc.). Phasing should be defined in the schedule and make clear the tangible output of each phase. If the project is to be completed in a single phase, it should be clearly defined that way with an explanation as to why the single phase is the most appropriate approach.

Projects may also be planned for a staged implementation approach or one where different parts of the project are delivered at different times. These should be clearly defined as part of the project schedule, with specific deliverables and success criteria for each stage. Generally, each stage must be successfully deployed before the next stage is delivered.

Usually, late or overbudget projects that are seen as failures are actually only estimating failures. This can happen when estimates, usually made in the early stages of a project, are based on inadequate or incomplete data and are used as the expected final. This is a major risk to any project and requires that the initiation phase be clearly defined and articulated as estimates only. One successful approach to mitigating this risk is to update the estimates at each phase of the project. This can even be incorporated as a deliverable at the end of each stage to set an expectation for management and provide valuable reviews to ensure the project still has full support from the organization. Insistence that unreasonable cost and time targets be met only results in a dispirited project team, unhappy customers, poor-quality outcomes, and yet another project failure.

Task: Determine Cost and Schedule Estimates	
Cost	
	Estimate one-time costs, including development, acquisition, and implementation
	Estimate maintenance and ongoing operational costs expected after project completion
	Determine anticipated benefits of the project (including tangible and intangible benefits, revenue generation, cost savings, cost avoidance, and other benefits)
	Explain funding, including funding resources, percentage by resource (if multiple resources apply), and any caveats or requirements of each funding source
	Identify the level of confidence in the estimates
Schedule	
	Identify high-level tasks for the project, their duration, decision points, and milestones
	Describe the phases of the project, what each phase will deliver, or explain why phasing is not appropriate
	Identify the level of confidence in the estimates
	Document project costs and schedule in the business case

8. Identify potential risks. Every project is full of risks that can be expected or may arise during the course of the project. It is prudent to perform and document an initial risk assessment to identify, quantify, and establish contingencies and mitigation strategies for high-level risks that could adversely affect the outcome of the project.

A *risk* is usually regarded as any unplanned factor that may potentially interfere with successful completion of the project. A risk is not an issue. An *issue* is something you face now, whereas a risk is the recognition that a problem might occur. By recognizing potential problems, the project team can plan in advance how to deal with these factors.

It is also possible to look at a positive side of risk. A risk may be seen as a potentially useful outcome that occurs because of some unplanned event. In this case, the project team can attempt to maximize the potential of these positive risk events should they occur.

Task: Identify Key Potential Risks	
	Identify high-level risks, both positive and negative
	Assess impact and probability of risks occurring
	Establish contingency plans and mitigation strategies for identified risks
	Document key potential risks and contingency plans/mitigation strategies in the business case

Initiation Phase Deliverables

Business Case

The business case is a business proposal. It is a statement of the opportunity with details about the problem it solves, the solution it provides, the cost of the solution, and expected benefits. Once the project sponsor, key stakeholders, and others involved in the project (e.g., departmental business owners, information technology staff, financial representative, privacy and security officer) accept it, the business case is presented to upper management (or a group appointed by them) for review and approval.

If the project is approved by a project steering committee or other appropriate review group, the initiation phase is ended and planning begins. During planning, the project team, along with additional staff as needed, will begin the work of creating the project charter and other project planning documents.

Phase II: Project Planning

Overview

Project planning follows the project initiation phase and is one of the most important stages in project management. Project planning is not a single activity or task, but instead is a process that takes time and attention. Project planning defines the project activities needed to complete the project and how those activities will be accomplished. Time spent up front planning the project, identifying needs of the project and project team, and the structure for organizing and managing the project, saves countless hours of confusion and rework in the execution and controlling phases of the project. Without proper planning, time and cost estimates are generally at risk even before the project starts.

Proper planning will result in:

- A clearly defined charter
- A detailed and well-defined project scope
- More detailed cost and schedule for the project and a higher confidence level of previous estimates
- A list of defined deliverables and delivery dates
- An organized work plan
- Project sponsor, team, and management acknowledgment of work to be accomplished
- A framework for review and control

Without proper planning, a project's success will be left to chance. The project team will have limited knowledge of its tasks and expected outcomes, project activities may not be well defined or in proper sequence, and resource requirements or skill sets required will not be identified or defined. Even if the project is finished, it may not be seen as a success because the expectations and deliverables were not clearly defined. Planning will involve identifying and documenting the project's scope, specific tasks, project schedule, risk and risk mitigation plans, quality requirements, and staffing needs. The planning process is not complete until as many of these details as possible are identified and addressed.

The planning process should include the following steps:

- Estimating the size of the project
- Estimating the scope of the project
- Estimating the resources required to complete the project
- Documenting a schedule with tasks to be completed and sequencing
- Identifying risks and a high-level mitigation plan
- Determining quality indicators

All of these steps are needed to complete the project plan. The planning process may take several iterations and may change throughout the planning process until a final plan is completed; however, the plan must be complete before the next project phase is initiated.

Activities

The following is a list of key activities required to plan a project:

1. Assign a project manager. Every project needs a leader. Without a leader, project activities are left to vacillate, unorganized, undocumented, and without drive.

Assigning a project manager should not be underestimated in its importance. The skills the project manager offers are a major contributing factor to the success or failure of the project. The project manager is seen as the face of the project and, as such, will be a direct reflection of the department's commitment and competence in project management. A project manager's responsibilities generally include:

- Making day-to-day decisions on critical project issues, specifically keeping the project within its scope, schedule, and budget
- Managing project resources
- Providing direction, leadership, and support to project team members
- Maintaining project documentation (e.g., project charter, scope, schedule, budget, requirements, and testing)
- Managing planning and control of project activities and resources
- Developing and managing contracts with vendors
- Reporting project status and issues to the project sponsor and executive (oversight) committee(s)
- Providing teams with advice and input on tasks throughout the project
- Resolving conflicts
- Influencing stakeholders and team members in order to get buy-in on decisions that will lead to success

Taking these responsibilities into account, it is easy to see that a project manager must be able to perform at a leadership level for the project team and cannot be selected based on function or longevity within the organization, but rather for his or her project management, organizational, and leadership skills. The following skills should be considered when selecting a project manager:

- Project management skills and experience
- Interpersonal and team leadership skills
- Business and management skills
- Strong communication skills
- Experience within the project's technical arena
- Respect and recognition among peers

Project managers who are selected to lead a project but were not involved in the initiation phase must review the project initiation phase documentation to get a clear picture of the project. Remember, the initiation phase defined the business need or opportunity and set the foundation for all future project work.

Task: Assign a Project Manager	
	Assign a project manager
	Project manager reviews business case and other initiation phase documents
	Project manager establishes the project planning team

2. Develop the project charter. Once the project is approved and a project manager assigned, a project charter should be developed. Much of the information for the charter will come from the business case.
3. Define product/project scope. The project scope will define what is, or is not, to be included in the project. Scope statements should be as concise as possible. If the project is to produce a product, a product scope may be created. If not, a project scope is appropriate. Remember:

   – Product scope is a description of the product or service that is produced as an outcome of the project.
   – Project scope is a statement of the work required to create and implement the product or service as well as the work required to manage the project.

   Project scope is documented at a high level in the project charter. It should include a discussion of the proposed solution and the business processes that will be used. Scope statements are generally written at a high level, with the detail described later in the charter document.

Task: Define Project Scope	
	Identify what is included in the project (expected deliverables)
	Identify what is not included in the project
	Determine the general approach used to complete the project
	Document the project scope in the project charter

4. Define project objectives. Project objectives are the specific goals of the project. These objectives, when properly defined and met, lead to the accomplishments outlined in the business objectives. While business objectives relate to the goals and objectives of the organization, project objectives relate specifically to the immediate goals of the project. For example, the project goal "implement a new time-tracking system" has no value in and of itself. That goal only brings value to the organization when it leads to accomplishment of

the business objective (e.g., "reduce costs and improve productivity through improved resource management").

Project objectives are used to establish project performance goals—planned levels of accomplishment stated as measurable objectives that can be compared to actual results. Performance measures should be derived for each specific goal and should be quantified to ensure the project is meeting its objectives. Using SMART (specific, measurable, achievable, realistic, and time-sensitive) goals is the best means of setting project objectives.

Project objectives can be described in two ways:

- *Hard objectives* relate to the time, cost, and operational objectives (scope) of the product or service. Was the project on time? Within budget? Did it deliver its full scope?
- *Soft objectives* relate more to how the objectives are achieved. These generally include overall customer satisfaction, team satisfaction, quality of outcomes, and so forth.

Focus should be on the full set of project objectives, both hard and soft, to lead to a more complete project success. Focus only on hard objectives can lead to a completed project but one that is less than successful because the customer and project team are not satisfied or accepting of the final product.

Task: Define Project Objectives	
	Define SMART project objectives as they relate to business objectives
	Define stakeholders' expectations for success
	Document project objectives in the project charter

5. Identify project constraints and assumptions. All projects have constraints, or limiting factors, that need to be identified in the planning phase of the project. Every project has some limitations, whether people, money, time, equipment, regulatory requirements, or business limitations. While these may be adjusted up or down, they are considered fixed resources by the project manager and form the basis for managing the project. Additionally, certain elements relevant to a project are assumed to be essential. For instance, it is assumed that the organization will make resources, both budget and human resources, available to the project manager. These assumptions need to be defined and acknowledged before the project moves to the next phase.

The project charter must include an acknowledgment of project constraints and major assumptions. These defined items are an essential part of the project.

Task: Identify Project Constraints and Assumptions	
	Identify limiting factors (people, money, time, and equipment)
	Describe major project constraints
	Describe major project assumptions
	Document project constraints and assumptions in the project charter

6. Determine procurement and sourcing strategy. Most organizations will not be able to supply all the necessary resources needed to complete a project, and therefore they must purchase these from outside vendors. Entering into a contract with an outside vendor is a necessary part of the project. Therefore, developing a procurement and sourcing strategy that identifies those needs as part of the planning phase of the project can avoid unnecessary delays later in project activation.

   When to procure:

   - *Make-or-buy analysis*: This is a simple method to determine the cost-effectiveness of creating a product in-house compared to the cost of buying the product or having it produced from an outside vendor. All costs, both direct and indirect, should be considered when performing a make-or-buy analysis. These costs should be compared with each other, reviewed with the project team, and a final decision made based on pros and cons of each option. There may also be opportunity to lease versus purchase certain resources, and again, the pros and cons of each option should be fully discussed in consideration of the project or product to be delivered. Many of these decisions will be based on the length of need for the item or service, as well as the overall cost. It is important to plan a schedule that includes time for whichever option is selected.

   How to procure (contract types):

   - *Fixed-price or lump-sum contract*: This is a contract that involves paying a fixed, agreed upon price for a well-defined product or service. Products should be well established and the requirements well defined to reduce the risk of purchase.
   - *Cost reimbursement contract*: This contract type refers to a reimbursement to the vendor for the actual cost of producing the product or service. Costs within the contract are classified as direct (e.g., salaries to staff, development or building of the product) and indirect (e.g., vendor

overhead costs, research and development costs, etc.). Indirect costs are normally based on a percentage of direct costs.

- *Unit price contract*: The contractor is paid based on a preset amount for each unit (e.g., $10 per item produced) or unit of service (e.g., $50 per hour of service). The contract equals the total value of all the units purchased.

How much to procure: Procurement of products or services should be planned based on the project schedule. For example, how much supply is needed at the beginning of the project, later in the project, or after the project is complete? Budget availability is another important consideration: When will budget dollars become available for the purchase of needed supplies or services? It is also important to consider in the contracting negotiation phase that opportunities to reduce purchase price may be driven by the time and amount of purchase of these resources.

Task: Determine Procurement and Sourcing Strategy	
	Determine what to procure
	Determine when to procure
	Determine how to procure
	Determine how much to procure
	Document the procurement details in the project plan and charter

7. Develop project schedule/work plan

Develop a work breakdown structure (WBS): The WBS is designed to break the scope of the project into multiple steps required to deliver the project with all the objectives previously defined. Remember in the business plan that a very high level plan was presented to articulate the major milestones needed to achieve the expected outcomes. The WBS further breaks down the activities into manageable ones and includes durations, work effort, and resources.

Identify activities and sequencing: The WBS reflects activities associated with the overall design of the project, its requirements, design, implementation, testing, training, operationalization, installation, and maintenance. The project manager is responsible for facilitating and documenting identification of all top-level tasks associated with a project, and then assembling the appropriate resources to ferret out the details of the top-level tasks.

WBS tasks are developed by determining what needs to be done to accomplish the project objective. The choice of how detailed the WBS becomes is subjective and reflects the preferences and judgment of the project manager based on his or her experience with similar projects. As levels of the WBS become more detailed, the scope, complexity, and cost of each subtask become more accurate. The lowest-level tasks, or work packages, are independent, manageable units that are planned, budgeted, scheduled, and controlled individually. However, while the project manager must be sure the appropriate level of detailed planning is done, creating a work plan that is too large and unmanageable creates unnecessary risk to the project.

In addition to identifying the tasks needed to reach project objectives, the order in which tasks must be completed is equally important, Activity sequencing involves dividing the project into smaller, manageable components (activities) and then specifying their order of completion. When creating the WBS, this may be simultaneously done so that the WBS is created in a logical sequence that makes sense to the project team.

Identify activity dependencies: The WBS creates a hierarchy of tasks and task relationships. Each task group rolls up into a higher-level group until all tasks are complete and ultimately project objectives are attained. Activity dependencies exist when tasks must be completed in order, or when one task must be completed before other tasks can begin. These are task dependencies (or constraints) and must be included as part of the overall project schedule.

Develop project schedule or work plan: After all project activities are identified, including their order of completion and dependencies, a project schedule or work plan can be created. The project schedule/work plan provides a detailed representation of tasks, milestones, dependencies, resource requirements, task duration, work effort, and deadlines. The project's master schedule links all tasks on a common timescale so that the full duration of the project to reach project objectives is clearly defined. The schedule/work plan should be detailed enough to show each task to be performed, who is responsible for that task, when it is expected to begin and end, and the full duration of the task.

Task: Develop Project Schedule/Work Plan	
	Identify activities and sequencing to complete the project
	Estimate each activity's duration, work effort, dependencies, and resource requirements
	Determine activity dependencies
	Create the project schedule/work plan

8. Establish milestones. A successful project includes milestones or key activities that must be completed throughout the project. These milestones are used

as checkpoints to ensure the project is progressing at a satisfactory level. The project manager will use the milestone events as a means of communicating project status with the project sponsor, and executive committee project milestones are recorded in the project plan and charter.

- *Phase exit criteria* are deliverables, approvals, or events that must occur before the project team is allowed to declare that phase complete. These are marked as milestones and reviewed with the team, executive steering committee, and project sponsor for agreement.
- *Phase entrance criteria* are materials, personnel, approvals, or other matters that must be available before the project team can begin the next phase. In some cases, project managers may need to get approval from the project sponsor and executive committee before moving forward to the next phase if budgeting or project approval is contingent on project progress and realignment with strategic business goals.

Task: Establish Project Life Cycle Phase Checkpoints	
	Establish milestones with clearly defined planned dates to measure progress
	Establish entrance criteria for each phase
	Establish exit criteria for each phase

9. Develop human resource requirements. In every project, a finite set of resources will be needed to complete the project. Once the project schedule is complete and resources are assigned to each task, the overall work effort needed to complete the project becomes evident. Generally, resources are a limited commodity and may require augmentation from external resources. One of the primary roles of the project manager is to identify all the required skill sets needed to complete the identified tasks in the project schedule/work plan and then to procure the people with those skills throughout the life cycle of the project. Resource planning then becomes the documented process to execute tasks in the order in which they are required to deliver the product required.

   Identify required skill sets by role: It is helpful in the planning process to develop a list of skills required, first for execution of the project and then for execution of each task. This skills list may then be used to determine the type of staff required for the task. It is helpful to create a roles and responsibilities document that generally describes responsibilities of key roles within the project. After assigning individuals to these roles, the project manager should review these roles with team members so that each individual understands expectations throughout the course of the project.

Acquire project team members: Organizations vary in the way in which resources may be assigned to a project. Some organizations may have a resource pool of available individuals who may be used for projects. Other organizations select from the entire organization to fill project roles. Regardless, understanding the skills needed to fill the needs of the project is essential.

The project manager has a primary role of securing necessary resources to complete the project, taking advantage of and maximizing skilled labor that is available. The project manager will be responsible for identifying any skills that are required by the project tasks but not available within the resource pool, and to build a plan that realistically accounts for those skills or lack thereof. Skill sets may not be the only deciding factor in assigning resources to the project team. The project manager must also ensure that team members will work well together and that conflicts are managed throughout the project life cycle. Additionally, team members may come and go throughout the project and may be part of the team only for the short time in which their skills are needed. Should available resources be unable to fill the required skill sets needed for the project, the project manager may have an option to hire the necessary talent or contract services to perform the work.

Update project schedule/work plan (e.g., load resources): Using the project tool provided by the organization, it is essential to capture the tasks and work assignments for each resource. This is a critical part of the planning process to ensure tasks have the appropriate level of resources, as well as ensuring the resources are available during the task duration to complete the task. This should be documented in the project plan.

Create human resource plan documents: The resource plan should consist of roles and responsibilities, to include project sponsor, executive steering committee, project manager, team leaders, and team members. Additionally, a hierarchal representation of how each team member is accountable should be constructed and reviewed with the team to ensure a clear understanding of communication and escalation paths.

Task: Define Project Organizations and Governance
Identify required skill sets by role
Assign/acquire project team members
Update project schedule/work plan (e.g., load resources)
Create human resource plan documents
Resource plan is accepted by project sponsor, team members, and executive committee

10. Identify other resource requirements. External to the human resource requirements, all project teams require the tools to successfully perform their tasks. In scheduling resources, the project manager must ensure that both people and equipment necessary to support the project team are available simultaneously. As part of the project schedule/work plan, the project manager must ensure all resources are available as needed.

> Workspace requirements: The project manager must recognize the needed workspace for people and equipment. It is desirable for all project team members to be housed in the same location whenever possible to facilitate interaction and communication. Team spirit and synergy are enhanced and chances for project success are increased when everyone is close together. While this may not always be feasible, it is a goal worth striving toward.
>
> Infrastructure, equipment, and material needs: In addition to workspace, equipment for the team should be included in the resource plan. Ensuring the availability of equipment at critical points in the project is key in planning a successful project. In some cases, there may be a need to procure and store equipment as part of the project; space must be made available for receiving, processing, and eventually deploying these products. When considering equipment, it is imperative that team members have the tools to do their jobs, so if additional equipment is needed for the team members, it should be part of the resource plan and secured as early as possible.

Update the resource plan document.

Task: Identify Other Resource Requirements	
	Determine facility needs
	Determine infrastructure, equipment, and material needs
	Update the resource plan document

11. Refine project cost estimate and budget. Budget planning is done in parallel with project schedule/work plan development. Remember, in the business case development, high-level budget planning was performed. During the project schedule planning, resource requirements are refined and budget adjustments may be identified. This is a crucial process in making sure that all costs associated with the project are identified and, if costs exceed the initial approved budget, that there is opportunity for review with the project sponsor and executive committee.

    Budgeting serves as a control mechanism where actual costs can be compared with and measured against the project budget. The budget is a constraint that must be continuously managed and reported on with the plan sponsor.

When a project schedule begins to slip, cost is proportionally affected. When project costs begin to escalate, the project manager should revisit the project plan to determine whether scope, budget, or schedule needs adjusting.

To develop the budget, the applicable cost factors associated with project tasks are identified. The development of costs for each task should be simple and direct and consist of labor, material, and other direct costs. The cost of performing a task is directly related to the personnel assigned to the task, the duration of the task, and the cost of any nonlabor items required by the task.

Budget estimates are generally obtained from the people responsible for managing the work efforts. They provide the expertise required to make the estimate and provide buy-in and accountability during the actual performance of the task. These team members identify people or labor categories required to perform the work, and multiply the cost of the labor by the number of hours required to complete the task. Determining how long the task performance takes is the single most difficult part of deriving a cost estimate. The labor costs should factor in vacation time, sick leave, breaks, meetings, and other day-to-day activities. Not including these factors jeopardizes both scheduling and cost estimates.

Nonlabor charges include such items as material costs, travel, cost of capital purchases, leasing fees (if applicable), software licenses, and other variable costs associated with tangible items.

All of this information is captured in the project budget and should be included as part of the business plan and project charter.

Task: Refine Project Cost Estimate and Budget	
	Identify the applicable cost factors associated with project tasks. The development of costs for each task should be simple and direct and consist of labor, material, and other direct costs.
	Identify people or labor categories required to perform the work and multiply the cost of the labor by the number of hours required to complete the task
	Include nonlabor charges
	Include all one-time and recurring costs
	Baseline approved project budget

12. Risk analysis: As discussed in the initiation phase, a risk is any factor that may potentially interfere with successful completion of the project. A risk is not a problem: a *problem* is a situation that has already occurred; a *risk* is the

recognition that a problem might occur. By recognizing potential problems (risks), the project manager can attempt to avoid or minimize their occurrence through proper planning or mitigation.

Risk analysis is a formal process for identifying potential problems, the probability of their occurrence, and actions that will minimize the chances of their occurring or minimize their impact to the project. In most cases, the project team will identify risks throughout the development of the project schedule.

Task: Risk Analysis	
	Identify potential project risks
	Assess impact and probability of risks occurring
	Determine a risk response, including any contingency plans
	Record risk data in the risk analysis plan document
	If a project management tool is used, document the risks and mitigation plans in the tool

13. Develop quality management plan. Providing a quality product or service is essential to every project. Often this most important aspect is left out of the project planning phase or does not have a documented plan with important customer acceptance. The purpose of using a good quality management plan is to ensure products and services meet the business plan objectives. Quality management consists of three very distinct processes: quality planning, quality assurance, and quality control.

During the business case planning, metrics to measure project success should have been established. These metrics should be documented and periodically measured throughout the course of the project. Additionally, during the development of milestones, key deliverables should be identified. Many times these milestones can be quantified and also serve as quality measurements.

The project team should discuss quality standards and how best to meet those. Product acceptance criteria should be part of the project planning and reviewed at routine intervals.

Successful quality processes always strive to see quality through the eyes of the end user (customer). Customers are the ultimate judges of the quality of the product they receive and will typically judge a project by whether or not their requirements are met. To ensure delivery of a quality product, the project team should ensure that requirements are addressed at each phase of the project.

Task: Develop Quality Management Plan	
	Define the quality standards that pertain to this project
	Describe how the project team is to meet those quality standards
	Define the audit process and schedule that will be used in the project to evaluate overall project performance
	Define the process that will ensure that customer requirements are met
	Document the quality plan as part of the overall project plan

14. Determine issue management strategy. The purpose of issue management is to provide a mechanism for organizing, maintaining, and tracking the resolution of issues that cannot be resolved at the individual level. This plan should consist of issue reporting, escalation path, tracking and reporting, and assigning priority to each problem. This important process should enable the project team to quickly report issues without waiting for other formal communication methods, and provide the project manager with a means of quickly assessing and addressing issues that may jeopardize the project.

Task: Issue Management Strategy	
	Determine issue management approach
	Define reporting and escalation procedures
	Define process for issue resolution

15. Managing scope change. Project scope management is a critical part of every project. Remember the mention of scope creep above, which can easily jeopardize a project. Having an established change policy and methodology for processing change requests is critical to every project manager. Often the project management office will have a documented change process that can easily be followed. It is imperative that the project team be educated on this process.

Task: Managing Scope Change	
	Define process for identifying and documenting change requests

16. Develop a project communication plan. Communication planning is a critical part of every project. Information exchange across all those

involved in the project is essential. From the project team members to the project manager, from the project manager to the stakeholders and executive committee and ultimately to the customer, communication is a critical success factor for every project. The communication plan, therefore, must identify which people need what information, when it will be needed, and how they will get it. Communication is the cornerstone of how work gets done among different parties within a project and must be free-flowing. Communications planning should incorporate how information will be shared and when it will be shared; set expectations for status reporting, issues management, problem resolution; etc. The communication plan should include defined steps to communicate with regularity with the project team, stakeholder, and executive committee, and provide a feedback mechanism for the customer and any end users that may be impacted by the product or service being developed, and may include marketing representatives as resources. This information is documented in the communication plan.

Task: Develop Project Communication Plan	
	Determine who needs what information and when
	Determine how to communicate information (memo, e-mail, weekly/monthly meetings, etc.)
	Document in the communication plan

17. Develop a project plan. The *project plan* is completed in the planning phase of a project and includes all the components discussed so far. For large projects, a team may be dedicated for the single purpose of creating the project plan, while smaller projects will likely be developed as part of the project whole. Project plans should be completed in cooperation with the project sponsor, key stakeholders, project manager, and team members, and ultimately reviewed with and approved by the customer.

The project plan is never a static document, but rather an iterative process. Each element of the plan is regularly reviewed for changes and refinements, based on further analysis and decisions made in developing other plan elements. This refinement also develops buy-in from the project team and stakeholders. However, once the project plan is finalized, any additional changes or adjustments must go through the change management process. It is critical to get buy-in to the project plan from the involved parties prior to actually starting the project. Approval of the plan commits the resources needed to perform the work.

Task: Develop Project Plan	
	Consolidate outcomes from planning phase activities
	Develop the project plan document; have it reviewed and gain approval
	Distribute the project plan according to the communication plan
	Project plan completed and approved

Deliverables

Project Plan

The project plan is a formal, approved document used to manage and control project execution. It is a compilation of text and stand-alone deliverables created during the initiation and planning stages. The level of detail should be appropriate for the scope, complexity, and risk of the project.

The following is a list of key components usually included in a project plan:

- Project charter
  - Project overview
  - Business objectives
  - Scope statement
  - Project objectives
  - Constraints and assumptions
  - Project deliverables and milestones
  - Project procurement and sourcing strategy
  - Project cost estimate and budget
- Project plan
  - Work breakdown structure (WBS)
  - Project schedule/work plan
  - Risk analysis
  - Quality management plan
- Project organization and governance
  - External resources
  - Internal resources
  - Roles and responsibilities
- Issue management
- Scope management
- Communication plan

Once the project manager completes the project plan, it should be reviewed and approved by the project team, including the business owners, project sponsor, and executive committee. The level and extent to which the plan will be reviewed is based on the size of the project as stated in dollars or period of time. Ultimately, the review process allows for executive management buy-in and approval of the plan. Once the project plan is approved and signed, the project manager is given the authority to complete the current project efforts and enter into the execution phase.

Phases III and IV: Project Execution, and Monitoring and Controlling

Overview

A project manager's responsibilities and skills really begin to be taxed once the execution phase starts. Because a project manager is responsible to internal and external stakeholders, the project team, vendors, executive management, and others, the visibility of the position is intensified because many of these people will now expect to see and discuss the resulting deliverables that were detailed in the planning phase. As a project manager, it is important to stay at the appropriate management level and not become task oriented beyond managing the overall project. Micromanaging at the project manager level will most certainly alienate the resource team and distract the project manager from the real goal of keeping the project moving forward and achieving its objectives on time and within budget.

Once a project moves into the project execution, and monitoring and controlling phases, the project team and the necessary resources to carry out the project should be in place and ready to perform their tasks. At this point, the team should be well prepared for the tasks ahead of them, recognizing their role and responsibilities, how to identify and report issues, and what quality control measures are in place, and be ready to move forward with confidence. The project plan should be complete and a baseline established from which to measure any variances that may occur. The project team should be focused on the project at hand and have confidence in their leader, the project manager.

Executing the project plan simply means taking the project schedule and completing the task. Monitoring and controlling the project is the primary responsibility of the project manager, in concert with the project team. Activities should be carried out effectively and efficiently, ensuring that measurements against project plans, specifications, and the original project feasibility concept continue to be collected, analyzed, and acted upon throughout the project life cycle. Particular attention must be paid to keeping interested parties up to date with project status, dealing with procurement and contract administration issues, helping manage quality control, and monitoring project risk. This is an important time for the project manager to be sure the team is working effectively together and achieving the desired results.

Project control involves the regular review of metrics and status reports in order to identify variances from the planned project baseline. These variances are determined by comparing the actual performance metrics from the initiation phase to the metrics achieved during project execution. Variances caught early and addressed immediately will help keep the project on track. The project schedule, including timing and resource alignment, may need to be periodically adjusted should unexpected problems or issues occur. In some cases, change management processes may need to be invoked to realign the schedule, resources, or budget. For example, a missed milestone date may require adjustments in resources for overtime or additional staff, which may result in budget overages. Project control also includes taking preventative action in anticipation of possible problems.

Activities

The following is a list of key activities required to execute, and manage and control a project:

1. Communication. The project communication plan is an important factor in the execution, and monitoring and controlling phases. Team members must effectively communicate with their team leader or project manager to keep the project on target. The project sponsor, internal and external stakeholders, and business partners expect to be kept informed of how the project is progressing. To that end, the project manager may employ several levels of communications:

   - The project manager should stay in constant communication with the project team, both formally and informally. Informal discussion is sometimes the best way to determine team morale, true project status, looming difficulties, etc.
   - Meeting minutes should be made available to stakeholders along with any "to do" lists that may have been generated during the meetings.
   - Routine (monthly) status reports should be offered to the project sponsor and other stakeholders as a means of providing a general overview of project status. These are generally generated by the project management tool being used.
   - A high-level project plan should be accessible to all stakeholders. This may be accomplished by providing access to a project management tool or providing routine updates.

– Joint project reviews are a good way to bring visibility to all areas of the project. They provide an opportunity to discuss important issues and make management decisions on the project with input from several sources. Joint project reviews can involve the project manager, project team members, project stakeholders, and department management, depending on the issues being discussed.

Task: Communication
Ensure that the communication plan is being executed as planned
Revise the communication plan based on feedback received from stakeholders and project team members

2. Risk management. Identifying new risks, monitoring known risks, and developing/implementing contingency plans are key tools for successfully completing a project. Part of controlling a project during the execution, and monitoring and controlling phases is to have implemented the risk management process developed in the planning phase. This process is a key component of project planning and should be kept current until the project is closed.

Risk management plays a vital role in the management of technology projects since the solution may include undeveloped or unproven technologies that may be critical to the infrastructure. For that reason, technology project managers must continuously monitor for unforeseen problems and be able to work with the project team quickly to identify potential solutions. These types of projects generally carry the highest level of risk and require the most skilled project team and project manager.

Task: Risk Management
Document all known risk in a project management tool
Include a risk summary in the regular status meetings—monthly status report
Providing consistent and ongoing evaluation of risk items and development of risk strategies
Identify new risks (e.g., risk assessment)
Evaluate new and existing risks (e.g., potential project risks)
Define/refine risk response strategies
Conduct regular follow-up risk assessments based on magnitude of the project

3. Schedule management. It is important for the project team to understand at all times exactly where the project stands with respect to the schedule (i.e., is the project ahead of or behind schedule?). The process used to communicate task status and then overall project status is critical to accurately depicting current work efforts and ensuring schedules are maintained.

Each team member or team leader should be expected to provide updates, including notes, quality issues, and work comments, for each of his or her responsible tasks in a project management tool. This real-time update provides invaluable information to fellow team members and the project manager for addressing schedule, quality, issues, and risks associated with the project.

Schedule control is one of the most difficult but important activities within the project control phase. The project schedule can be affected by any number of issues, including resource issues, funding, and vendor performance external influences, among others. The ability of a project manager to manage the schedule and keep the team focused is a critical part of his or her responsibilities.

Schedule issues may come from a variety of sources, but schedule changes should be dealt with consistently. If a potential schedule problem occurs, the problem should be immediately investigated and the cause determined quickly. Once the schedule problem is uncovered, an immediate plan should be created for correcting the problem in the shortest allowable time with the least impact. The promptness with which this occurs may directly affect the ability to recover with minimal amount of impact; however, every schedule change should be analyzed for potential risk to the project and overall budget.

It is standard practice to baseline the schedule at the start of the project. This allows all schedule changes to be displayed against the original project schedule/work plan. If schedule slippage becomes significant, adjustments to the baseline may be advisable. Any change to the baseline should be done only after the change management process has occurred.

Every project is constrained by its scope, schedule, and budget; however, stakeholders may see meeting the schedule as the prime imperative. If this is the case, change control for the schedule and communication of the change is imperative to keeping the customer and stakeholders satisfied. It is a good idea for project managers to hold regular project schedule/work plan reviews with the team and to update stakeholders as frequently as may be needed to ensure their comfort level with the project. Large or complex projects may have several schedules being managed at a deliverable or functional level; therefore, having the "owners" of these schedules meeting at regular intervals is critical to the overall project schedule remaining on track. The project manager is responsible for integrating these project schedule/work plans and making them understandable for all of the project's stakeholders.

Task: Schedule Management	
	Collect and validate schedule status
	Validate work effort to ensure that the schedules are accurate
	Conduct regular project schedule/work plan review meetings. Large or complex projects may require more frequent meetings
	Identify potential schedule problems
	Investigate potential schedule problems and uncover the cause as soon as possible
	Develop a plan for correcting schedule problems in the shortest allowable time with the least impact
	Make the customer aware whenever a schedule change occurs
	In the event of severe schedule slippage, re-baseline the project schedule/work plan

4. Document work results. Work results are the end results of each task. To stay on schedule, each work effort should be updated to show when it is completed, any issues associated with the work effort, quality indicator results, work effort required, and costs. The project management tool should be updated with this information to allow appropriate performance reporting.

Tasks: Document Work Results	
	Project deliverables are produced and work products are tracked

5. Scope management. Project scope should have been specifically stated as part of the project charter, and therefore contains the requirements of the project. Scope management is thus ensuring that all elements in the scope are carried forward so that any changes that could impact the scope, either to increase or to limit scope, are immediately addressed. Scope control, therefore, is avoiding scope creep as well as controlling scope reduction.

Scope changes will come from the perceived need for a change in a project deliverable that may affect its functionality and in most cases the amount of work needed to perform the project. A scope change is critical.

Scope changes most likely will require a change in project funding, resources, or time. All scope change requests should be submitted in writing and must be approved by the project sponsor, stakeholders, and customer. A committee that consists of stakeholders from all areas of the project should be willing to convene and discuss the potential change and its anticipated impact on the project. This group of stakeholders should be a predefined cross section of people that will have the ability to commit their interests at a strategic management level. Once a decision is made to increase or reduce scope, the change must be authorized by all members of the committee. Any changes that are agreed upon must be documented and signed as a matter of formal scope control.

For technology projects, scope control is critical, especially when producing a product. It is not uncommon when team members are doing their development testing or implementation work for them to try to get creative or give the customer something other than, or in addition to, the original stated requirements. Doing any work that is outside or beyond the stated work, as called out in the original requirements, is considered scope creep.

Task: Scope Management	
	Identify potential scope change
	Evaluate impact of potential scope change
	Determine if additional project funds, resources, and time will be required
	Ensure that the scope change is beneficial
	Convene a committee to review the scope change
	Update planning documents with scope change
	Communicate change to the project team

6. Quality management. Quality control involves monitoring specific project results to determine if they comply with quality standards and seeking ways to eliminate unsatisfactory results. It is expected that quality control be performed throughout the course of the project. Quantifiable results, such as deliverables, and management results, cost and schedule performance, should all be part of quality control. In some organizations a specific group of staff may be assigned to do quality control for projects, although this is not a requirement for quality management to be in place.

Task: Manage Quality	
	Monitor specific project results to determine if they comply with relevant quality standards and to identify ways to eliminate causes of unsatisfactory results
	Establish quality management awareness and training program
	Project team members accept responsibility for quality

7. Budget management. Budget management is a critical part of the project manager's responsibility. If the project has been appropriately planned in the initiation and planning phases, the necessary budget to complete the project is available. The project manager, then, must ensure that costs do not exceed those approved, and he or she must follow a strict change control process. Often, budget overages are not the result of a single issue but rather a compilation of smaller problems that accumulate over time. Staying on budget is often seen as the most critical constraint for a project and must be managed accordingly.

Cost control involves understanding why budget variances occur, in both the positive and the negative. It requires the same diligence in management as scope control, schedule control, and quality management. Setting budget limits and monitoring variances must be done early in the project and repeated often. Budget problems tend to compound themselves if left unattended. On a technology project, more money could be spent trying to fix budget, scope, or schedule issues near the end of a project than should have been spent on the entire project. In many cases the budget is a fixed amount, so if other actions fail to bring the project's costs into budget alignment, the scope must be reduced.

Task: Manage Costs	
	Monitor cost performance to detect variances
	Document variances between the scheduled and actual costs
	Inform appropriate stakeholders about authorized changes

8. Issue management. Issue management is the process of organizing, maintaining, and tracking issues and their resolution. Issue management should consist of controlling issues identified through the course of the project, prioritizing to ensure those issues with the greatest risk of impact to the project are worked on first, and using sound problem-solving techniques to reach resolution.

The issue management process should give everyone involved with, or affected by, the project a way to report issues or problems. Usually a project management tool is provided to capture issues, but something as simple as a shared Excel worksheet will provide the same level of documentation. Some issues may remain throughout the project if they are determined to be of minimal impact, and the cost to resolve the issue will pose risk to the project. In some cases, issues may be escalated to the executive team if they are of great significance or pose risk to the schedule, scope, or budget.

Task: Issue Management	
	Maintain a repository of project issues
	Review issues on a regular basis
	Track all issues until they are resolved

9. Conduct update meetings. The project manager plays a key role in the communication process and, as such, is required to coordinate a number of communication opportunities or meetings. The project team should meet routinely to provide an opportunity to update the work effort, communicate problems and issues, and understand the overall project schedule, budget, and quality. Additionally, the project manager is responsible for communicating outside the project team, with stakeholders, both internal and external, the project sponsor, and the executive oversight committee. Communication may take the form of an informal review or may be a formal process, based on the size and complexity of the project.

A standard requirement of all projects is to provide status reporting. Although the format and frequency of these reports may vary, they should include specific information to address project constraints of scope, budget, and schedule, along with risks, issues, and quality controls. In order for reports to be accurate, however, team members must update the project tool.

Communication should be directed to three distinct audiences:

- *Project*—Status meeting includes the lowest level of detail and provides an opportunity for the project team to discuss the current state and for the project manager to discuss the overall project status, issues, and to escalate problems or risks. For large, complex projects with multiple project teams, this level of meeting should be about bringing the teams together for a collaborative update.
- *Sponsor*—Sponsor meetings are a venue for the project manager to discuss key project issues and escalation points with the sponsor. The sponsor is generally there to help resolve key or organizational issues and provide general direction to the team.
- *Executive steering committee*—The executive steering committee meeting is intended to be a forum for the committee to evaluate the overall progress of the project and hear updates specific to scope, schedule, and budget. If the sponsor is part of the executive steering committee, these meetings may be combined to avoid duplication.

Task: Conduct Update Meetings	
	For large or complex projects, each project team leader conducts a weekly status meeting with his or her team
	The project manager conducts weekly status meetings with team or team leaders
	Conduct monthly meetings with project sponsor, including providing status reports
	Conduct monthly executive steering committee meeting using status report to identify key issues

10. Review project life cycle checkpoints. The project manager, along with the project sponsor, executive committee, and stakeholders, ensures the project is progressing appropriately by reviewing key milestones and critical checkpoints throughout the project. In some cases, completion of a phase may require approval to move to the next phase of the project.

Task: Review Project Life Cycle Checkpoints	
	Review exit criteria and associated deliverables of completed phase
	Review deliverables and milestones
	Failing projects are stopped or corrective action is taken
	On-track projects are authorized to continue

11. Administer vendor contracts. The project manager is responsible for management of vendor contracts throughout the duration of the project. Vendor management includes ensuring the vendor is delivering quality services on time and within the cost constraints agreed upon. The project manager must be responsible for the vendor, as he or she is for internal resources, and must obtain the same information from the vendor as he or she would from other project team members.

Contract administration is the process of ensuring that the vendor's performance meets contractual requirements. This is accomplished by monitoring the vendor's performance, obtaining progress reports and project plan updates, inspecting for quality, and approving deliverables.

Setting up procedures for contract control is vital to dealing with unexpected situations during project development, testing, and implementation. Without procedures in place, issues can go unresolved or result in project delays. It is important that the project manager have a strong communication plan with the vendors during the course of the project.

Task: Administer Vendor Contract	
	Project managers will also be responsible for tracking, reviewing, and analyzing the performance of contractors on a project
	Participate in oversight and review of any contract changes that will affect the project
	Ensure vendor adherence to application development and project management methodologies

12. Update project documents. During the execution, and monitoring and controlling phases, the project plan is implemented and may be changed as

needed. Modifications may be needed as a result of work still to be done, changes in scope, resource changes, or other unforeseen circumstances.

Assuming project baselines were created, changes may be necessary to formally reflect approved changes. Project documentation should include updates to the budget baseline, schedule baseline, risk documents, and project tool.

Task: Update Project Documents	
	Revise project plan baselines (through formal change control process)
	Revise other project documentation as needed

Deliverables

Project Status Reports

Routine status reports should communicate the following:

- Current schedule status
- Significant accomplishments for the current reporting period, including deliverables and milestones
- Planned activities for the next reporting period
- Financial status
- Present issues, concerns, and risks

Updated Planning Documents

Deliverables in this stage include consistent and updated planning documents, such as the project schedule, budget, scope, issues, risks, communication plan, etc.

Project-Specific Deliverables

Deliverables and milestones identified during the planning phase of the project and documented in the project charter should be documented as to their completion date and any issues remaining from the deliverable.

Phase V: Project Closeout

Overview

The last major stage of a project's life cycle is project closeout. The project closeout is completed once all defined project tasks and milestones have been completed and the customer has accepted the project's deliverables.

When planning for the closeout, the project manager should consider that, even though all project tasks may be closed, the project closeout cannot occur until there is formal acceptance by the executive committee, project sponsor, and key stakeholders. Documentation presented for the closeout meeting should include evidence of all project deliverables and acceptance of those deliverables, remaining open project issues and recommended action plan for closure, and a formal acknowledgment document.

Key activities to be conducted as part of the project closeout should include return of resources to their primary positions, closeout of any financial requirements, including internal budget review, and outstanding requirements from the vendor. A formal review meeting to identify lessons learned throughout the project should be conducted and documented in the project management tool. Project documents should be finalized and archived as part of the project closure. Finally, always celebrate project successes with the project team, stakeholders, and affected parties.

Activities

The following is a list of key activities required to close out a project:

1. Conduct final acceptance meeting. The issue of primary importance with project closure is the acceptance of the product or project by the customer. The best way to secure this is by holding a final meeting with all necessary stakeholders to review the product delivered against the baseline requirements and specifications. Any deviations from the established baseline should have been documented and approved, but it is still necessary to document any variations from the scope, schedule, or budget for stakeholder review.

   The final deliverable of this meeting should be an acceptance statement created by the project manager describing the project's final deliverables and requiring the stakeholders' signatures.

Task: Conduct Final Acceptance Meeting	
	Obtain formal acceptance from stakeholders and executive committee
	Evaluate project to determine if business and project objectives and benefits were achieved

2. Conduct final contract review. Vendor contract closure is another critical process in closing out a project. Vendor meetings should be conducted to finalize acceptance testing of the product and to verify all terms of the contract have been met. Contracts may have been for the duration of the project or may be extended to include operational coverage well beyond the terms of the project.

Contracts can be brought to closure for a variety of reasons, including contract completion, early termination, or failure to perform. Regardless, closure of the contract term, even if it is beyond the scope of the initial project, should be performed.

Task: Conduct Final Contract Review	
	Review contract and related documents
	Validate that the contractor has met all of its contractual requirements
	Resolve contractor variances and issues
	Terminate current contract

3. Conduct outcomes assessment. An outcomes assessment meeting is an essential part of closure for the project team. It provides an open discussion to review project strengths, weaknesses, and challenges. The project team is able to put closure to any remaining open issues and discuss opportunities for improving the project process.

The outcomes assessment meeting should include the project team, sponsor, stakeholders, and vendors. Items of discussion should include customer satisfaction, final budget, scope and schedule reviews, open issue review, and risk review. It is equally important for the team to provide feedback for what went well in the project and opportunities to improve the process.

A final project report is generally completed to document the full project through all phases, ending in a final review of the triple project constraints of scope, schedule, and budget. This report should also include recommendations from the team for improving the project and specifically improving project processes. Sharing this report among other project managers is a key to continuing to improve project methodology in the organization.

Task: Conduct Outcomes Assessment	
	Document project successes and failures
	Determine the extent that business and project objectives, and benefits were achieved
	Compile lessons learned
	Complete the final project report

4. Conduct knowledge transfer. All documentation that has anything to do with the product itself (including design documents, schematics, technical manuals) that has not already been turned over to operations should be completed and turned over during an operational transition meeting.

All documentation pertaining to the project should be compiled. This includes contracts, meeting minutes, project plans, charter, and other materials not archived in the project tool. Generally the project management office maintains all materials related to projects. Summary documentation, such as technical specifications, technical documentation, operations manuals, and the like, will be turned over to the operations group. Project documentation should be stored in an archival fashion, either through the project tool, on CD, or in a project binder for future reference. Contracts should be archived as a part of the project unless it is to be maintained for operational purposes, in which case a copy should be retained with the project documentation and the original turned over to operations.

Task: Conduct Knowledge Transfer	
	Turn all documentation related to the product over to operations
	Confirm all end users have been adequately trained
	Create an archive for project documentation

Deliverables

Project Closure Document

The project closure document summarizes the agreement with the project sponsor and stakeholders and confirms:

- The product meets requirements and specifications as outlined in the charter
- Deviations are documented and approved with applicable action plans
- Issues are closed or have been acknowledged with an action plan
- Agreement to the project closure by the project sponsor and key stakeholders

Final Project Report

The final project report creates a historical look at the project and includes both planned and actual scope, schedule, and budget summaries. Any quality metric outcomes should be documented along with open actionable items. Final assessment documentation, including lessons learned, should also be included in the project report.

Conclusion

This chapter has reviewed the methodology a project manager should use during the initiating, planning, managing, controlling and executing, and closing stages of every project. The described phases, tasks, and deliverables suggested for each phase are only a proposed method for reaching a successful project implementation. Repeatable methodology more often than not leads to success.

References

1. David I. Cleland, Roland Gareis. 2006. *Global project management handbook*, 1–4. McGraw-Hill Professional.
2. HIMSS Project Management Task Force, Nancy Stetson, JoAnn W. Klinedinst. 2008. *Why have a project management methodology in healthcare? How to deliver successful projects*. Chicago: HIMSS.

Chapter 4

Nursing Roles in the Implementation of Clinical Information Systems

Terry Moore

Contents

An electronic health record (EHR) is a standardized, efficient, and accessible way to provide information to clinical staff across the continuum of care. A clinical information system (CIS) is the foundation of the EHR. Most healthcare institutions have embraced the 1999 Institute of Medicine report *To Err Is Human: Building a Safer Health System*. This study identified that faulty systems or processes most commonly cause errors.[1] Follow-up studies from the IOM, *Crossing the Quality Chasm*[2] and *Keeping Patients Safe: Transforming the Work Environment of Nurses*,[3] address the role systems play in safe, quality care. Driving forces for CIS implementations include clear documentation, real-time access, timely execution of orders, and quality care consistent with best practice.[4] Successful implementation relies on identifying key clinical champions and defining their specific role in the implementation. While all clinical stakeholders are important to the implementation, nurses can play a unique role in each phase, and at every level, of the implementation. Including nurses in the selection, design, and implementation teams and giving them a significant role is one key to a successful implementation. Nurses can facilitate end-user engagement, enhance system design, provide education, sponsor change management, and effectively communicate to all other stakeholders. Because their focus is patient-centered care, they can support most clinical disciplines where tapping into this pool of experts is a recognized way to successful implementation.

Implementation Roles

There are many roles in a CIS implementation. Different levels of experience are needed and responsibilities vary for each role. Since system implementation has many phases and each phase requires different knowledge and skills, the roles and responsibilities vary at each phase. The phases include system selection, design and go-live, and system optimization. Implementation roles include executive sponsor, project director, team leader, clinical system analyst, educator, and super-user.

One important team in the process is the executive steering committee, which assumes responsibility for the project, ensuring that the vision is identified and communicated, and escalated issues are resolved. The committee members provide top-down, visible support to the team members. Very often the chief nursing officer (CNO) and the chief information officer (CIO) co-chair this committee, and additional members attending this committee include the chief financial officer (CFO), chief medical officer (CMO), chief medical informatics officer (CMIO), and department chairs. The executive steering committee will resolve any issue that cannot be resolved by the project teams, where typically these issues relate to resources or budgeting concerns.[5] During the course of the project, the teams may need additional resources since some steps in the project plan may take longer than anticipated to complete. In addition, the team may uncover a more complicated process that could delay the go-live date. These issues will be resolved by the executive steering committee, led by the executive sponsor.

Executive Sponsor

Deciding who will be the executive sponsor is a critical step in the implementation. The CIO oversees the entire project, and the role of executive sponsor is one that bridges the gap between the technical and the clinical environments. The person in this role ensures that the clinicians are fully engaged in the implementation. The executive sponsor will help align system design with clinical outcomes and will establish implementation goals that will support the organization's mission, vision, and values. The sponsor will also determine strategic and business objectives, communicate the vision to stakeholders,[6] and help define the scope of the project, ensuring that mission-critical applications are given highest priority. Finally, the executive sponsor reports project progress to senior leadership and to the board of governors.

Project Director

The project director is responsible for overseeing all of the teams associated with the implementation. These teams will be application specific and can include such areas as clinical documentation, order entry, pharmacy, or radiology. Each team will have its own project plan with tasks and milestones that are specific to the application. There will also be some items, such as selecting point of care devices, system security, and printing options, on each of the plans that are common to all of the applications. The project director must be able to coordinate multiple project plans and ensure that milestones in the plans are met. Each of these plans must be synchronized across all applications so that common milestones are addressed once for all teams. Each of these plans will roll up to the main project plan for the entire implementation, where the responsibility of the project director is to ensure that the project milestones are met.

The project director must have the respect of end users as well as administrators, as they align the organizational goals to the project goals. This individual is generally a person who is comfortable with both the technical and clinical aspects of the system. The director will develop the project plan and direct every aspect of the project,[7] where his or her responsibility is to ensure that the team is meeting the project goals and following the project plan, which includes resolving issues within or across applications. Meeting project milestones, identifying regulatory changes that will affect the design, and monitoring the budget are key components of project direction, and the director ensures that an effective change management strategy is in place. While the executive sponsor will identify and communicate vision, it is up to the director to manage the teams and keep the vision aligned at all aspects of the project plan. Finally, the project director should be an active member of the project steering committee, reporting on project progress, team accomplishments, and issues, and will work with the vendor to manage the project timeline.

Team Leader

Since there may be multiple applications and multiple teams in the implementation process, an additional role to be filled is that of team leader. This person fills the role of managing one application, or team, provides oversight to the individual application team, keeps the team members on vision and team goals aligned with the vision, and matches resources to each task.[7] The team leader generally reports to the project director and is responsible for the daily operations of the members of the application team. The team leader is generally well versed in departmental operations and has detailed knowledge of the application and can apply both a technical and a clinical focus to it. Part of his or her task is to assign a clinical system analyst to project tasks, ensuring the analyst has the competence to complete the assignment. The team leader will also coordinate with the other team leaders on duplicate tasks across the entire project, chair team meetings, provide updates to the project director, and resolve individual issues within the application and escalate to the project director those that cannot be resolved.

Clinical System Analyst

The application team is responsible for bringing the finished product to end users[8] and completing the tasks associated with the application project plan. Working together are representatives of all disciplines, including nursing, physical therapy, dietary, respiratory therapy, medical records, and finance. Members can be either permanent or *ad hoc* team members, where the permanent members of this team are called clinical systems analysts (CSAs).

The CSA reports to the team leader and focuses on workflow analysis, software requirements, and design of the application to meet organizational specifications.[6] The CSA conducts an assessment of existing workflow and the current operational process and receives education on the system from the vendor. The education will provide the CSA with knowledge of system functionality and how to design the system, where upon completion, the analyst will be the expert on the application. In collaboration with clinical staff, the analyst will evaluate how the system can be adapted to meet clinical outcomes and departmental and organizational goals. The department manager, in collaboration with the project director, will identify resources for the evaluation, and the CSA will work with these resources, who will be experts on the current operational process.

Educator

New system implementation requires competent users. To ensure this, end users will need formal education to develop the skills to use the system since no matter how well designed the system is, if the end user does not learn the system, the implementation will fail. The educator will determine when training will be conducted,[5] and the project director, in collaboration with the executive sponsor, will identify the additional trainers, class location, and logistics. The selection of the staff to train end users will depend on the applications to be implemented, and the educator will have a detailed knowledge of how the system works and the operational process of the end users.

The project director and the educator will develop the education plan that determines logistics, such as number of educators, appropriate class size, process for scheduling end users, and identification of clerical support services. The educator will be responsible for development of lesson content, the process to measure competency, and skills validation. The lesson content will include both application procedures and workflow redesign, and the educational session will be concept based rather than task oriented. Ultimately, the emphasis will be on integrating technology and workflow.

Super-User

Another important member of the team is called a super-user. Super-user refers to peers who will help train and support their colleagues in the implementation process.[9] They are active members of the implementation team and will provide input into the design of the system. Super-users generally possess excellent communication skills, expert knowledge of department operations, and are a coach to their peers. The super-user, as nurse champion, facilitates communication in two directions: articulating nursing needs to the CSA and explaining technology solutions to the nursing staff.[10] Super-users help decrease dependence on the CSA, are a department-based resource, and have expert skills in the use of clinical applications.[11] The super-user should be flexible and understand the internal chain of command for resolution of issues. Additionally, he or she will provide input into policy revision and procedure redesign. The CSA will follow super-users through their workday and log each of the steps and document each task and how the task is completed. This will provide the basis for documentation of the current workflow. The CSA compares the current workflow and applies it to the design of the system, where the super-user offers guidelines for documentation, participates in system selection, completes system testing, and trains and supports his or her colleagues.[12]

The Phases of Implementation

Once the implementation roles are defined for the institution, it is up to the executive team to match the appropriate clinician to the role. Each role actively participates in all phases of the implementation. Nurses should have a prominent role as champions on the implementation team given their professional experience and knowledge.[10] Nursing roles include the CNO, informatics nurse specialist, nurse educator, and staff nurse. Involving nurses in education, go-live support, and system optimization is one of the key factors to success.[13] This concept is supported by a study that concludes that successful implementations are ones that are owned, sponsored, and championed by the nursing team.[13]

There are several phases in the life cycle of an informatics project: selection, implementation, which includes design and go-live, and postimplementation system optimization. In the selection phase, the focus is finding the right system for the institution. In the design phase, technology and workflow will be integrated to facilitate best practice, and in the go-live phase, support for new users of the system will be the priority. System optimization prepares the clinicians for less intense activities of maintenance and enhancements, where they will eventually fully own the system, with the project team transitioning to a supporting role.

System Selection

In the role of executive sponsor, the CNO has a strategic position in system selection. In collaboration with the CIO, CMO, CFO, and CEO, the CNO identifies and communicates the organizational vision for management of information.[14]

The CNO will be actively involved in selection and implementation of information systems, a policy that is supported by The Joint Commission (TJC), which requires nursing involvement in the selection process.[15]

The executive steering committee determines the budget for the project, identifies the participating disciplines, and approves the standards by which vendors will be evaluated. The committee will ensure that organizational goals are congruent with the system and evaluate the vendors from a macro perspective. By networking with their peers, the committee will be able to compare vendor solutions for systems that are functioning at similar institutions. The executive team will also approve the request for information (RFI) and request for proposal (RFP) documents. Members include administrators from nursing, medicine, pharmacy, information technology, operations, and finance.

Ideally, a nurse with clinical, informatics, and implementation experience is an ideal candidate for the role of project director given his or her broad background across a variety of processes in the healthcare spectrum. An informatics nurse specialist is a nurse who is formally trained in the practice of informatics. This involves the management and utilization of information and technologies. Responsibilities for this role include development of systems, research to support information systems, and making information systems usable for nurses.[16] The informatics nurse synthesizes informatics standards into every aspect of the implementation. With an American Nurses Credentialing Center (ANCC) certification in nursing informatics, project management certification, or as a *Certified Professional in Healthcare Information and Management Systems* (CPHIMS), the project director will have the knowledge and skills necessary for this role. The ability to follow a plan, identify barriers, and resolve issues is a common skill in nursing practice. The director has experience in managing multiple patient priorities that enables him or her to manage multiple application project priorities.

The project director completes the RFI and RFP documents. The director, in collaboration with directors from other disciplines, will identify requirements from a technical and clinical perspective, where functional requirements are included in these documents. He or she will also include information about the institution, such as number of beds, facility structure, annual admissions, and annual outpatient visits. This will allow the vendors to better prepare a proposal. Those vendors who cannot meet basic functionality are eliminated from the selection process.

Evaluation of the systems that make the first cut will give an end-user view of how the systems function in day-to-day operations. This will allow the selection team to further narrow down the field of systems. The final evaluation will ensure that patient-centered care is maintained through electronic documentation, improved accuracy of documentation, and clinical decision support.[15] The project director completes a functional needs assessment that details the necessary functions a system should have. The functions will be based upon regulations, policy, and best practice. The director will then develop the assessment listing the key components for the system, specific to the institution that identifies the "must haves" for the system (Table 4.1). For example, does the system allow standard tables/drop-downs across modules? The director will determine if this is a requirement or an option. Each system is evaluated by the functions, and a decision is made once all system evaluations are complete. The functional assessment is combined with other factors, such as cost and technical requirements, to identify the top choices. The next step is to identify the team to see the top choices in action. The director will coordinate the site visits and ensure that all disciplines are represented on the visit. Once the site visits are complete, and the assessments are made, the director will prepare a recommendation to the executive team.

The next step in the selection process involves the staff nurse and front-line direct caregivers. This is when the top vendors will come to the institution to demonstrate their system. The staff nurse as super-user can be a valuable asset at this stage. The team will want to see how the systems work in their own environment. Staff nurses will help prepare a script of the typical patient encounter at the institution. The systems should be evaluated across the patient care continuum and include the most common patient populations. The best way to accomplish this is to use the system to follow the patient experience through orders, documentation, and follow-up care. Enabling direct caregivers to walk through the system will provide an opportunity to "test drive" it. Designated staff nurses will become engaged in the selection process, where they will be the early adopters and help create a pool of super-users who will assist through the next steps of the implementation. Once the site visits and demonstrations are complete, the selection team will complete

Table 4.1 Example of a Functional Assessment for Clinical Documentation

System Functionality— Clinical Documentation	Present Yes/No	Required Yes/No	Description/ Comments
Does the system allow standard tables/ drop-down menus across modules?			
Can documented information be pulled from encounter to encounter?			
Can documentation in all encounters update information in history?			
Does the system support multidisciplinary documentation?			
Are problem lists supported?			
Can documentation generate a charge to the financial system?			
Can documentation generate acuity?			
Can alerts be generated based upon documented fields?			
Can sets of information be required?			
Can documentation be set up to specific patient populations?			
Can documentation trigger orders?			
Can documented problems generate orders or interventions?			
Can problems be prioritized?			
Can the system prevent future documentation?			
Are there templates for progress notes, op notes, etc.?			

evaluations of each of the vendors and the director will compile the results and make a recommendation to the executive committee.

At this point, contract negotiations will be held. The project director will evaluate the contract for inclusion of requirements identified in the functional assessment. The chief counsel, CIO, CNE, and CFO will complete the negotiation team, and they will have the final decision and take all aspects of the selection steps into consideration. The signing of the contract will start the next phase, system implementation. See Figure 4.1 for a stepwise illustration of the entire process.

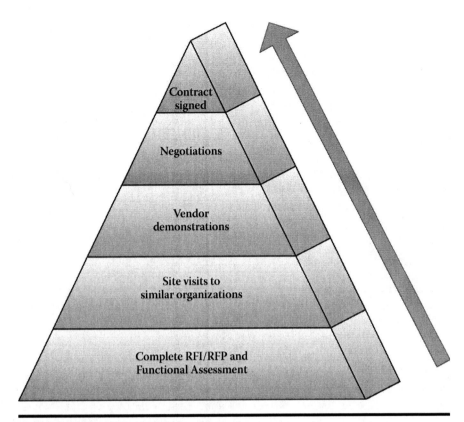

Figure 4.1 The steps of system selection.

System Implementation: The Design Phase

After the contract is signed, the executive steering committee identifies the team for the implementation phase. The executive sponsors' primary responsibility is to facilitate end-user engagement in the design. The executive steering committee team will determine the scope of the project and identify which applications will be implemented first. The implementation team members will be assigned to each application based upon their clinical expertise. The application team will assess the needs of the end users, and a formal needs assessment will capture their basic requirements for system functionality. The assessment will include collecting information needs, workflow process, and functional requirements, where the requirements indicate what must, must not, may, or should be included in the design of the system.[17]

The team should meet frequently with the super-users in this phase, where the CSA designs the system and provides feedback on the design to the super-users. As executive sponsor, the CNO focuses on the administrative aspect of the design, keeping in mind the strategic goals, mission, vision, and values, making certain that the best candidate is assigned to the role of the project director.

Much of the high-level implementation activity is the responsibility of the project director. The director applies project management and informatics standards, integrating nursing science, computer science, and information science. Project activities include analyzing, testing, and implementing systems to support patient care. The project director will have communication, change management, and business and application knowledge,[16] and the director will guide the application teams through the steps of system design.

The director is also responsible for multiple teams and multiple applications. The scope of the project will determine the required skills of each CSA and the number of analysts needed per application. If the implementation consists of many applications, team leaders will be assigned to each application. The director ensures that the project plan is developed and that the team stays on track for the expected go-live date. Key milestones and target dates will be identified, and it will be the responsibility of the project director to keep the team on target. Ultimately, the CSA will follow the plan and complete the tasks in the application plan.

Success in system implementation will depend upon the nurse having a prominent role in change management, with nurse champions on the team.[10] The CSA will review basic system functionality and match it to the clinician workflow, and will identify and review all departmental policies and procedures that relate to the implementation. He or she will evaluate the screens provided in the basic system and tailor them to end-user specifications. The CSA also collaborates with super-users to identify and incorporate best practices into the system, where system design should include standard terminology and required minimum data. Required data are the essential information that must be included for completion of the process. In this case, the user cannot leave a computer screen without entering the information. This guarantees that minimum data are collected.

The nurse in the CSA role documents the current operational workflow associated with the application, which takes place over several days in various ways. Workflow process analysis leads to a clearly defined diagram of how tasks are completed by the clinical staff. This step requires frequent interaction with the clinicians. These interactions include a formal interview to detail the step-by-step process needed to complete the task. Time to shadow the clinician is also necessary to verify the accuracy of the documented process. Super-users comfortable with the current documentation process will be the primary resources for documentation of workflow, where several episodes of shadowing are necessary. The CSA will follow the super-users through their workday and keep a log of the steps documenting what they do and how they do it, and complete the diagram of current process. The goal is to integrate the current best practice, new functionality, and technology into one seamless process.

Workflows will be created for each of the operational processes associated with the functions in each application. For nursing workflows, this will include the medication administration process, documentation of patient assessments, vital signs, intake and output, and care planning, where all details will be included. As each

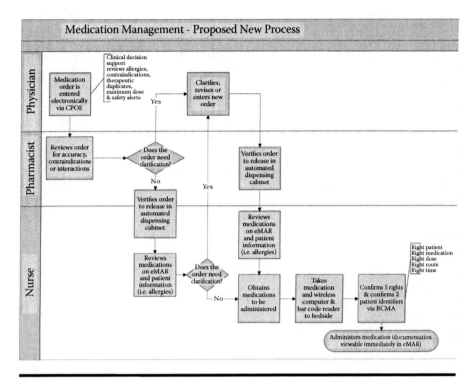

Figure 4.2   Medication management proposed new process for CIS implementation.

workflow is documented, the appropriate administrator will sign off to validate the accuracy of the documented workflow. The CSA will then compare the current process to the functionality in the system and will also take into consideration any new point of care devices or steps that will be added to the workflow at implementation. A proposed new workflow will be diagramed to show how the new system will change the process.

Figure 4.2 shows a typical new medication management workflow for a physician, pharmacist, and nurse after implementation of the CIS. The new process will build safety into each step with the addition of computerized physician order entry (CPOE), clinical decision support system (CDSS), point of care (POC) technology, and barcoding for medication administration (BCMA). Automated dispensing cabinets will improve turnaround time and provide another level of safety. For physicians, CPOE with CDSS will provide patient-specific recommendations to assist in making clinical decisions.[2] For nursing, it is important in this phase to recognize the implementation as practice redesign. Current processes and workflows will change in order to implement a new evidence-based practice model.[13]

The CSA designs the system based upon the details in the new workflow. After completing the screen builds, data entry fields, and tables, the CSA compares the current process to the proposed new process, where the comparison of the two workflows will generate an impact analysis. The executive sponsor and appropriate department leaders then review and sign off on the new process and the impact analysis, which will be used to prepare the end users for the new system. It will form the key items to stress in education for the end users. The super-user will communicate the new process prior to formal education to better prepare the end users for the change, and will champion the new workflow as one that is beneficial to delivering patient care.[11] Holding regularly scheduled sessions with the super-users will provide them with the information to validate and communicate the change. Figure 4.3 shows the process for identifying and detailing the current process, proposed new process, and impact analysis.

Upon completion of the new workflows and revisions to the system, the CSA will start the testing phase and complete individual testing within each application. This will verify that the application build works as intended. Then the CSA will test across applications, where once the verification at this level is complete, the super-users will test for usability and accuracy. Testing should be integrated to include hardware, interfaces to ancillary systems, and the billing process. Testing new point of care devices will identify any network issues, and if the network is unreliable, the devices will not consistently be available for the end user.[18] Super-users from all disciplines will participate in the final level of testing, and they will sign off on the workflow and screens. The project director then confirms all is ready to start training the end users.

Ideally, classes should start shortly before the staff is scheduled to begin using the system. Planning too far ahead may result in users forgetting what they were taught.[5] Together, the project director and the educator will develop the education plan. It should be kept in mind that classes should be scheduled at times that are convenient for the end users. This will require a large pool of educators who can conduct classes on all shifts, seven days a week. Managers will be responsible for maintaining minimum staffing levels on their units while sending staff to class, and the educator will select and train the class instructors. Super-users are generally excellent choices for instructors given their expert knowledge of the new workflows and the system. The educator will monitor class attendance to ensure the majority of users are educated prior to go-live, and completion of class will be mandatory prior to granting access to the system. Each attendee will be expected to demonstrate competency by completing a test on the new workflows and system, where once education is complete, the end users are ready to use the system. Figure 4.4 shows the process for the steps up to go-live, including education and issue resolution.

System Implementation: Go-Live

The go-live is the date on which the staff will begin using the new system. The date is one set by the executive team from the recommendation of the project director. Consideration for the decision includes availability of resources to support the

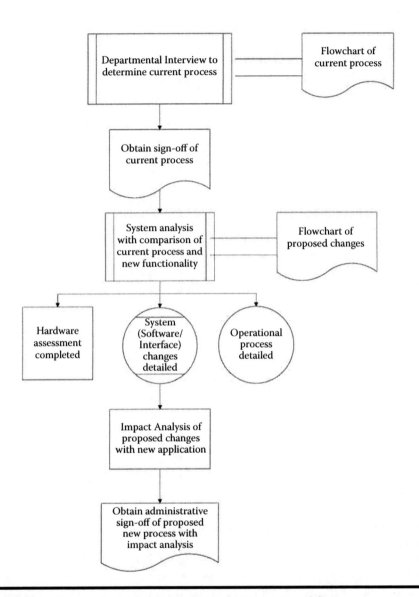

Figure 4.3   Process for current, proposed, and impact workflows.

go-live and organizational initiatives that could divert resources or attention from the go-live. At this point, education of end users must be complete and the system must have passed integrated testing.

The executive sponsor and project director must be sure that the support for go-live is adequate. Whether the go-live is a pilot on one unit or whole house, users must be adequately supported. This implies that requests for assistance must

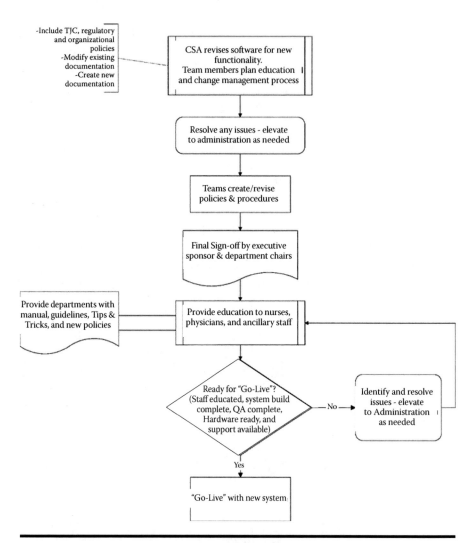

Figure 4.4 Steps in go-live phase of implementation.

be responded to in real time and the entire implementation team will be available to support all users. The super-user will provide on-unit support for basic trouble-shooting and resolution of operational issues[5] and will triage more complex issues to the support team stationed in a go-live command center.

During the go-live period, a log should be kept of all calls to the support team. The information that will be logged includes name and location of the caller, description of the issue, category of issue, responsible party, and resolution of the issue. The issues will be identified into three categories: operational, technical, or educational, where the category of the issue will determine who will be the responsible party to resolve. The issue log will provide a mechanism for trending analysis and will help the team to determine if they are isolated events or part of a more global problem. The log should be posted for all end users to view, which will allow them to see the response and to reach out to the responsible party with any questions. In the case of educational or operational issues, it can also help prevent the issue from occurring again by another user.

The support team located in the command center will be a combination of vendor support staff, CSA, team leaders, and the project director. Additional support will take the form of a roaming team of super-users on the units to resolve operational and educational issues. Support will be 24/7 and will remain in place for as long as calls are coming into the command center. The number of staff needed for support will decrease after the first week, and then the team should be able to transition the support to the super-users and normal support staff. The transition from active 24/7 support to standard support operations will be determined by the CIO, executive sponsor, and project director. Nursing administration will take the lead in establishing a team for ongoing operational support for the end users, where this support team will answer questions about documentation, provide advice on how to improve new workflows, and continue to log and trend issues. The post-go-live super-users will be well versed in the CIS and new processes.[19]

The executive sponsor and the members of the executive steering committee should have a visible presence during the go-live, in the command center and on the units. The executive sponsor and project director's responsibilities are to ensure that the transition for the front-line staff is seamless. The executive sponsor will empower the clinicians to take ownership of the system and the new process. Finally, the CNO should understand the impact of the implementation on all levels of the organization.[15]

System Optimization

Following the go-live period, the project team will begin the optimization phase, at which time they will evaluate enhancements to be implemented. These enhancements may be suggestions or noncritical issues from the issue log. They could also be items that were deferred during system design due to time constraints. The project director will prioritize the enhancements and the team leaders will implement the solutions.

The executive sponsor and the project director will determine the metrics by which the implementation will be measured. Some of the critical success factors include staff satisfaction, patient satisfaction, increased time at the bedside for the nurse, increased accuracy in documentation, the timeliness of information, and the accessibility of information. The pharmacy and pathology areas will measure turnaround time, number of clarifications, and number of prevented errors by clinical decision support alerts.

Staff satisfaction should improve with the implementation of more efficient and effective workflows. To measure this, a satisfaction survey should be conducted after some time has elapsed following the system rollout. Typical questions in this survey include ease of documentation, speed of response by the support team, and turnaround time for recommended changes.

Another way to evaluate success is to monitor the quality and completeness of documentation, where the minimum required data identified in the planning stage could be used as indicators for performance monitoring. Accuracy and completeness should be key elements considered. The evaluation should be simple since computerized data are more accessible and retrievable than handwritten documentation. Other evaluations should then be completed based upon quality of documentation, assessment of national patient safety goals (NPSGs), TJC standards, and organizational policy. Completion of documentation, such as assessment and reassessment of pain, within specified time frames can be measured.

The executive steering committee will prioritize and allocate resources for monitoring the effect of implementation on the clinical workflow and patient outcomes. The implementation will also streamline and automate the process for reporting of public data. The team can use the driving forces for the implementation to assess their performance.[4] See Figure 4.5 for a stepwise illustration of the process.

Conclusion

The implementation of a CIS is a process that requires teamwork. Assembling the best teams will ensure a successful transition to new workflows, automated processes, and real-time clinical decision support, where the teams must represent all disciplines. The inclusion of nurses at all phases and in key roles of the implementation will help ensure for end users that the implementation will be patient centered. The selection phase will allow the team to see the systems in action being used by their peers. The design phase is the best opportunity to get buy-in from nurses and other disciplines, which includes understanding the current process and integrating technology into best practices to redesign clinician workflow. Education is a very important consideration in this phase.

In order to achieve a smooth go-live rollout, dedicated staff support by the implementation team is necessary. The team, in collaboration with administration, will decide the day the clinicians begin to use the new system, where well-trained and supported users should begin to utilize the new platform. In the optimization phase, the team will evaluate the implementation, where feedback will include a staff satisfaction survey. The team will monitor documentation for accuracy and completeness.

Implementation of a CIS should ultimately increase accessibility and improve the accuracy of documentation. In the end, an implementation is costly, time-consuming, and resource-intensive, but the return on investment should be

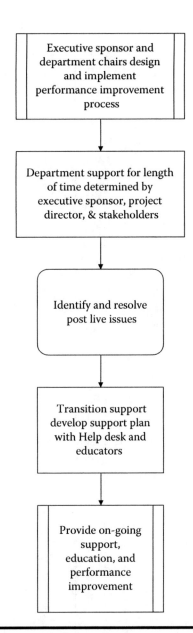

Figure 4.5 Post-go-live processes for system optimization.

worthwhile given the positive impact on clinical outcomes. Including new technology in the redesigned workflow will improve safety with real-time clinical decision support, improve quality with more complete documentation, and improve satisfaction by increasing nurse time at the bedside. Having nurses in key implementation roles will ensure that the patient is the primary focus of the implementation.

CLINICAL INFORMATICS: A CASE STUDY

The journey toward a safer system for one large medical center in northern New Jersey began in 1992 with the creation of the Department of Clinical Informatics. At that time, nursing administration recognized the role technology would play in the delivery of patient-centered care. Nursing also recognized that clinical input was absolutely essential to the success of any system used to support patient care. The decision was made to temporarily assign two staff nurses to work side by side with system analysts in the design and implementation of a clinical information system. The nurses and the system analysts were responsible for system design, workflow redesign, end-user education, and support. In 1993, order entry and results reporting were implemented across the organization. The use of nurses in an informatics role was so successful in supporting nursing that the assignment was made permanent and the department was expanded to a total of seven nurses. Their primary focus was to collaborate with system analysts in the design, support, and education of clinical staff on computerized processes. The department continued to report to nursing but was responsible for the computer needs of clinical departments. The nurses in the informatics department were selected due to their diverse skills and experience, including inpatient, adult, pediatric, outpatient, and admission services. This diversity added a global perspective to the design of the system. Their experience ensured that the system would address the continuum of care. The department worked very closely with information technology on each phase of implementation. Together, the team implemented clinical documentation, electronic medication administration records, computerized physician order entry, and ER patient tracking. The nurses and analysts collaborated on clinical application selection, design, implementation, and performance monitoring. The informatics nurses were the liaisons between the analysts and clinical staff, but their primary focus evolved into the education and support of clinical staff.

In 2008, the organization selected a new clinical information system to replace existing applications and to enhance those applications toward the goal of a comprehensive EHR. The plan is to have an integrated electronic solution across the continuum. One step toward that goal was to consolidate resources under one umbrella. The department of clinical informatics transitioned to the department of information technology, with the title of clinical systems. The primary focus is now the design and implementation of the new clinical information system. The clinical systems team now includes twenty-four members from all clinical disciplines. The director is a registered nurse with a master's in nursing informatics. She has ANCC certification in nursing informatics and as a nurse executive. There are two team leaders, both registered nurses. The clinical system analysts include one advanced practice nurse, eleven registered nurses, two pharmacists, one medical technologist, two health information experts, one dietitian, one respiratory therapist, one OR coordinator, and one radiology technologist. All have diverse experience, both clinical and technical. Although the team reports to information technology now, there is a strong bond with the clinical disciplines. The motto of the team is that "behind every transaction, whether it is an order or a charge, there is a patient."

References

1. Kohn, L. T., Corrigan, J. M., and Donaldson, M. S., eds. 1999. *To err is human: Building a safer health system.* Washington, DC: Institute of Medicine Committee on Quality of Health Care in America, National Academy Press.
2. Institute of Medicine Committee. 2001. *Crossing the quality chasm: A new health system for the 21st century.* Washington, DC: National Academy Press.
3. Page, A., ed. 2003. *Keeping patients safe: Transforming the work environment of nurses.* Washington, DC: Institute of Medicine Committee on the Work Environment for Nurses and Patient Safety, National Academy Press.
4. Mustain, J. M., Lowry, L. W., and Wilhoit, K. W. 2008. Change readiness assessment for conversion to electronic medical records. *JONA* 38:379–85.
5. Maffeo, R. 2000. Project implementation: A tailored approach. *Semin Nurse Managers* 8:51–52.
6. Hassett, M. 2006. Case study: Factors in defining the nurse informatics specialist role. *JHIM* 20:30–35.
7. Staggers, N. 1998. Notes from a clinical information system project manager: Requisite survival skills. *Computers Nurs* 16:244–46.
8. Souther, E. 2001. Implementation of the electronic medical record: The team approach. *Computers Nurs* 19:47–55.
9. Ball, M. J., Hannah, K. J., and Edwards, M. J. A. 1999. *Introduction to nursing informatics.* New York: Springer.
10. Kirkley, D. 2004. Not whether, but when. *JONA* 34:55–58.
11. Boffa, D. P., and Pawola, L. M. 2006. Identification and conceptualization of nurse super users *JIHM* 20:60–68.
12. McNeive, J. E. 2009. Super users have great value in your organization. *Computers, Informatics, Nursing,* May/June, 136–39.
13. Murphy, J. 2009. The best IT project is not an IT project. *JIHM* 23:6–8.
14. Brokel, J. 2007. Creating sustainability of clinical information systems. *JONA* 37:10–13.
15. Simpson, R. L. 2007. The politics of information technology. *Nurs Admin Q* 31:354–58.
16. American Nurses Association. 2008. *Nursing informatics: Scope and standards of practice.* Washington, DC: American Nurses Publishing.
17. Brady, M., and Hassett, M., Eds. 2000. *Clinical informatics.* HIMSS Guidebook Series. Chicago: HIMSS.
18. Huvane, K. 2008. Trouble at the bedside. *Healthcare Inform* 25:32–35.
19. Shedenhelm, H. J., Hernke, D. A., Gusa, D. A., and Twedell, D. M. 2008. EMR implementation and ongoing education. *Nursing Management,* July, 51–53.

Chapter 5

Architecting Computer Physician Order Entry (CPOE) for Optimal Utilization

James F. Keel and D. Arlo Jennings

Contents

Computer physician order entry (CPOE) is an electronic means for physicians and other clinical providers to place patient orders. CPOE is not keyboarding orders as free text into a word processor, but rather it is the process of retrieving orders from an electronic order catalogue by matching specific catalogue orders to the desired order intent as conceived. CPOE additionally provides the means to make available defined order sets that support integrated tasks into a common complex clinical action.

Because CPOE deviates markedly from the traditional paper-based ordering format, the proposed transition to CPOE has commonly spawned significant physician resistance to its utilization as a new technology platform. This resistance, common with many new users of technology, is generally in reaction to a change in their daily routines forced upon them by the use of the proposed technology. In 2009 approximately 10% of the five-thousand-plus hospitals in the United States had ventured into the world of CPOE. Two factors have inhibited a stronger adoption rate of CPOE: the expense of the implementation and a resistance to adoption on the part of stakeholders. However, given the reputed benefits attached to the utilization of these systems, there is a strong national consensus building that makes it likely that CPOE will become the standard instrument for executing clinical orders.

The implementation of CPOE creates added expenses to hospitals' bottom lines. These expenses derive from the considerable effort needed to effect this major cultural and clinical transformation, including planning, expectation setting, implementation of preparatory, prerequisite applications, deployment of adequate computers for access, downtime contingencies, design and build of an ordering process physicians will accept, education, go-live support, and management of post-go-live requests for changes and updates. Each of these will be discussed in some detail in this chapter.

How then should a hospital's information technology (IT) team work with clinicians to orchestrate the best approach to ensure a well-functioning system that is readily accepted by physicians and that works efficiently for clinical support staff? The IT team must include a strong chief medical information officer (CMIO) position to interface among the design and build team, the administration, and physicians to guide the transformation process and to provide clinical guidance to the design of the system. IT must also have experienced nurses on the informatics staff to help with design and build, but without physician input, acceptance will be limited or completely denied. The ultimate success of the implementation depends upon the interaction among the administration, support departments, and physicians. The hospital must then devise a project scope, develop a formal implementation plan, and budget appropriate resources, utilizing formal project management methodology. Finally, the hospital administration must fully recognize that this is not "just another project." This kind of transformation is unique and requires uniform leadership alignment, persistence, collaboration with medical staff, and an unwavering commitment to follow through with stated intentions.

Background: Perceptions, Costs, and Outcomes

CPOE presents a perception both enlightening to administration and threatening to physicians. Hospital administrators react positively to moving in this direction because of the potential savings that might be gained and the potential reduction of medical errors assumed to be attributable to CPOE.

As regards potential savings, measurement of return on investment from CPOE is complex and fraught with pitfalls. Hospital executives may be tempted to significantly underestimate both capital and expense costs of implementation. Global changes in dashboard outcomes for the organization, such as length of stay, cost per case, mortality, and morbidities, are confounded by many factors, including shifting acuity, seasonal variations, adjustments in market share, impact from multiple other projects, changing reimbursement plans, and so on. In addition, reduction in medical errors, particularly those with harm, is commonly cited as a benefit of CPOE, but is notoriously difficult to quantify, primarily because of problems inherent in voluntary reporting. Finally, hospital executives must keep in mind that CPOE will not be the final product to justify their goal integration of information technology into the provision of healthcare. CPOE should be viewed as one of many pieces that will form the foundation of an electronic underpinning to replace an antiquated and highly limited paper-based system. Although the final solution may be expected to facilitate and yield enormous improvements in hospital care, too much should not be expected of or attributed to CPOE alone. Nevertheless, a careful process should be put in place prior to implementing CPOE to facilitate a careful analysis of investment costs tied to clinical and operational outcomes.

Medical Error Reduction Proposition

Much has been written about medical errors and CPOE. CPOE has been touted to decrease medical errors by several mechanisms. On the surface, CPOE eliminates errors and problems associated with misinterpretation of illegible orders. Illegible handwritten prescriptions introduce the potential for additional errors at patient discharge. CPOE also holds the potential to make orders more explicit and less vulnerable to misinterpretation resulting from errors in construction and syntax in the creation of handwritten orders. Furthermore, orders may be implemented more consistently as a result of properly imbedded clinical decision support at the point of order entry. This includes such devices as the attachment of commonly used, appropriate order sentences to medication orderables, the development of computer-based order sets that may act as prompts to prevent errors of omission, and the judicious use of rules and alerts to guide safe and proper execution of orders. Although CPOE holds great promise for reducing medical errors, it should be kept in mind that other processes for ensuring safe administration of medications, such as barcoding or radiofrequency identification tying patients to dose dispensing of medications, may be equally important in this regard.

CPOE processes have the potential to do more than decrease medical errors; they may improve outcomes directly through the embedding of best practice standards as decision support at the point of order entry. It is tempting for the hospital and medical staff to grossly underestimate the resources necessary to design and build a complete orders environment that will meet these expectations, which are necessary to achieve the anticipated benefits of a successful implementation. Furthermore, these benefits assumptions have been challenged by conflicting reports in the literature that include wide ranges in outcomes following CPOE, most likely resulting from variations in vendor technology, orders design and build, and implementation strategies. Finally, measuring benefits from CPOE is a shifting proposition, owing to changes and improvements in hardware and software technologies that make prior reports of outcomes rapidly obsolete.

Preplanning for CPOE: Analysis and Documentation of Clinical Processes and Workflow—Current and Future State

In order to be successful, the process should begin with reengineering both clinical and business processes. This should always begin with a careful workflow analysis of all clinical processes from the bedside through all of the clinical support departments both for current state and as expected to be leveraged in the future state.

As an organization, you must think in terms of how physicians, nurses, clinicians, and clinical support staff work, and how a patient needs to be processed through the hospital, regardless of health issue, and inclusive of all clinical departments. A structured approach is necessary to construct an effective analysis:

- Initially, an up-front systems analysis detailing workflow must be accomplished that will address current state and future state after implementation of CPOE.
- Workflow must be considered at all points in the clinical process. A detailed process and data flow diagrams should be designed for each clinical process, clinical unit, and clinical support department to indicate patient flow, patient data flow, and detailed workflow processes for all staff. Foremost, the patient must be considered at the center of the process.
- The flow diagrams may now be used to examine weaknesses in the current environment and then pose possible solutions for improving patient care and data flow, creating new flow diagrams. Comparing current state with the new flow diagrams allows users to easily visualize and become more creative in seeing new opportunities.
- Finally, a subsequent flow diagram may be constructed, depicting how workflow could be improved if electronic systems were in place to support the needed functionality. To achieve optimal process improvements, one must "get outside the box in thinking." This process provides an important time to pause and carefully consider, not to redesign your current system—it already exists and will not meet your future needs—but rather to think future, think workflow, think process, and think reengineering. Most of all, think in terms of optimal patient care.

Most hospitals may be tempted to make the mistake of expending valuable resources redesigning what they are already doing, thereby missing this vital opportunity to reengineer processes and better leverage information technology. No hospital can take advantage of computerized applications if the objective is to continue to do things the way they have always been done. Design teams must think outside the box. Once current workflow, a desired workflow, and reviewed processes that must be reengineered have been defined, workflow may be aligned to the order entry applications design and build.

CPOE Methodology for Adoption: The Transformation and the Product

The Mission Hospital Experience

Mission Hospital in Asheville, North Carolina, underwent a relatively smooth implementation of CPOE in 2008 with 100% adoption by the medical staff. Below will be described the features of the CPOE implementation at Mission, including what worked, what was most important to the success of the project, and some of the most difficult challenges along the way. We will discuss CPOE implementation from two distinct perspectives: (1) the product, meaning the design and build of the ordering environment, and (2) the transformation, meaning the preparation and process of transition of the clinical culture. Although CPOE impacts the entire hospital organization as a consequence of its downstream impact on all departments, we will focus in this chapter primarily on the transformation necessary for the physicians and other providers who are users of CPOE.

Some vital statistics about Mission Hospital are useful to understand the context of this implementation of CPOE. Mission is a community hospital in structure with 764 licensed beds and 700 physicians on staff. The hospital serves as a referral hospital for a network of sixteen smaller regional hospitals. Significantly, 93% of our physicians are employed in private practices, with the corollary that administrative executive decisions are often not well received, putting adoption of new technology at risk. In addition, Mission employs very few residents (family practice and ob-gyn only) so that the attending physicians are not shielded from the chore of entering orders and taking inpatient calls.

Prerequisites

Before engaging in a discussion of the transformation, there are a number of prerequisites regarding the computer system that should be solidly in place before undertaking CPOE. Also, certain clinical and departmental processes should be standardized to incorporate evidence-based best practice and limit unnecessary variability through the use of structured, standard protocols, procedures, and orders sets (usually on paper initially), prior to implementing CPOE. These concepts are very useful and are discussed subsequently in more detail.

Clinical Access to Computer Workstations

There must be ample access to computers for clinical care distributed in a way that supports efficient clinical workflow. This requires a structured walkthrough of the nursing units and areas where physicians normally congregate to discuss patient care. This analysis will definitely mean adding more computer workstations and telephones to ensure appropriate workflow. The adequacy of computer access points must be carefully assessed prior to a live rollout through careful inspections of the demand for computer terminals during peak rounding hours. Demand for computers will not decrease with CPOE implementation. These observations should be followed by augmentation of those areas in the system that may become deficient when CPOE goes live. Observations should also be conducted to identify any areas that may need renovation to accommodate the required number of devices. New devices and renovations should be budgeted, acquired, and deployed, with follow-up analysis to confirm the sufficiency of the remedy. It is critical to observe how physicians make rounds. If part of the patient chart is on paper, physicians will want a place to sit and enter information, where mobile access devices may not be first choice.

Downtime Procedures

There must be carefully designed downtime procedures, including appropriate backup software and workflow processes in place. All downtime solutions should be tested by regularly scheduled drills to ensure familiarity with downtime procedures and to identify potential gaps in the process. We learned quickly that having paper forms available on each unit for downtime (but secured during normal uptime) will expedite continuing patient care by all providers during downtime occurrences.

Computer Authentication Login and Performance

Computer login efficiency and performance should be assessed and optimized with appropriate network, hardware, and software installations that will facilitate rapid screen-to-screen times. Computer processor utilization on the backend as well as user screen-to-screen timings on the front end should be monitored and reported at regular intervals. We learned no matter how fast the back end processing might be, the ease and quickness of screen response on the front end, in fact, defined the physicians' perception of satisfactory computer performance.

Use of Computer Order Entry by Hospital Staff in Advance of CPOE

Optimally the electronic order entry system should be built and in active use by hospital unit secretaries and clinical support personnel prior to turning the order entry process over to physicians. This permits significant opportunity to improve any issues with the computer orders design prior to physician use. Also, the hospital staff will then become knowledgeable and adept with usage of the system, making them an excellent resource for support to physicians at go-live.

Deployment of Departmental Clinical Support Applications in Advance of CPOE

Clinical department-based applications that will support the deployment of orders downstream from the physician orders should be implemented, fully tested, and functional prior to CPOE. This includes laboratory, radiology, nursing documentation, rehabilitation services, respiratory care, nutrition services, and so on. Most importantly, medication process applications that will support pharmacy filling and verification functions, medication dispensing functions, and the electronic medication administration record should be live and functioning smoothly prior to CPOE to ensure a complete, safe, and effective medication delivery process. Finally, applications supporting surgery, emergency department services, scheduling, registration, and patient management are additional IT building blocks that are best implemented prior to moving to CPOE.

The Transformation

Preliminary Steps

The first step should be to get physicians on the computer in advance of CPOE. Part of preparing the medical staff for using CPOE should focus upon leading physicians to engage the computer in their daily clinical workflow. We facilitated this transition in two ways:

1. Making the postdischarge chart available only via the computer. This was accomplished by first implementing a robust document imaging product. We then transformed the processing of all medical records by our health information management department such that all paper documents from the inpatient record were scanned into the electronic medical record within twenty-four hours of discharge. This had the effect of forcing physicians to go to the computer to retrieve any patient's old record, whether retrieving a chart for a patient returning for subsequent care or completing medical record postdischarge deficiencies. This change in workflow proved to be an extraordinary asset to physicians. First, physicians found that they could access the old chart in seconds instead of twenty to forty minutes when evaluating return patients, thereby greatly improving their workflow. Second, physicians discovered that they could review and complete charts at any time from any location. The dividend from this transition was that all physicians not only became rapidly adept at using the computer, including keyboard and mouse point-and-click activities, but also became familiar with navigation of the electronic patient record. A final, and perhaps the most important, dividend was that physicians for the first time experienced concrete benefits in their daily workflow directly attributable to the electronic patient record. This represented a first critical step in the pathway to adoption of CPOE.

2. Making results available online. This step was accompanied by a simultaneous implementation to make all or nearly all results and documents immediately available in the electronic inpatient record in real time through direct feeds

and interfaces with dictation/transcription, lab, electrodiagnostics, radiology, PACS (Picture Archiving and Communications System), electronic medication record, home and in-hospital medication lists, vital signs, ICU flow sheet data, family contact information, active provider lists, and nursing documentation. Once physicians became familiar with accessing patient information in the electronic postdischarge record, their ability to access comprehensive, fully up-to-date patient data through a single process from any location provided a second revolutionary improvement in their workflow. As a result, physicians quickly transitioned voluntarily from a paper to an electronic process for chart review in their inpatient rounds every day. This provided a second giant step in the movement toward CPOE.

The second step is to develop paper orders sets. Many years prior to CPOE we began down the path of developing order sets on paper to facilitate admission orders, postop orders, and titrations of complex patient care modalities and medication drips. We reached a point in time where we had created a plethora of redundant and personalized order sets. Recognizing that order sets should be evidence based where possible and minimize unnecessary variations in care, we set up a process by which all order sets in the system must:

- Be initially developed or reviewed by specialty- and subspecialty-based committees with input from physicians and staff stakeholders
- Be reviewed and approved by a single multidisciplinary committee, with physician, nursing, pharmacy, medical records, risk, and informatics oversight, before they could be made active in the ordering environment
- Be evidence based where possible
- Be reviewed and updated not less than annually

This important transition resulted in:

- Improved, highly refined, and streamlined order sets throughout the system, using a common style guide format familiar to all providers
- A comprehensive array of paper order sets, supporting admissions, consultations, titrations, and perioperative/procedure processes
- Improved compliance in general use by all physicians
- A strong platform for conversion of these order sets into an electronic format to facilitate an efficient transition to CPOE

Physician Transformation

Physician Resistance

Understanding how to successfully approach transformation begins with an appreciation of the reasons physicians often resist the transition to CPOE. Some of the most commonly expressed concerns include:

"It will take me too long to enter my orders."

"I will be spending more time in front of a computer than in front of my patients."

"We are just trading one system of errors for another."

"There is conflicting literature on the efficacy and safety of CPOE."

"You're asking me to do the work of a secretary."

A review of the 2008 data from KLAS (a leading research company that focuses on healthcare technology) shows how serious this issue of physician adoption has become. KLAS reported in 2008 that only 17.4% of hospitals greater than two hundred beds had implemented CPOE at some level. At these sites, only about 60% of orders on average were entered using CPOE, and tellingly only 3% of physician users reported increased satisfaction with use of CPOE. Our argument is made more difficult by the small number of published reports in the literature that have provided objective data supporting the case for CPOE adoption. Furthermore, available information indicates that CPOE does indeed take clinicians more time to enter orders than using the traditional handwritten paper process.

A Physician-Driven Project

CPOE failure may occur for several key reasons, but at the top of the list is failure to engage physicians in the process. *Hospital administrators, often pushing an IT-driven initiative from a business proforma, decide to implement CPOE systems with insufficient involvement and collaborative cooperation on the part of the medical staff.* It is unwise to succumb to the notion that adequate physician engagement cannot be practically achieved. Physician involvement may be facilitated by the inclusion of physician champions very early in the formative process of decision making. *In fact, engaging physician champions to primarily initiate and drive the process toward CPOE for reasons of improved patient care is by far the best approach to achieving medical staff adoption.*

Recommended Steps to Achieve a Successful Transformation

The transformation of the medical staff may be broken down into a number of components, ranging from the development of an initial, basic understanding of the CPOE process to the formulation of implementation strategies. These will be discussed in the following paragraphs.

The Rationale for CPOE

The first step in transformation is to help physicians and clinical support staff understand the rationale behind the decision to proceed with CPOE. This argument may be summarized as follows:

- CPOE resolves the chronic problem of deciphering physician handwriting that has plagued healthcare since its inception, which can lead to countless errors.

- A properly built CPOE system provides the opportunity for unmatched clarity and standardization in order entry format, which in turn removes much of the ambiguity found in handwritten orders, even when they can be easily read.
- CPOE ordering has the advantage of not being confined to one location and one chart, such that orders can be implemented from any computer access point.
- CPOE represents not just the simple rote process of effecting the entry of orders, but instead involves the deployment, notification, coordination, and completion of algorithms, checklists, and safety elements for all departments downstream of these orders.
- CPOE has been repeatedly demonstrated to significantly shorten the time of order implementation as a result of both the clarity of orders and the speed of order transmission, resulting in a system that provides for reliable execution of the intended orders in far less time than in the paper world.
- Perhaps most importantly, CPOE holds the promise of leveraging true clinical decision support to influence clinical decision making. By deploying well-designed, evidence-based clinical order sets, appropriate rules and smart alerts that fire only when an unsafe or undesirable action is invoked, and a series of prompts and reminders, such as prepopulating medication orders with the most commonly used medication order sentences, clinicians are provided with state-of-the-art decision support tools. These tools allow physicians to practice medicine at an enhanced level of performance not otherwise achievable.
- Finally, CPOE is one of the fundamental components that can make up a searchable clinical data repository, permitting analysis of practice patterns and resource utilization tied to clinical and financial outcomes. This process, in turn, creates the opportunity to engineer true continuous quality improvement.

Anticipated Impact of CPOE on Workflow

Another early essential step in transformation is the building of a realistic expectation of how CPOE will impact physicians and staff, and a clear explanation of how it may be expected to affect workflow in their daily lives. They should be made aware that they are likely to experience both improvements and difficulties with the new system. Anticipated advantages of CPOE include:

- Improved legibility and clarity of orders, leading to fewer misinterpretations and fewer callbacks for clarification.
- Orders may be entered and reviewed from any location, permitting physicians to provide care without calling the unit or waiting for someone else to finish with the paper chart.
- Order sets will be immediately available on the computer, obviating the necessity of locating needed order sets in drawers, or requesting staff to find more because the sets you seek have been depleted.
- Physicians will have more decision support available to support safer and more effective order entry than is possible with the paper process.

■ Physicians can expect more prompt action on orders with CPOE compared with a paper process.

On the other hand, it is important to be frank with physicians regarding perceived disadvantages of CPOE:

■ Orders may take longer to enter than paper handwritten orders.
■ Orders may be more difficult to locate in a computer order catalogue due to terminology in the catalogue that is foreign to the physician's thought about how the order might be named.
■ Orders may be accompanied by alerts and pop-up reminders that physicians may find annoying, impeding, and distracting.
■ Some ordering formats may be poorly designed by the software vendor or the hospital staff, making clear order submission difficult.
■ Physicians may find that they are vulnerable to new types of medical errors not present on paper, such as accidentally picking an incorrect, adjacent order from a list.
■ Physicians will face the difficult task of learning a new and foreign method for completing a very familiar task.

Communicating an Appropriate Expectation

The goal of communicating CPOE expectations may be accomplished by an initial communication of the intention to move to CPOE through presentations in meetings, posters, e-mails, intranet/Internet postings, mailings, and informal discussions. These efforts should be accompanied by the presentation of a series of scheduled, structured, live demonstrations of CPOE to all practice groups. In our experience, these demonstrations were well attended when folded into regularly scheduled group practice meetings. Interest in the subject matter and live demos could be described only as very high, with the result that many questions and much discussion followed at each encounter.

Some groups requested follow-up presentations. As these presentations were rolled out, physicians' preconceived notions of CPOE (almost uniformly negative) were successively replaced by an educated and more realistic understanding of the actual facts of the matter. In this regard, the importance of being brutally honest about the expected impact of CPOE on the workflow of the providers cannot be overemphasized. Overselling or overmarketing may be perceived as disingenuous, which could result in creating loss of confidence in those putting forward the effort. These initiatives to build understanding and an appropriate expectation will take a significant period of time. This time should be factored into the cost and the timeline for CPOE. Any plan to minimize this component of the preparatory process is likely to lead to serious problems with adoption later in the course of the project.

Engaging Physicians in the Process

A very important step is actively engaging practicing physicians with the CPOE design and implementation processes. Initially there was perceived reluctance to impose upon physicians and request their time to help with CPOE. It was wrong to be reluctant. In most cases, there were ample physicians who were willing to step forward and become involved in many aspects of the project. Some of these aspects included participation in leadership roles, site visits, assistance with the design of orders and order sets, assistance with the design of specialty-specific folders of order collections, and participation in CPOE pilots and go-live support. In virtually every case, their participation improved the execution of the project and led to improved adoption.

Physician Leadership

Any project of this magnitude and controversy will require strong leadership. The role of the physician leadership in the design and support of CPOE implementation is a critical element in the success of the project. If the implementation is to proceed with high adoption, the project should be primarily led by the physicians themselves. This begins with the need for a lead physician and a chief medical information officer (CMIO) or leader in a similar role who is afforded the necessary time and resources to effectively organize and lead the overall process. Our CMIO enlisted a group of interested physicians to form what may be termed an information technology clinical advisory committee to review and make formal recommendations to the hospital and the medical staff on clinical IT initiatives. These physicians termed themselves the Physician Information Group (PIG). The role of the PIG proved critical in both guiding the process and providing the most visible nidus of physicians to lead the initiative.

The chief and vice chief for medical staff played pivotal roles in the leadership effort for CPOE. Their clear and articulate understanding of the value of CPOE and their willingness to aggressively support the aim of the project were very important. These individuals, in turn, worked to provide the medical staff service lines and departmental clinical leaders, usually during meetings of the medical executive committee, with presentations and opportunities for input and decision making that directed the implementation.

Four Critical Questions for the Physician Leadership to Address: A Crossroads Decision for the Leaders

During this process the chief and vice chief of medical staff addressed a number of critical questions to the Medical Administrative Committee:

1. Whether they should endorse the decision to proceed with CPOE and, if so, over what time frame.

2. Whether CPOE should be mandatory or optional for all providers. In this regard, the leadership must be apprised of a comprehensive list of pros and cons. Among these was careful deliberation of the patient safety risks inherent in a protracted dual process (paper and computer) in any optional adoption strategy. The group recognized that a dual process represents an ongoing patient safety risk and workflow consideration, not only for clinical review of implemented orders, but also for the dual deployment of orders to downstream departments should an optional strategy be chosen.
3. Whether CPOE should be implemented by a "big bang" or a sequential go-live process, again with consideration of the potential risk associated with dual ordering methods during a prolonged sequential approach.
4. Whether physician education would be a sufficiently important factor in promoting a smooth and safe transition from paper to electronic order entry to justify requiring that CPOE education be mandatory, including a requirement that all providers who intend to enter orders spend significant time in class.

In our institution these questions were bitterly debated for months in our medical staff leadership meetings and in the hallways. After phone conferences with other hospitals, site visits, and reviews of published reports, the physician leadership eventually agreed to the following decisions:

- CPOE would be implemented in an appropriate time frame with the caveat that any patient care and workflow issues be resolved prior to go-live.
- CPOE would be mandatory for all providers. This decision was backed by appropriate changes in medical staff policy requiring full adoption as a stipulation for membership on the active medical staff for all physicians who provide patient care.
- CPOE would be implemented with a big bang strategy. This was perhaps the most controversial decision and was later modified significantly, as will be explained in greater detail later.
- Education prior to CPOE use would be mandatory for all users who ever intended to enter orders in the inpatient environment.

These decisions represented the most important ingredients in the recipe for a successful implementation of CPOE with full adoption by the medical staff. They incorporated the critical role of physician leadership with the necessary mandatory elements to bring along those members of the medical staff who inevitably would resist the transformation. Without these decisions, as has happened in many hospitals where optional participation was permitted, a significant percentage of physicians on staff would almost certainly have persisted indefinitely with paper order entry.

In any major organizational change, there is usually a bell-shaped curve plotting willingness to adopt new technology against number of providers. The curve typically ranges from a relatively small number of ready adopters to a much larger number of individuals who are less opinionated and assume a wait-and-see attitude, to the deeply entrenched, highly resistant, and regrettably, highly vocal naysayers. The challenge is how to bring along even the most resistant elements without allowing the naysayers to convince the much larger group of "undecideds" to also become resistant to the proposed change. One element proved critical in disabling an effective resistance to the CPOE implementation: the fact that the process had been driven by and voted upon by the elected medical staff leadership. Following the decisions of the medical staff leadership, rules and regulations were amended to incorporate the mandatory components, including clauses that would specify accountability and accompanying consequences for noncompliance.

Project Organization, Management, and Budget

In coordination with physician leadership, the hospital administration and board of directors must be also be fully informed, engaged, and uniformly aligned in their commitment to the success of the project. Their roles include ensuring the development of an appropriate organizational structure for project design and implementation, a credible scope of project, an implementation plan with milestones and oversight, an appropriate budget, and a large bully pulpit from which to engage and support the effort across the organization.

In terms of organizational structure, a number of teams should be created to address each of the core elements necessary for the design and implementation of CPOE. These include teams for computer access, downtime, performance, completion of any software support for online viewing of results, functionality (the design of build of the product), clinical process mapping for current and future states, and transformation, including communications, education, policy, rules, bylaws, pilot strategy, and go-live support. Each team should be assigned a team leader and begin by developing a scope document and plan requiring sign-off at the executive level to be incorporated into an overall project plan. Team leaders should meet regularly to report on progress of the plan, to coordinate with other teams, and to raise, escalate, and track issues. At Mission, each team was assigned two sponsors, a physician and a clinical vice president, who advised the team and acted on their behalf within the organization. The teams should report in turn to a CPOE executive committee. At Mission, that committee consisted of the CIO, the CMIO, the CMO, the COO, and the informatics project manager. This committee was responsible for general oversight, review of milestones, and issues resolution.

A lesson learned early in the implementation of CPOE at Mission focused on the need to anticipate a solid budget for the project. Because of the cost and complexity of CPOE design and implementation, specific funding should be allocated to the project and formal project management methodologies should be applied, including development of scope of project, a managed project plan, a transparent listing of milestones, and an appointed project manager, who would be responsible not only for the overall management of the project, but also for management of the budget.

The Product

The product consists primarily of all of the orders, order sets, rules, alerts, and formats forming the basis of the computerized order entry tool. The goal is to construct a product that is fast, elegant, and easy to use. In IT terminology, one could say the system must possess speed, usability, and breadth of functionality. Stated yet another way, if the product does not work well, no amount of transforming will lead to adoption.

The most basic element of the build is the individual orderable. We built approximately sixty-two thousand such orderbles. Each orderable contains within it a set of detailed options and values, also known as order entry formats, that allow each order to be easily modified to suit individual patient needs. The rules for the construction of orderables are fairly simple, but clearly the design, build, and testing of this massive compendium of orderables demand a considerable effort to complete, depending on the amount of work preformatted from the vendor. Several key features that should guide a correct approach to orderable build are listed below.

Synonyms

First, orderables must be easy to look up, as they are generally not entered as free text, but rather are matched to the terms within a search catalogue. Stated differently, ease of lookup means that as the provider begins typing in the name of an order, the search engine successfully matches and converts the provider's idea into a standard prebuilt order. This requires that each orderable name be listed under a variety of commonly used aliases or synonyms, mandating careful attention to completeness in the catalogue build. Consider, for example, an order for a CT of the chest. At Mission, this orderable is listed variably with synonyms as "CT chest," "chest CT," "CT thorax," and "thorax CT." Thus, the orderable catalogue must be comprehensive to include nearly any order that may be imagined. In this approach, as the physician thinks of the name of the test, he or she may expect to get a positive match with a prebuilt orderable from any reasonable search.

Modification of Order Details

Modification of orders should be easy for physicians to complete and should have the fewest possible required fields for order completion. Some required fields are necessary to capture all relevant information to construct a clear and complete order. The number of required fields may be minimized using several techniques. One of the most important fields is a listing of prepopulated order sentences attached to each medication orderable. The most common sentences for all formulary and many nonformulary medications should be prebuilt so the provider may easily select the closest one to the desired order sentence required for the order, thereby avoiding the completion of additional required fields specifying dose, dose unit, route, and frequency. These prepopulated order sentences also serve another important function. They provide real-time decision support at the point of order entry by prompting the provider to choose from the most commonly used and safest order sentences, thereby preventing errors by providers who may inaccurately recall a medication order sentence.

In the case of some orderables, many useful order details that would otherwise need to be completed by the physician may be pulled from information already present elsewhere in the system. For example, when ordering a radiology examination, relevant details for mode of travel, monitoring, oxygen support, nurse escort, pregnancy status, and others may be pulled from daily nursing assessments into the order details without querying the physician for this information. A more complete description of the design and build of orderables will depend upon the format and software design from each particular vendor. Nevertheless, the point is that the ease and speed of order entry, facilitated by a smooth search, and the inclusion of all relevant information within the order are critical components in the successful adoption of CPOE.

After successful order entry, efficient and effective order fulfillment must follow. The design and build of the downstream deployment of orders must include the clear and proper communication of the order intent, the provision of all necessary accompanying information, and careful design of processes needed to facilitate order completion and documentation. The design of these elements is best facilitated, as previously stated, by constructing a detailed analysis of current and future state workflow processes for each clinical support department.

Order Sets Design and Construction

Another necessary element in the build of the product is the creation of a useful array of order sets. An *order set* may be defined as a set of related orders required for the management of a series of integrated clinical tasks. Common uses for order sets include the admission process, transfer, and pre- and postoperative processes, adapted to the needs of each specialty. In addition, diagnosis-specific order sets may be constructed. Others may be used to facilitate safety measures, such as vaccinations or venous thromboembolism prophylaxis. Order sets may also be constructed to guide the administration of complex medications, such as titrated drip medications requiring additional orders for monitoring labs or titration algorithms. These may be additionally supported by relevant guidelines, reminders, supporting lab results, nomograms for administration, and dose calculators.

Occasional high-risk medications require the provider to address a list of indications and contraindications prior to use. These may be incorporated into required ordering formats for specific medications. Other order sets may be constructed to support the performance of bedside procedures or the ordering of groups of related tests. Order set utility may be further enhanced by the inclusion of nested order sets and sequenced order sets. Clearly, order sets are highly useful, not only for the purpose of saving time for the user, but also for the provision of real-time decision support to guide ordering precision, consistency, and reliability at the proper point along the continuum of care. We developed more than five hundred order sets in preparation for CPOE. Physicians from each service line were involved in the construction, revision, and approval of all order sets in advance of CPOE.

Refining the Product: Usability Testing

Following design and build, the product must be refined and polished prior to productive use. This critical phase involves extensive testing. In a system as complex as the practice of medicine involving more than sixty thousand orders, each with numerous ordering options, and with more than five hundred order sets, many millions of ordering options are assembled. Therefore, great care must be exercised to avoid errors in this process in order to ensure their safe application to patient care. In addition to customary unit testing, application testing, and integration testing, we recommend an additional category of testing that we shall refer to as *usability testing*.

Usability testing consists of making scanned copies of thousands of handwritten paper orders. These images of actual orders were stored on compact discs in order that they may be viewed exactly as they had been written by physicians. Testing consisted of tasking informatics personnel with converting these handwritten orders into electronic orders. Each user recorded on standard forms any difficulty or impedance he or she may encounter, however minor, to the successful computer entry of these orders. All such order defects were reviewed by a change control committee, charged with evaluating each complaint and recommending appropriate action to amend and improve the order.

Usability testing began at Mission one year prior to go-live and was conducted in four separate waves. The first attempt resulted in a finding that 72% of orders tested had some form of defect or imperfection. After making the necessary corrections to the build, a second wave conducted three months later showed the defect rate had been reduced to 46%. A third wave reflected further improvement to 18%, and a final wave conducted two months prior to go-live revealed a much more satisfactory 2% rate. We should state there was considerable resistance on the part of many of our clinical testing staff to the performance of usability testing. We remain convinced, however, especially in retrospect, that this testing was a critical factor in CPOE adoption. Physicians may be expected to exhibit a low tolerance for defects in the build of the product. Other elements concerning the refinement of the build of the orders will be addressed subsequently.

Education

Because CPOE differs substantially from paper order entry, and because many elements of the process are not entirely intuitive, the issue of formally educating the medical staff and hospital staff must be addressed. Our education process began with the development of an interactive computer-based training (CBT) module. Our CBT was internally developed by our education staff and several physicians using a CBT software development tool. For interest, we created a mock patient care scenario consisting of the case of a woman who presented to the ED with abdominal pain, required admission, went to surgery, experienced complications, improved, and was eventually discharged home.

The CBT offered examples in the use of single orders, order sets, conditional orders, order modifications, rules and alerts, formulary issues, and so on. Some of the ordering steps were automated while others required interactive participation. The CBT took approximately two to three hours to review. The CBT was made broadly available via the Internet and intranet links, and was also mailed in the form of CDs to all providers. Although review of the CBT was not mandatory, it was strongly encouraged for preparation for classroom education.

Because CPOE could be enabled (turned on or off) for each individual provider, all providers were advised that failure to complete CPOE training would result in the loss of all ordering privileges, both paper and computer, until their education could be completed. Classes were scheduled months in advance of class sessions to permit physicians adequate time to adjust their clinical schedules. The format of the classes consisted of an introduction, followed by a recapitulation of the content of the CBT, but in the format of a paper-based manual that contained the same order entry steps as the CBT. In this format the provider was expected to execute each individual keystroke and mouse click to effect entry of each required order. The classroom experience lasted four hours, with each physician working from separate computer workstations. Several educators circulated during the class to offer assistance to answer questions, and attendance was documented. They also examined the physicians' final completed orders to ensure that the orders had been entered correctly. Although admittedly tedious, by the time physicians had completed this classroom activity, they were able to independently execute a broad range of basic order entry functions.

We did include a provision to permit providers to test out of the manual exercise. Providers who had carefully studied the CBT prior to class were offered the option of taking a forty-five-minute competency test. Those who passed the test were not required to perform the manual exercise and were able to complete their educational requirement in less than the allotted four hours. Beyond the education classes, we offered supplemental evening classes for selected groups of physicians who requested additional assistance with order entry education specific to the needs of their specialty. In addition, we set up practice patients in our electronic training domain with the entire order catalogue available online so that providers would have the opportunity to work independently on their own for additional order entry practice. We also posted educators in our physician lounges who were available to help with questions and assist with useful tips and tricks. Because we broadcast an expectation that the go-live experience would be seriously challenging for those not sufficiently familiar with the order entry application, many physicians, concerned about the impact to their workflow, took advantage of these additional options.

CME Credit

In one medical staff conference, the question was asked: Given the CPOE was likely to take providers more time than paper order entry, what advantage was there for providers in embracing this transition? The response was: Other than the expected benefit to patient care and cost efficiency for the hospital, there was no other perceived benefit to the provider. This response was poorly received. In searching for a means to give back some token of appreciation to the medical staff for going through this process, we investigated the possibility of securing continuing medical education credit for physicians. With the assistance of our local Area Health Education Center (AHEC) organization, we were able to secure a hospital-funded initiative that would allow all physicians who went through the CPOE implementation process to be awarded eight hours of category I continuing medical education (CME) credits. In addition, for those physicians who agreed to undergo a three-phase documentation plan to assess agreed-upon outcome variables that the physicians would review and provide a written conclusion for, we could award twenty-eight hours of CME credit. We had thirty-two physicians who availed themselves of the twenty-eight-hour option. All the remaining physicians who completed CPOE training and implementation were awarded eight hours each.

Only six out of approximately six hundred physicians on staff who required ordering privileges failed to comply with training and were subsequently denied their ordering privileges. These six subsequently completed training within two weeks of go-live and their privileges were reinstated at that time.

Building Physician Favorites Folders

Because physician specialties tend to select from a limited range of commonly used orders, allowing physicians to build individual favorites folders containing frequently used or complex-to-build orders prior to go-live was expected to be useful. Training for favorites folder build was included in our physician education program. In addition, selected members of the medical staff assisted in the build of folders of orders specific to each of their clinical specialties. These folders were useful for assembling collections of specialty specific orders and also served as templates to assist some physicians in the construction of their personal favorites folders. To accommodate the need for physicians to build orders into their personal favorites folders, we devised a technique allowing physicians access to the production domain prior to go-live in order to build their favorites folders, but without allowing them to sign and implement orders until the scheduled go-live. Having a prebuilt favorites folder available to use on the day of go-live proved helpful and reassuring to many physicians.

The Pilot

Ultimately a structured physician pilot for CPOE was implemented that served several purposes preceding the primary go-live. First, the pilot served as a final proof of concept for the order entry process. This proof of concept was closely watched by the entire medical staff, as they observed their piloting colleagues' reactions throughout their CPOE transition for signs of failure. Second, the pilot served as a final "polishing" of the product orders to clear up any final identifiable defects in the build prior to the main go-live. Issues with orders and processes were carefully recorded by informatics personnel assisting the pilot physicians and sent to the change control team for analysis and remediation. Finally, the pilot served as a proving ground for workflow effectiveness as orders from a variety of service lines were deployed downstream from the order entry position.

There was substantial discussion regarding how to structure the pilot and the transition leading up to the main go-live. Some had advocated a more complex, sequential pilot leading up to the main go-live, whereas others had advocated a simplified pilot shortly followed by the big bang main go-live. In the end, the former approach was implemented in that we planned for a relatively protracted, twelve-week sequential pilot phase that involved a significant percentage of the medical staff, followed by a big bang day that capped the end of the pilot, incorporating the remainder of the medical staff. The first group to pilot CPOE was the emergency department. All physicians in the ED went live twelve weeks ahead of the rest of the hospital. This was followed five weeks later by an orthopedic pilot that consisted of five orthopedic surgeons going live over a two-week period. In the final phase we had planned to add five new physicians per week over five weeks, representing a broad range of specialties to test workflow and usability across diverse services. We had limited this number to five new physicians per week based on a limited number of qualified personnel to assist the physicians in the pilot phase. To my surprise, within a few days vice presidents were calling on behalf of physicians from a number of services requesting that we include additional physicians in the pilot. The vice presidents committed to provide for the rapid training of additional, qualified informatics assistants who could support the additional interested physicians, allowing them to participate as pilots as well. By the week prior to go-live, there were 107 (out of 650 eligible physicians) of the heaviest users of the inpatient service live on CPOE and with most physicians performing very well.

The Main Go-Live

The movement toward go-live was afforded additional momentum by the increased number of physician pilots across a broad range of specialties who were finding the CPOE process reasonably easy to navigate and use. The day of go-live proved remarkably uneventful with few unexpected complications. For the go-live, we staffed every clinical unit with two to three nurse super-users. In addition, we maintained a staff of roaming support personnel who could be deployed to any area where the super-users had trouble keeping up with the flow. We also maintained a fully staffed command center of eight to twelve individuals for two weeks, utilizing a rotating phone system to take calls requesting assistance. Nighttime staff coverage was reduced to two individuals. On the day of go-live we received 380 calls to the command center. By the end of two weeks, this figure had dropped to about thirty-five calls per day. Most issues fielded could be dealt with through educational reinforcement. A smaller percentage required more detailed analysis by the change control team, of which only about 4% required some type of change in the build of the orderable or order set. Within two weeks, with an absence of major issues or adverse events, and with rapid response to identified problems, CPOE was well on the way to cementing itself into the new culture of the electronic support of clinical patient care.

Change Control and Long-Term User Support: Final Polishing of the Product

Over the first three months following CPOE implementation, we observed a gradual decrease in calls for assistance with CPOE ordering and an increase in calls for improved functionality in terms of order set modifications and advanced decision support, particularly as the strain of new processes in downstream departments and services surfaced. These pressures were enhanced by impending Centers for Medicare and Medicaid Services (CMS) and Joint Commission reviews. Post-CPOE support was by phone, which was initially maintained 24/7 by an on-call team of trained users. Ordering issues were registered through these calls and through the work of service line and departmental staff responsible for order sets development. Issues were captured using an intranet site dedicated to CPOE. Issues were routed through a relatively small change control group consisting of two physicians, two nurse liaisons, a pharmacist, two clinical informatics staff, one IT staff member, and others from specific departments only as needed for dealing with problems relevant to their particular areas.

Over a three-month period the change control group addressed more than thirty-eight hundred requests for change. Approximately three-fourths of these issues were educational or redundant in nature. Of the remaining quarter, about three-fourths were problems requiring changes in operational processes within services and departments downstream from the orders. About 4% of the issues required actual change in the build or design of the orders. The majority of these changes were remediated in a timely fashion. Fewer, but more frustrating, were issues with the performance of the software from the vendor, which took significantly longer to resolve.

As a final note, we are now sixteen months into CPOE and the substantial majority of providers have acclimated well to the new system. We are in the process of studying the impact of CPOE on a variety of processes, including safety, clinical, and financial outcomes. Our study also includes a time motion analysis of the order entry process for providers pre- and post-CPOE, as well as an analysis of the order completion time for departmental services. The measurements for the post-CPOE arm were completed in the spring of 2009, one year following go-live. We look forward to sharing the outcomes of these studies in the coming year.

Summary of Salient Recommendations

■ Build a logical case for the necessity to move to CPOE.
■ CPOE ideally should be physician led.
■ Involve the medical staff at the beginning of the process and have physicians champion innovations at each step along the continuum.
■ Focus on and develop teams to support CPOE prerequisites: performance, ease of use (functionality), provision of supporting results and documentation, access to computer workstations, adequate downtime procedures, communications, policies and regulations, education, and go-live support.
■ Take whatever time is necessary to carefully document your current processes in the present state and then in the future state using process flow diagrams in order to properly integrate and positively leverage IT changes into clinical workflow.
■ Provide features that save time, effort, and cost, and that improve quality of care, drawing providers to engage and use the system. Measure and publish outcomes.
■ Engage physician assistance in leadership, in implementation strategy, design and build, piloting, and go-live support, including the involvement of physician champions.
■ Create collaborative alignment among physicians, clinical support staff, administration, and board of directors.
■ Develop an appropriate budget for CPOE. Treat the design and implementation as a formal project management initiative.
■ Create evidence- and consensus-based order sets for all clinical specialties and departments, initially on paper and then transition to support CPOE.
■ Communicate an honest, realistic expectation for CPOE in terms of workflow. Listen to and answer questions and concerns raised by the medical staff.
■ Mandate participation in the use of CPOE.
■ Mandate education for all users prior to go-live.

- Create educational support to make the process as efficient, yet comprehensive as possible, including computer-based training, classroom-based education, *ad hoc* targeted education, a training domain for users to practice, and support staff in physician lounges or other easy-to-access locations to answer questions.
- Enable and encourage the build of orders into favorites folders for users in the production domain prior to go-live.
- Offer category I CME for all users who go through the education and go-live process.
- Apply liberal usability testing to ensure that the CPOE orderables and order sets work smoothly and efficiently.
- Utilize a progressive pilot strategy, followed by a bang go-live.
- Employ liberal support for all users at go-live. Taper support over two to three weeks.
- Employ the use of a command center, tapering to phone support, to provide rapid responses to questions that cannot easily be fielded by on-site super-user support personnel.
- Develop a mechanism to capture all problems, issues, and requests for change.
- These issues should be triaged, analyzed, and referred for remediation as needed by a change control group that can provide prompt turnaround on requests for change.

Don't deviate too much from the list above if you want a successful implementation. The key is that physicians must use the system, so physicians must be involved in its development. Finally, remember the process of order entry is not completed until the order is initiated and follow-through is achieved by nursing and clinical support departments downstream for patient care. After all, this is about patient care.

Bottom line: Don't implement CPOE because other hospitals are doing it or because there are stimulus dollars attached. Implement CPOE because it is right for the care of your patients.

Chapter 6

Knowledge Translation and Informatics in Healthcare

Ann McKibbon

Contents

Introduction

Knowledge translation is the process whereby research findings, or any new and worthwhile knowledge, are integrated into everyday practice. Louis Pasteur summed up this important aspect of research and development by saying:

> To him who devotes his life to science, nothing can give more happiness than increasing the number of discoveries, but his cup of joy is full when the results of his studies immediately find practical applications.

Pasteur did not, however, include in this statement how important this movement of research into practice is for those of us who stand to benefit from the research findings—or how difficult it is. In the healthcare world, estimates of the size of the gap between what we know about the best possible care from research and what we receive from health professionals is significant. Estimates of the size of the gap translate into the fact that on average, Americans receive only 55% of their recommended healthcare services.[1] This care gap is comprised of both care that is received that should not be given and care that should be administered and is not.

Woolf and Johnson make a strong statement about the magnitude of the effects of not using health research efficiently.[2] They provide substantial evidence that suggests we need to put more money and effort into determining the most effective methods of implementing existing knowledge rather than to fund additional basic and clinical research and other projects designed to discover new knowledge. Their estimate of the relative amount of research investment between basic science and other research and implementation is likely (100:1), favoring the discovery of new knowledge. Until we can insure that new and important knowledge is integrated into our healthcare system in a timely manner, lives will be lost, care will be substandard, funding will not be optimized, and the healthcare system will continue to be inefficient and possibly even dangerous.

The gap between best possible care and actual care, or between evidence and practice, occurs because of many factors:

- Ever-increasing growth of new knowledge that leads to information overload.
- Growth in the complexity of healthcare and the need to document this care fully. The potential for litigation is also a factor here.
- Increasing demands on the time clinicians have to interact with patients. (For this chapter, the term *clinician* refers to a health professional who helps make clinical decisions for and with patients—usually physicians, nurses, and pharmacists, although others are often included.)
- Structural issues related to disincentives to improve care (e.g., financial penalties to provide advice by e-mail rather than clinical visits).
- Organizational issues related to things like an inappropriate skill mix to address patient needs, lack of facilities, inadequate staffing, or outdated equipment.
- Peer group pressures (e.g., local standards that tend toward less than optimal care).
- Individual deficits in health professional knowledge, skills, and attitudes.
- Individual deficits in patient and family knowledge, skills, and attitudes.
- Patient expectations that are not aligned with best care (e.g., direct to consumer advertising or expectations related to antibiotics).
- Basic human nature and our inclination toward resistance to change.

Many people across disciplines, domains, countries, and time periods are interested in optimizing knowledge translation to close the gap between evidence and practice. Consequently, multiple terms referring to knowledge translation exist; see http://whatiskt.wikispaces.com/ for a list of one hundred terms related to the concepts of knowledge translation. For this paper we use the term *knowledge translation* as defined by the Canadian Institutes of Health Research (CIHR):

> Knowledge translation is a dynamic and iterative process that includes synthesis, dissemination, exchange and ethically sound application of knowledge to improve the health of Canadians, provide more effective health services and products and strengthen the health care system.
>
> This process takes place within a complex system of interactions between researchers and knowledge users which may vary in intensity, complexity and level of engagement depending on the nature of the research and the findings as well as the needs of the particular knowledge user.
>
> **Source: http://www.cihr-irsc.gc.ca/e/29418.html**

In its role to improve knowledge translation, CIHR has supported publication of a 2009 book on knowledge translation in the health sciences that can be used by those who want more information on the topic.[3]

Knowledge translation and its techniques are vitally important for researchers as well as developers and entrepreneurs in all knowledge domains. This chapter will concentrate on knowledge translation and health information technology. Shekelle and colleagues summarized published evidence and showed that health information technology can be cost-effective in improving the quality and efficiency of healthcare. These authors also present challenges to the health informatics community.[4] Their report is summarized as follows:

> HIT [health information technology] has the potential to enable a dramatic transformation in the delivery of health care, making it safer, more effective, and more efficient. Some organizations have already realized major gains through the implementation of multifunctional, interoperable HIT systems built around an EHR. However, widespread implementation of HIT has been limited by a lack of generalizable knowledge about what types of HIT and implementation methods will improve care and manage costs for specific health organizations.

The following content of this chapter describes the interventions and actions that are most likely to improve and speed the flow of research evidence into practice, and how informatics applications can enhance the probability that patients and their families obtain the best care possible.

The informatics world needs to understand how to optimize knowledge translation for two reasons. First, we need to produce tools and services that will best serve the needs of health professionals to optimize their care process. We need to produce systems that can ensure quick, efficient, and accurate implementation of appropriate new advances and promote or block discontinuation of outdated care. Once we produce these tools and services, we must work to ensure that they are adopted, implemented, and sustained by the intended users, utilizing the most effective change strategies. Without this knowledge translation by informatics practitioners our tools and projects will not be used to their fullest potential.

Strategies for Improving Knowledge Translation in Healthcare

What tools and techniques are effective for behavior change of clinicians and their institutions and organizations? Knowledge translation in the domain of healthcare deals with changing the behavior of individual clinicians and how clinics, hospitals, cities, municipalities, states and provinces, and even countries respond to the challenge of making health decisions based on evidence in a cyclical, ongoing manner so that care provided is the best currently available. Once we know what changes behavior, we can determine if and how the informatics applications we implement can enhance these interventions. Bero and colleagues summarize the evidence on interventions or actions that close the gap between research and practice.[5] They summarize their findings of eighteen separate review articles assessing interventions for health professionals into three categories: what works, what might work, and what does not work. Although this article is somewhat dated, the general categories of what works and does not work remain applicable.

The first category is interventions that consistently change behavior: those that are supported by strong evidence that shows improved care across multiple studies and time periods.

- Educational outreach visits of an expert to discuss certain aspects of care, especially prescribing issues in North America. The drug companies use this technique quite effectively. Data show that 35% of the staff of pharmaceutical companies are employed in marketing departments, many of whom visit physicians, sponsor conferences, or provide educational sessions to emphasize drug adoption.[6]
- Computerized or manual reminders of care to be done or not done for a patient in a specific situation.
- Multifaceted interventions (combinations of two or more of audit and feedback, reminders, local consensus processes, or marketing).
- Educational programs that are interactive—those that require discussion, role playing, or practice by health professionals in workshops or similar programs of active learning.

The second group of interventions are those that show variable effectiveness. In some instances studies of these interventions have shown positive changes, and some have been associated with no changes or detrimental outcomes.

- Audit and feedback of actual performance of the individual, often compared with group norms (e.g., surgical infection rates for a given individual that are 10% higher than those of the other surgeons in the hospital).
- Use of local opinion leaders (those in a group, such as a hospital or multi-physician clinic, who are identified by their colleagues as being asked often for advice or guidance in care situations).
- Local consensus processes that involve practicing clinicians in a geographic area or group who work together to establish care norms or procedures for a specific situation or care issue. These documents have been called care maps or clinical practice guidelines. They can be for a small group such as a hospital ward or reflect the standard of care for national practice.
- Patient interventions whereby information is provided to them, and they in turn use the information to change clinician knowledge or behavior, e.g., direct to consumer marketing.

The third category is also important. These interventions have little or no effect on clinician behavior:

- Educational materials in paper or electronic format (not individualized).
- Didactic educational meetings, e.g., lectures, and most standard conferences with featured speakers or researchers presenting papers to peers in lecture format.

Areas of Health Professional Needs That Can Be Addressed by Health Informatics

The remainder of this chapter will discuss challenges that clinicians have in improving their care of patients (ensuring the best possible care) and how various existing or new health information technologies can aid the knowledge translation process. The chapter ends with cautions for informaticians.

Information Overload

Information overload for clinicians is a real dilemma. The problem of too much information is evident on a number of fronts in the clinical world. Clinicians deal with approximately eleven thousand different diseases and conditions, and most of these have multiple overlapping signs and symptoms. (For clinicians, symptoms are what patients report during a clinic visit, and signs are what clinicians find when using their hands and tools, such as thermometers, blood pressure cuffs, and stethoscopes.) Adding to this information that a clinician needs to synthesize and use for decision making is the information from the published literature. Medline, the major health database, contains approximately 17 million citations and publishes more than twelve thousand articles per week. Of these, three hundred are likely to have information relevant to clinical care.[7] In addition, the web contains an estimated 25 billion pages as of July 2009. All of these factors provide tremendous pressure and tax an individual's ability to cope. One way to alleviate this information overload is through the utilization of health informatics applications.

Point of care information systems are designed to address the flow of new information or can provide information backup when a clinician feels that he or she needs more information. These point of care systems provide access to e-resources using several communication means, including handheld devices. Prendiville et al. describe a study of Irish pediatricians using handheld devices to answer questions that arose during hospital care.[8] The summarized conclusions below depict the importance of these point of care informatics resources for this group of physicians.

> The study received 156 completed questionnaires, a 66.1% response. 67% of pediatricians utilized the internet as their first "port of call" when looking to answer a medical question. 85% believe that web-based resources have improved medical practice, with 88% reporting web-based resources are essential for medical practice today. 93.5% of pediatricians believe attempting to answer clinical questions as they arise is an important component in practicing evidence-based medicine. 54% of all pediatricians have recommended websites to parents or patients. 75.5% of pediatricians report finding it difficult to keep up-to-date with new information relevant to their practice.

Another study of question answering using health information technology was done in Ottawa, Ontario. Handheld devices were given to hospital physicians and physicians in training to provide information support. These devices were programmed to provide electronic communication to an information service provided by librarians.[9] The librarian service was designed to provide fast and efficient answers and to determine if the twinning of the librarian with the mobile devices was more effective than the devices with only access to online information resources. At the end of the study, more than 85% of the participants favored having direct access to a librarian to provide answers to clinical questions. Most of the physicians in the study felt that the service improved the care they provided. As another example of information support at the point of care, Cimino and colleagues developed information systems embedded within electronic health record (EHR) systems. They provide strategically placed electronic "infobuttons" in systems in the EHR to indicate a probable information need. This might involve an issue such as an abnormal laboratory finding or some patient data suggesting a potential change in medication. The infobutton is actually a link to context-specific information or another information resource that will likely address that abnormal finding or trend.[10]

EHRs also provide great value in helping clinicians with their information overload in other areas. A well-designed EHR will collect and integrate information from multiple sources, such as hospitals, clinics, the workplace, and pharmacies, for a given patient. A strong EHR will also enable important information to be collected just once, and then make it available thereafter. For example, questions related to allergies, medications, home address, next of kin, and previous pregnancies are often asked and recorded multiple times during patient care encounters. This information should be collected once and then made available for all other recognized care providers. EHRs are also ideal tools for collecting and synthesizing sequential data and presenting them to depict time trends or abnormal patterns. Most chronic diseases such as heart disease, diabetes, and asthma rely on analyzing multiple data points and making decisions based on trends. The literature on EHRs is extensive: Häyrinen and colleagues have produced a systematic review of the definition, structure, content, use, and effects of EHRs.[11]

Clinical (or computerized) decision support systems (CDSSs) are also useful tools to help clinicians deal with information overload. CDSSs by definition are systems that integrate data from two separate sources. They store patient-specific information, either entered by the user or from EHRs. These patient-specific data are then integrated into a database of clinical knowledge rules or patterns (using an "inference engine"). This inference engine then produces suggestions for actions related to the diagnosis, treatment, or monitoring for that particular patient case—one of the main functions of CDSSs. The clinician can choose to act according to these recommendations or make other decisions. Open Clinical (an international organization that promotes the utilization of decision support and other knowledge-based technologies) provides a more detailed summary of the characteristics of CDSSs (http://www.openclinical.org/dss.html). Perreault and Metzger list the functions of CDSSs, including the previously mentioned clinical support:[12]

> Four key functions of [C]DSSs are outlined: (i) Administrative: Supporting clinical coding and documentation, authorization of procedures, and referrals. (ii) Managing clinical complexity and details: Keeping patients on research and chemotherapy protocols; tracking orders, referrals follow-up, and preventive care. (iii) Cost control: Monitoring medication orders; avoiding duplicate or unnecessary tests. (iv) Decision support: Supporting clinical diagnosis and treatment plan processes; and promoting use of best practices, condition-specific guidelines, and population-based management.

Haynes and his group are updating an important review of the evidence of the effectiveness of CDSSs,[13] which will be published in late 2009 or early 2010.

In addition to the point of care information systems and CDSS, almost all informatics applications have components that assist clinicians with information overload. Many of the systems are designed to collect and analyze large quantities of evolving data across systems and from research studies or patients in general, and their functionality continues to evolve. Areas of ongoing development for enhanced functionality for informatics include interoperability, intelligent information retrieval, automated or manual (people-centered) mechanisms to keep information resources current with the standards of best practice, and better integration of research findings into EHRs.

Clinician and Patient Deficits in Knowledge and Skills

Clinicians, patients, and caregivers can have deficits in knowledge and skills that can impede obtaining, providing, or acting on the best possible care. For the general public, an example of the magnitude of these deficits is a review of the literature on public knowledge of the risks for and signs and symptoms of stroke. Strokes are common, carry considerable disability, and fast access to care lessens the potential suffering. In a study that addressed levels of knowledge in select communities regarding the risks of strokes, Nicol and Thrift found that between 20 and 30% of the people surveyed did not know a single risk factor for stroke despite considerable marketing of this information.[14] Another example of clinician knowledge revealed that more than 75% of Australian family physicians felt that their knowledge of breastfeeding was inadequate.[15] Informatics applications can identify gaps in knowledge and provide learning based on these gaps. For example, residents are taught how to identify pathology abnormalities and conditions, as well as report writing, using intelligent tutoring programs at the University of Pittsburgh. The system uses natural language processing and other informatics tools to identify when the residents show they have mastered a given set of content, or if the student needs more practice in identifying certain diseases or content areas.[16] Computer tutoring (individualized education) is on target to become even more highly used to educate undergraduate medical and nursing students and residents. Individualized educational programs that evaluate the learning achieved and direct further learning for patients have also been shown to be effective. For example, nursing researchers are building computer-mediated, web-based, individualized educational programs for women with ovarian cancer. Both format and content are based on the authors' analyses of data in forty studies of computer education for women with cancer and chronic diseases.[17]

Fordis and colleagues showed that online continuing professional education is as valuable for providing education as in-person continuing education. Continuing education is vital to health professionals for two major reasons.[18] First, because so much information is changing, health professionals must be lifelong learners to provide the best possible care. Second, health professionals must report formally

on their learning to maintain their clinical certification. An added benefit of online courses and point of care learning systems over traditional learning is that the credential benefit (continuing education credits) of the course can be captured in a format suitable for submission to certifying bodies such as the American or Canadian Medical Association. Some professional organizations are actively pursing automatic reporting of credit hours for certification via online systems. Keeping track of continuing education to support ongoing certification manually is time-consuming and often inaccurate.

In addition to identifying knowledge gaps, health information technology can also detect errors. The U.S. Institute of Medicine has estimated that between forty-four thousand and ninety-eight thousand deaths occur in the United States annually because of errors in care.[19] One of the most important areas in healthcare where errors occur, especially in hospital and long-term settings, is with medications. Errors can occur during ordering (for patients in hospitals) or prescribing (for patients meeting health professionals outside hospitals). Because children are given doses based on weights and ages, some people estimate that pediatric patients have prescribing error rates three times higher than those for adult patients.[20] Ordering and prescribing can be improved using health information technology with things like provider order entry systems (see below) to deal with poor handwriting, systems to block inappropriate dosing, or prompt when a prescribed drug may be one to which the patient has allergies. Dispensing can be improved by using barcode systems that notify the nurse giving the medicine that the barcode for the medication is not the same barcode that the patient has on his or her wrist. Monitoring of the patient to ensure that the drug is given in sufficient quantities to provide the proper effect and not cause adverse reactions is also available using information from EHRs. AGRAWAL provides more information on medication safety using health information technology.[21] Another, more specific example is illustrated in a study which discusses the benefits of physician order entry on prescribing in pediatrics intensive care units.[22] It concluded that the systems reduced prescribing errors, but these errors did not reduce the rate of adverse drug reactions or mortality.

Time Pressures

Time is an important factor for current healthcare providers. Although clinicians perceive that EHRs, with or without personal health record (PHR) components, consume more time than paper records, they do offer some time-saving features.[23] Examples where EHR or PHR systems or other devices, like tablets in waiting rooms, can save time are if they enable patients to book their own appointments and provide data on current issues before clinic visits. The patients and caregivers can state the reason for the scheduled visit plus signs and symptoms, provide detailed lists of prescribed and over-the-counter medications, and update information on addresses and insurance coverage. The time that is available for the appointment can then be spent analyzing the data and formulating decisions and care plans. EHRs that integrate data from multiple caregivers and settings (e.g., primary care clinics, nursing homes, specialists, and hospitals) also save time during patient visits. Complete records can also alleviate the need for duplicate diagnostic or evaluation studies if all the patient data are successfully aggregated in a timely manner and available for all caregivers and all locations of care.

CPOE

Another informatics application designed to save time as well as improve information flow and reduce errors is computerized physician (or provider) order entry (CPOE) systems (also mentioned above in the error section). Using a CPOE system, healthcare professionals place their orders for such things as medications, diagnostic tests, appointments with specialists or generalists, or discharge instructions online rather than verbally or on paper. These online orders are then quickly distributed without transcription and its inherent errors to those who can ensure that the tests are booked, carried out, and the results reported back to all who are involved. CPOE systems can not only speed care but check and verify that the data are accurate, actions are appropriate, their booking is efficient, and communication is facilitated and recorded. A study by Wietholter et al. illustrates the time-savings potential made possible by CPOE systems. The study compared processing time for prescriptions (time from the initial order by the physician or nurse until it is prepared and delivered by the hospital pharmacist) with and without automated systems. Processing time for prescriptions showed a mean time of 115 minutes before automation, compared with 3 minutes to process the same drug order after the introduction of CPOE for prescribing.[24]

Workflow Applications

Workflow is vitally important for clinicians in all care settings and has often been overlooked or underappreciated by system developers. Workflow refers to the processes and their time sequencing when patients, healthcare professionals, and their system interact. Often physicians have different ways of working than do nurses. New systems, either online or not, must respect and adapt to these differences. For example, in a teaching hospital, the physicians in charge "round" each morning bringing along the care team of medical students, residents, and sometimes pharmacists, social workers, or librarians. They meet as a team with each patient assigned to their care, ascertain his or her progress and needs, and plan for next steps. Each patient is completed and orders are given to address all of the needs—a patient-centered workflow. Nurses in hospital units deal with patients

differently. For example, one nurse provides all of the medications for patients several times per day. The nurse wants the information in an EHR to be focused only on the needed medications and presented in patient order—needed medications for the patient in room 1 bed 1, for the patient in room 1 bed 2, and so on. Those who schedule diagnostic testing or assign operating room time to physicians or teams need to see the clinical information in another format, as do the administrative team who maintain supplies and equipment. Informatics professionals must ascertain the flow of people, tasks, and information, the workflow and how it differs for different groups of people, before planning for new systems.

Zahra Niazkhani of the Institute of Health Policy and Management in the Netherlands provides a summary of what is known about the effects of CPOE on workflow.[25] Computerizing a system with existing poor workflow has been the downfall of many systems. Also, not recognizing and respecting the existing workflow as well as the culture of an organization has proven costly and frustrating for system designers during implementation.

Computer Reminders

Manual or computerized reminder systems have been shown to be one of the most effective methods of improving clinical behavior, clinical practice, and knowledge translation. Reminders originally were provided in the form of paper notes on paper charts for such things as missing childhood vaccinations, influenza shots, and mammographies. The next implementation came in the form of e-mails. These e-mails were often more general reminders, such as notice of a new hand sanitizer solution system to be implemented into a hospital, or to consider generic instead of brand name drugs. Paper- and general e-mail-based reminders are not as effective as those that are patient specific and delivered at the point of care from within an EHR. Shojania and colleagues produced a Cochrane Review of point of care reminders delivered by a computerized decision support system within an EHR. They reviewed twenty-eight original studies that showed consistent increases in actions when the reminders were provided across a range of conditions, practitioners, and settings.[26]

Reminder systems within EHRs are important in many applications. The twenty-eight studies in the Shojania review described the settings and content areas of the thirty-two comparisons in these studies:

> Of the 32 comparisons that provided analyzable results for improvements in process adherence, 21 reported outcomes involving prescribing practices, six specifically targeted adherence to recommended vaccinations, 13 reported outcomes related to test ordering, three captured documentation, and seven reported adherence to miscellaneous other processes (for example composite compliance with a guideline).

Reminder systems can work for patients also. For example, Puccio and colleagues studied whether reminders via cell phones would improve adherence (taking their medications) with HIV and AIDS medication in adolescents and young adults.[27]

Producing New Knowledge from Data

Another opportunity for increasing efficiencies in healthcare is that data stored and generated by powerful integrated EHRs and PHRs, hospital information systems, and insurance collections can be mined via quantitative analytic techniques to extract information and produce new knowledge. This new knowledge can, and will, direct an increasing number of patient-specific decisions. Currently our limited data collection and analyses capabilities could create knowledge only on groups of people (i.e., populations) rather than individuals. These new data will likely have an impact on being able to predict prognosis for an individual (the likely path that a person's disease or condition will take). This is very useful information for the patient, health professionals, and insurers. For example, data mining of information on 258 variables from 16,604 patients with heart-lung transplants showed associations between variables that could be used to predict survival in the patients, where traditional statistical analyses of data sets with that many variables could not yield these results.[28]

In addition to data mining and knowledge discovery, advances in bioinformatics can link a person's health and family history data with his or her genomic data for decision making. This information will allow for better targeting of treatments: some drugs work well for some people and not for others. Strong data collection and analyses will be able to sort this puzzle out. Thervet and colleagues provide a summary of the promise of tailoring drugs based on genomic data.[29]

The production of new data is not really a classical knowledge translation task, but it is one that will become more important over time as our data collection methods become stronger and more genomic data are available. Our systems will continue to play an increasing role in the application of new and proven knowledge to maintain optimal healthcare, especially in the production and integration of new patient-specific information.

Challenges

Challenges exist in producing systems and projects designed to improve patient care through knowledge application. These challenges relate to the complexities of care, its ever-changing and advancing knowledge base, and the size of the healthcare enterprise. We also are held back by funding limitations. Despite the significant resource allocation by governments to health information technology, there is still not ample funding to produce ideal systems that integrate across the multitude of

people and organizations. We also must deal with multiple players, conflicting local, national, and international standards and regulations, and the fact that patients differ in their preferences, resources, and attitudes. Whenever clinicians, patients, or both seek individualized and tailored care, complexity creeps into our design specifications. Another challenge is that although our systems often change care processes and improve some intermediate outcomes such as knowledge or skills improvement, many of our projects are like those of Egberts et al.: the process changes do not always improve clinically important outcomes such as reducing mortality.[22] Despite all of these challenges, the opportunities are vast in the health informatics arena, where collaboration with our health professional peers will likely improve care.

Summary

Clinicians involved in healthcare struggle with changing practices, procedures, and the complexities of care in an ever-changing world. Patients and their conditions, insurance providers, threats of litigation, and local organizational issues are factors that must be considered in managing resources in this dynamic environment. Clinicians need all the help that informatics has to offer in its quest to keep current with advances in care where effective implementation of new knowledge or knowledge translation is essential.

Enabling effective knowledge translation is an important and exciting challenge in the development in informatics. As we build and complete projects we need to think about the knowledge translation challenges our clinicians and other partners have in their quest to stay up to date and provide optimal care. We need to remember that some interventions such as timely, useful, and context-specific reminders; decision support systems and CPOE within EHRs; individualized and continuing audit and feedback; combined interventions including patient training; and educational interventions that allow interaction and reflection work well at improving care and bring care closer to the ideal.

References

1. McGlynn, E. A., S. M. Asch, J. Adams, J. Keesey, J. Hicks, A. DeCristofaro, and E. A. Kerr. 2003. The quality of health care delivered to adults in the United States. *N Engl J Med* 348:2635–45.
2. Woolf, S. H., and R. E. Johnson. 2005. The break-even point: When medical advances are less important than improving the fidelity with which they are delivered. *Ann Fam Med* 3:545–52.
3. Straus, S. E., I. D. Graham, and J. Tetroe. 2009. *Knowledge translation in health care: Moving from evidence to practice.* Oxford: Wiley Blackwell and BMJ Publishing.
4. Shekelle, P. G., S. C. Morton, and E. B. Keeler. 2006. Costs and benefits of health information technology. *Evid Rep Technol Assess (Full Rep)* 132:1–71.

5. Bero, L. A., R. Grilli, J. M. Grimshaw, E. Harvey, A. D. Oxman, and M. A. Thomson. 1998. Closing the gap between research and practice: An overview of systematic reviews of interventions to promote the implementation of research findings. The Cochrane Effective Practice and Organization of Care Review Group. *BMJ* 317:4658.

6. Angell, M. 2004. Excess in the pharmaceutical industry. *CMAJ* 171:1451–53.

7. Glasziou, P. P. 2008. Information overload: What's behind it, what's beyond it? *Med J Aust* 189:84–85.

8. Prendiville, T. W., J. Saunders, and J. Fitzsimons. 2009. The information-seeking behaviour of paediatricians accessing web-based resources. *Arch Dis Child* 94:633–35.

9. McGowan, J., W. Hogg, C. Campbell, and M. Rowan. 2008. Just-in-time information improved decision-making in primary care: A randomized controlled trial. *PLoS One* 3:e3785.

10. Del Fiol, G., P. J. Haug, J. J. Cimino, S. P. Narus, C. Norlin, and J. A. Mitchell. 2008. Effectiveness of topic-specific infobuttons: A randomized controlled trial. *J Am Med Inform Assoc* 15:752–59.

11. Häyrinen, K., K. Saranto, and P. Nykänen. 2008. Definition, structure, content, use and impacts of electronic health records: A review of the research literature. *Int J Med Inform* 77:291–304.

12. Perreault, L., and J. Metzger. 1999. A pragmatic framework for understanding clinical decision support. *J Healthcare Inform Manag* 13:5–21.

13. Garg, A. X., N. K. Adhikari, H. McDonald, M. P. Rosas-Arellano, P. J. Devereaux, J. Beyene, J. Sam, and R. B. Haynes. 2005. Effects of computerized clinical decision support systems on practitioner performance and patient outcomes: A systematic review. *JAMA* 293:1223–38.

14. Nicol, M. B., and A. G. Thrift. 2005. Knowledge of risk factors and warning signs of stroke. *Vasc Health Risk Manag* 1:137–47.

15. Brodribb, W., Fallon A. B., C. Jackson, and D. Hegney. 2009. Breastfeeding knowledge— The experiences of Australian general practice registrars. *Aust Fam Physician* 38:26–29.

16. El Saadawi, G. M., E. Tseytlin, E. Legowski, D. Jukic, M. Castine, J. Fine, R. Gormley, and R. S. Crowley. 2007. A natural language intelligent tutoring system for training pathologists: Implementation and evaluation. *Adv Health Sci Educ Theory Pract* 13:709–22.

17. Dumrongpakapakorn, P., K. Hopkins, P. Sherwood, K. Zorn, and H. Donovan. 2009. Computer-mediated patient education: Opportunities and challenges for supporting women with ovarian cancer. *Nurs Clin North Am* 44:339–54.

18. Fordis, M., J. E. King, C. M. Ballantyne, P. H. Jones, K. H Schneider, S. J. Spann, S. B. Greenberg, and A. J. Greisinger. 2005. Comparison of the instructional efficacy of Internet-based CME with live interactive CME workshops: A randomized controlled trial. *JAMA* 294:1043–51.

19. Kohn, L. T. 1999. *To err is human: Building a safer health system.* Washington, DC: National Academy Press.

20. Kaushal, R., D. W. Bates, and C. Landrigan. 2001. Medication errors and adverse drug events in pediatric inpatients. *JAMA* 285:2114–20.

21. Agrawal, A. 2009. Medication errors: Prevention using information technology systems. *Br J Clin Pharmacol* 67:681–86.

22. Egberts, A. C. G., C. W. Bollen, F. van Rosse, B. Maat, C. M. A. Rademaker, and A. J. van Vught. 2009. The effect of computerized physician order entry on medication prescription errors and clinical outcome in pediatric and intensive care: A systematic review. *Pediatrics* 123:1184–90.
23. Ash, J. S., and D. W. Bates. 2005. Factors and forces affecting EHR system adoption: Report of a 2004 ACMI discussion. *J Am Med Inform Assoc* 12:8–12.
24. Wietholter, J., S. Sitterson, and S. Allison. 2009. Effects of computerized prescriber order entry on pharmacy order-processing time. *Am J Health Syst Pharm* 66:1394–98.
25. Niazkhani, Z., H. Pirnejad, M. Berg, and J. Aarts. 2009. The impact of computerized provider order entry systems on inpatient clinical workflow: A literature review. *J Am Med Inform Assoc* 16:539–49.
26. Shojania, K. G., A. Jennings, A. Mayhew, C. R. Ramsay, M. P. Eccles, and J. Grimshaw. 2009. The effects of on-screen, point of care computer reminders on processes and outcomes of care. *Cochrane Database Syst Rev* 3:CD001096.
27. Puccio, J. A., M. Belzer, J. Olson, M. Martinez, C. Salata, D. Tucker, and D. Tanaka. 2006. The use of cell phone reminder calls for assisting HIV-infected adolescents and young adults to adhere to highly active antiretroviral therapy: A pilot study. *AIDS Patient Care STDS* 20:438–44.
28. Oztekin, A. A., D. Delen, and Z. J. Kong. 2009. Predicting the graft survival for heart-lung transplantation patients: An integrated data mining methodology. *Int J Med Inform* 78(12):e84–e96.
29. Thervet, E., D. Anglicheau, C. Legendre, and P. Beaune. 2008. Role of pharmaco-genetics of immunosuppressive drugs in organ transplantation. *Ther Drug Monit* 30:143–50.

Chapter 7

Self-Service Technology in Healthcare

Tomas Gregorio

Contents

For years self-service technology has been utilized throughout the commercial spectrum. We find it in financial organizations in the form of automatic teller machines and in retail establishments and supermarkets in the way of self-checkout. It is used by hotels for checking guests in and out, and airlines utilize it to self-check passengers when they arrive at airports. Food chains are also starting to do bill payment for food up front, such as in Atlantic City, where patrons can pay before they go into a buffet at restaurants in the casino. According to NCR, a global technology company whose main product lines include self-service kiosks, point-of-sale terminals, ATMs, check processing systems, barcode scanners and business comsumables, the self-service movement continues to expand. Their study found that in 2007, 77% of consumers enjoyed using self-service technologies, where in 2008

145

that number jumped to 86%. Self-service technology will account for 58% of all customer service interactions by 2010. Consumers will spend $1 trillion using self-service technology by 2011. Retailers show that there is a 6 to 8% incremental increase in sales when kiosks are placed in the store; by the end of 2007, eight hundred thousand customer kiosks will be installed in North America, increasing to 1.2 million by 2009.[1]

Cross-industry results show 11% of customers select a retailer because of self-service checkout, 38% of customers are more likely to dine at quick service restaurants, 41% of customers are more likely to stay in a hotel with self-service, ATM machines generate $2.5 billion in fees, and airlines drive 8 million passengers per month with self-service facilities at the airports around the country. When you consider the labor optimization benefits of utilizing self-service kiosks in putting the power of the work in the consumer's hands, you realize that ATMs cost $0.27 per transaction versus $2.93 a transaction conducted with a bank employee. Airlines saved $3.52 per passenger, utilizing self-service kiosks; retailers estimate that up to 250 cashier labor hours a week are saved by utilizing self-service. When you consider how the Internet has revolutionized our shopping habits and its ability to communicate on a global scale, it's easy to see how putting the power of technology into a consumer's hands assists with expediting and reducing costs for transactions that would otherwise have to be managed by another person on the other side of the counter. NCR, the industry leader in self-service kiosk technology, commissioned the study that yielded the results (presented by NCR at the Self-Service Universe Conference, Orlando, FL, 2008) found in charts A and B. It included the following questions:

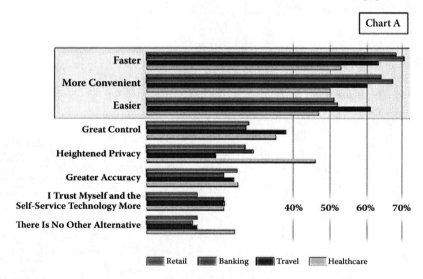

Q: Why would you choose self-service over personal assistance?

As chart A depicts, the three major reasons why a consumer would choose self-service are the speed, convenience, and ease of conducting and completing the transaction in lieu of an individual managing the process.

Interestingly enough, the respondents also found a heightened feeling of privacy in managing those transactions in the self-service environment. In analyzing the category of trustworthiness in self-service technology transactions ("I trust myself and the self-service technology more") the follow-up question was asked:

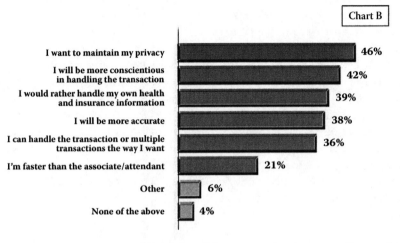

Chart B

I want to maintain my privacy	46%
I will be more conscientious in handling the transaction	42%
I would rather handle my own health and insurance information	39%
I will be more accurate	38%
I can handle the transaction or multiple transactions the way I want	36%
I'm faster than the associate/attendant	21%
Other	6%
None of the above	4%

Q: Why was "I trust myself and the self-service technology more" one of your top choices?

Chart B depicts the results, which clearly indicate that privacy dominated the responses.

Self-Service Technology and Privacy in Healthcare

Privacy and *healthcare* are almost synonymous terms. The Health Insurance Portability and Accountability Act (HIPAA) was enacted by the U.S. Congress in 1996. According to the Centers for Medicare and Medicaid Services (CMS), Title II of HIPAA, known as the administrative simplification (AS) provisions, requires the establishment of national standards for electronic healthcare transactions and national identifiers for providers, health insurance plans, and employers. This is intended to help people keep their information private. The administration simplification provisions also address the security and privacy of health data. The standards are meant to improve the efficiency and effectiveness of the nation's healthcare system by encouraging widespread use of electronic data interchange.

Privacy is clearly at the forefront of everyone's thought process when considering personal health information. Providing patients with a vehicle to manage that information on their own is in line with not only the provisions set forth by the federal government, but also the wishes of our patients.

Self-service kiosks are more private. There are many topics a patient may not want to communicate to another person. Self-service platforms enable individuals to stand in a booth and utilize the intelligence built into the software. They can register themselves financially as well as inquire about their condition or their medications without having to involve anyone at all.

The utilization of self-service technology is quickly gaining market share in healthcare. The healthcare market is growing in leaps and bounds and showing enormous potential for reducing costs associated with mundane transactions that would otherwise have to be managed by an individual or caregiver. The penetration of Internet users around the country and a well-empowered and -informed consumer makes the healthcare industry right for the opportunity for patients to play an active role in their medical management and well-being. Also, future iterations of kiosk technology will make relevant information more accessible, and experts believe that providing that expertise up front to the patient upon arrival to a hospital clinic, doctor's office, or emergency department will provide for increased patient adherence to treatment protocols and reduce the frustrations associated with long wait lines and voluminous paper consent forms.

According to IHL Research, which affirms a September 2007 IBM study that showed consumers becoming more and more comfortable with self-service as a way to access additional resources when it is convenient for them:

- Eighty-one percent of consumers indicated their reasons for choosing to use self-service technology over human interaction is that it allowed them to access information and services outside of normal business hours.
- Sixty-nine percent said they expect more and more businesses to offer a self-service option.
- Fifty-two percent revealed they are very comfortable using self-service technology, with roughly 50% indicating their usage of self-service devices had gone up during the past year.
- Almost half of consumers would use self-service technology in lieu of human interaction to get more personal information, such as accessing human resources or benefits information at work (45%) and checking in and reviewing medical history at a doctor's office (40%).
- More than 33% of consumers said they would like additional resources available to them while they shop.

Venture Development Corp. (VDC) recently stated in its *Kiosks for Self-Service and Interactive Applications: Technical and Vertical Market Analysis* report that kiosk solutions exceeded $524 million in 2007 and are expected to grow at a compounded annual growth rate of 22% through 2010. More than 200,000 kiosk units were deployed in 2007, VDC reported.[2]

Combined with a robust electronic medical records software solution, the self-service kiosk technology can serve as a valuable bridge to electronic health records and to obtain up-to-date prescription information and other customer data products and services.

Self-Service Technology Projects at Newark Beth Israel

Newark Beth Israel Medical Center (NBIMC), an affiliate of the Saint Barnabas Health Care System, is a 671-bed regional referral teaching hospital with specialized programs, including heart, lung, and kidney transplantation, cardiac surgery, oncology, and maternal/child health services. It is home to the Children's Hospital of New Jersey, the state's premier hospital for treating ill and injured children from newborn through adolescent years, including more than thirty pediatric specialties. The Saint Barnabas Health Care System is New Jersey's largest healthcare provider.

NBIMC's Information Technology and Services (IT&S) Department serves as one of the Saint Barnabas Health Care System's technology incubators and focuses on creating an environment of care where clinical staff members can maximize their time and have patient information at their fingertips, regardless of where they are in the medical center.

In 2004, NBIMC contracted with two vendors to revolutionize the patient experience at the medical center. We purchased an enterprise scheduling system to uninstall the old outdated system we had in place, as well as a self-service technology solution (kiosk) to improve patient satisfaction and the overall patient experience. We were looking for self-service to provide a good return on investment. Our organization used to print over twelve pages per patient of registration documents and consents to put in every patient chart. We were also looking to shorten our lines and free up our registration staff to focus more on our patients with special needs and their financial concerns. Given the complex front-end requirements associated with registering a patient, our goal was to leverage the self-service successes found in other industries, put that power in the patient's hands, and reduce the bottlenecks associated with taking care of patients as they arrived at the various outpatient areas around the hospital.

Much like the bank customer who walks up to an ATM, rustling through his or her wallet for the plastic bank card and swiping it for access to some fast cash, we wanted patients presenting at the hospital's registration areas to walk up to a kiosk, check themselves in, confirm a preexisting appointment or enter the reason for their visit, and then take a seat. Registrars would then call patients to the counter, where all of their consent forms are presented for electronic signature and demographic components of their visit are updated.

Since we were using two different systems to schedule and register patients with self-service technology, we had to build complex interfaces between the two in order to link appointments and push registration information from one system to the other, validate scheduled appointments, and upgrade accounts in the patient management system. All of those data points were completed by April 2005, and by September 2006 we were up and running with four areas on the new scheduling and self-service kiosk technology. Over those two years a significant amount of development and testing were put in place to make sure that we lost no patient appointments and we had full integration across all of our systems. From September 19 through December 11, 2006, we decided to put on the big push and complete the scheduling project across twenty-seven areas of the hospital. In order to implement the technology across all areas we needed to do the following:

- Dedicate a project manager/system administrator
- Redesign the registration process for each registration area
  - Document current workflow
  - Document proposed workflow
  - Perform a gap analysis
    - Focus on changes to registration, scheduling, and check-in processes
- Load future appointments
- Make changes to the hospital information system (Siemens Invision)
  - Add fields pertinent to the patient appointment
  - Create HL7 interface between SMS Invision, Scheduling.com, and self-service technology
- Upgrade our desktops
- Expand our wireless infrastructure
- Test, test, test
- Change the culture
  - Get management/staff buy-in
  - Give up paper
- Change behaviors

It was a tall order to complete in such a short time frame; fortunately, the team was able to band together and accomplish this daunting task. As a result of that positive experience, we took the same approach and dovetailed the kiosk installation into the scheduling implementation process described above. The four departments that were live with the self-service technology had a full registration application for the patients to enter everything from demographics to insurance information on their own on a total of eight screens. The steps involved were:

- Develop a full kiosk workflow (review demographic information and sign)
  - The early adopter departments using kiosks:
    - Preadmission testing—full workflow
    - Same-day surgery—full workflow
    - Cardiac services—full workflow
- The components of the full workflow consisted of:

- Patient presented at kiosk with scheduled appointments for that day only
- Patient presented with eight screens
  - Choice of two languages:
    - English
    - Spanish
- Four validation screens: demographics, next of kin, emergency contact, insurance
- Maximum of four forms for signature, as applicable
■ Forms print with a signature
■ Forms completed field sent back to the patient accounting system
- Forms during first visit on account
- Forms are not presented to patient again on subsequent visits
- Avoid duplication of effort, paper, and patient signature
■ HIPAA privacy (one time only)

While we were doing the big push implementation, we found that the full workflow might be a bit overwhelming for the patients to use, so we came up with a modified workflow to try and benchmark one against the other in order to determine which was the best method for a patient to be checked into the hospital. The new workflow consisted of:

■ Patient presented at kiosk with scheduled appointments for that day only
■ Patient presented with four screens
- Choice of two languages:
  - English
  - Spanish
■ Current appointment is listed and patient is asked to validate
- After validation patient is asked to have a seat—patient called by registrar
■ During registration patient is presented with a maximum of four forms for signature, as applicable
■ Forms print with a signature
■ Forms completed field sent back to patient accounting system
- Forms during first visit on account
- Forms are not presented to patient again on subsequent visits
- Avoid duplication of effort, paper, and patient signature
■ HIPAA privacy (one time only)

The end result was the workflow shown in Figures 7.1 and 7.2.

■ Patient validates appointment time and is directed to be seated
■ Once completed, a series of registration questions are then validated in a series of subsequent screens as described in the earlier two pages referencing the two types of registration workflow

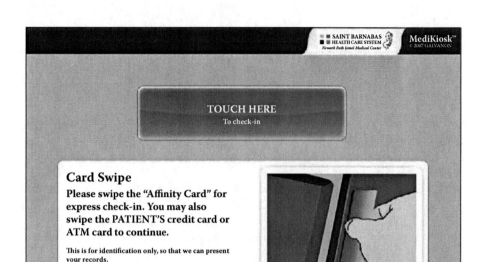

Figure 7.1 Patients touch screen name and DOB or swipe a hospital-issued patient access card to begin authentication process.

■ Patients read, complete, and sign general consent, patient rights, HIPAA Notice of Privacy Practices, and Medicare utilization form (Figure 7.3)

Outpatient Check-In Staff View

The activity monitor depicted in Figure 7.4 provides real-time patient status, just like the airport:

■ Schedule time, arrival time, registration throughput
■ Who is completed and "to be seen"
■ Comments
■ Date and time stamps for each process step

Project Goals

Our project in the outpatient areas was a resounding success; the following outcomes were goals and results achieved during the project:

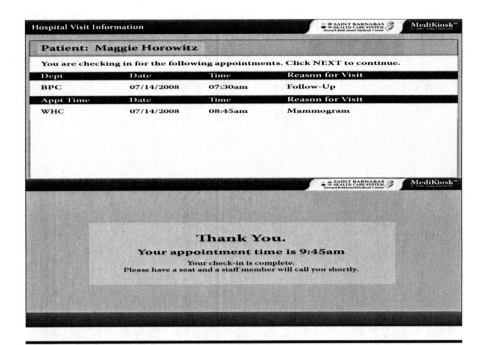

Figure 7.2

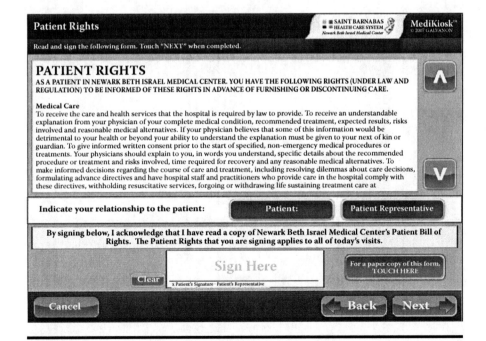

Figure 7.3

GALVANON
The Patient Experience Company™

CVM Enterprise Server™   Change Password ☒ Log Out

Activity Monitoring

| Home | Member Manager | Activity Monitoring | Appointment Manager | Reports Manager |

Sign-In-Sheet | Activity Log | To Be Registered | To Be Seen

Key

● = Checked-In/Information OK/Consent   ● = Checked Information/No Consent   ● = Record Saved/Posted

Wed Oct 28, 2009 4:18 PM

Search Activity By

Date / / 🔢

Activities for : Wed Oct 28, 2009   Search

✓ Edit Member ◉ Delete Activity(s) ✓ View Member ✓ Scan Card ✓ Forms ✓ Scan Docs ✓ Update Status   -Select- ▾

A C F R W N S Q	MRN	Acct	Name	Appt	Arrival	Kiosk Start	Kiosk End	Status Time	Status	Reg End	Visit Type	Clinic Code Desc	Resource	Roomed Start	Roomed End
●●●●	908070	289379738872	Orange, Apple	02:30 PM	2:49 PM	02:49 PM	2:49 PM	2:49 PM	ICVL		MRI	MRI	Smith, John	2:45 PM	
●●●●	2344	2893723231232	Suv, K	02:30 PM	2:41 PM	02:40 PM	2:41 PM	2:41 PM	ICVL		CT	CT	Vengal, Raj	2:45 PM	3:42 PM
●●●●	2344	289373878773	Suv, K	02:30 PM	2:41 PM	02:40 PM	2:41 PM	2:41 PM	ICVL	2:49 PM	CT	CT	Jones, Jen	2:42 PM	3:40 PM
●●●●	23000	2893722398728	Best, Friend	02:30 PM	2:39 PM	02:39 PM	2:39 PM	2:39 PM	ICVL		MAMM	MAMM	Dr. Doctor	2:48 PM	3:16 PM
●●●●	2344	289379989399	Suv, K	02:30 PM		02:40 PM	2:41 PM	2:41 PM	ICVL	2:41 PM	DXUS	DXUS	Jones, Jen	2:54 PM	3:12 PM

Figure 7.4

- ■ Improve patient satisfaction and the overall patient experience
    - – Behaviors are changing
    - – "Wait" experience changing: Kiosk limits check-in to thirty minutes prior to appointment; patients are coming on time
- ■ Decompress central registration areas
    - – Reduce amount of areas registering centrally
    - – Line shifting or reduction
    - – Patients called by appointment time in central registration rather than FIFO
- ■ Increase patient throughput
    - – Appropriate documentation (forms)—less printing
    - – Printed paper reduction
- ■ Centralized system for scheduling
    - – Automate manual process, improving efficiencies
- ■ Improve workflow in central registration—redesign the registration process to allow for more preregistration

Since our health system was an early adopter of kiosk technology, we discovered that the user interface needed to be simpler to use. The kiosks are touch screens, so we wanted the user interface to be closer to that of an ATM, where large buttons prevent one from accidentally pressing the wrong key. On the kiosk, the early user interface buttons were much closer; therefore, it was easier to make mistakes. The vendor created a larger button/user interface, which was part of our ER project. Later, kiosks in the existing twenty-seven hospital locations were retrofitted to the updated user interface, reducing touch-screen errors across the campus. In order to get to the next level, it was important for patients at NBIMC to be comfortable using the technology. Our patient population needed to get accustomed to using the self-service features before we could expand to more robust features. As described earlier, the technology has empowered our patients and increased operational efficiencies.

Kiosk Self-Service in the Emergency Department

In November 2007 we began using self-service technology for patients to check themselves in when they arrive at the emergency room (ER). Our experience company-wide with the technology was a critical factor in deciding to implement the platform in an area where 70% of the hospital's admissions originate. We wanted to be at the forefront of technology and the first hospital in New Jersey to deploy self-service kiosks in its emergency department to streamline the check-in and triage process. The vendor we use from Galvanon, an NCR company, estimated 48% of emergency care departments are at or over capacity, according to the 2007 Survey of Hospital Leaders released in July 2009 by the American Hospital Association.

Self-service kiosks help staff to quickly determine which patients are experiencing the most pressing medical needs, which assists with patient volume.

If a patient presents in the ER with a high-priority complaint, he or she is immediately taken to an exam room. The kiosk technology has an activity monitoring tool that uses priority rules based on the severity level of the patient's condition. If a patient presents at the kiosk and indicates he or she is having chest pains or other high-priority medical complaints, the system automatically moves that patient to the top of the queue and alerts a member of the medical staff via the activity monitor, for all triage nurses to see that the patient requires immediate attention.

In the past, a patient would come into the ER and sign his or her name on a log attached to a clipboard. The hospital clerk would call the patient's name from the list in the order it was entered and the patient would go to triage. The list was static and there was no way of prioritizing patients. So, if patient A presented before patient B, but patient B was having chest pain or difficulty catching her breath, patient A still would have been seen before patient B. There was no effective way of understanding what was on the paper list, other that reading down the names and calling out the next name in sequence. With kiosk technology, we have eliminated the list.

A noteworthy area where kiosks increased our efficiency was in the number of patients seen. Previously, some patients did not make it into triage in a timely manner. Our ER implementation increased the number of triaged patients seen from six to ten patients per hour the day we went live with the self-service kiosk.

Once a patient is checked in, a hospital staff member at the registration counter manages the activity monitor (as in Figure 7.5), and if a patient needs assistance, the clerk will assist him or her at the kiosk (much like what a home improvement store or grocery store employee does when someone experiences problems at a checkout kiosk).

The hospital's kiosks are set up much like an airline's kiosk, where a patient in the queue is directed by the technology to where he or she needs to go. The kiosks used in the ER have a basic user interface that was previously developed at another emergency department prior to the NBIMC implementation, and was enhanced with input by the on-site clinical management team. The technology shows a diagram of a patient's body (Figure 7.6), and the patient taps on the screen indicating where he or she is experiencing discomfort or pain.

Tangible Benefits Experienced by System Stakeholders

The triage environment at our medical center has changed because of the self-service technology. In the past, after a patient signed in on the clipboard, he or she typically had a twelve-minute wait to sign in on paper, unless he or she was in need of immediate care; now, there are six self-check touch screens in the ER waiting room, and a technician escorts patients to a kiosk. Three are attached to the wall,

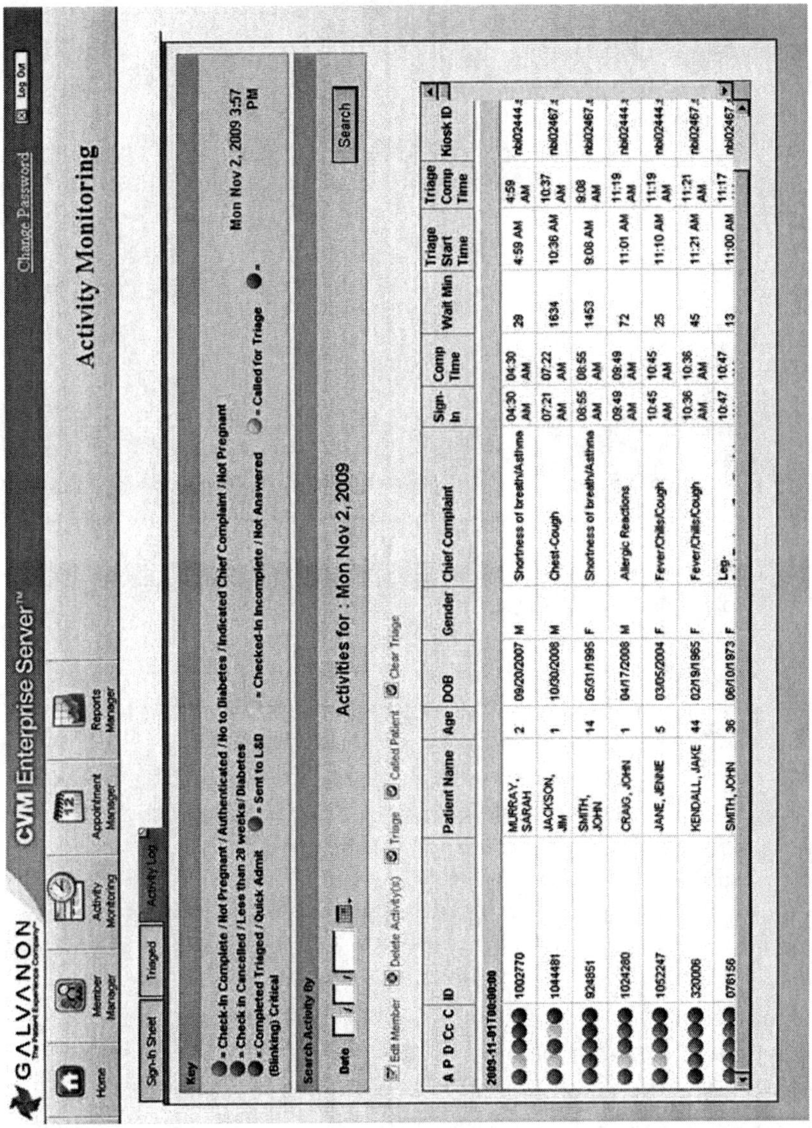
GALVANON
CVM Enterprise Server
Activity Monitoring
Activities for : Mon Nov 2, 2009
Search

Figure 7.5

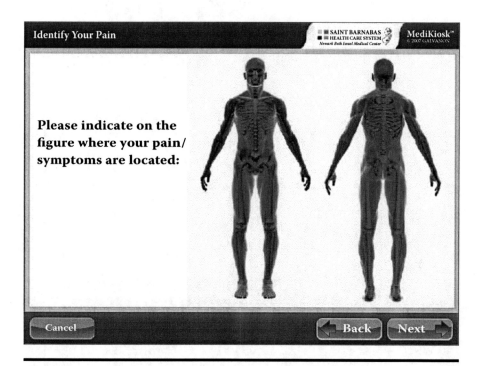

Figure 7.6

each with its own booth and privacy screen. Three other portable, wireless tablet PCs are available, primarily for people in wheelchairs. Patients take an average of forty-five seconds to answer up to fifteen yes/no on-screen questions, which are designed in a simplistic manner, where the patient checks himself or herself in at the kiosk and indicates his or her primary ailment/reason for being there, so we know how to navigate patient traffic more efficiently. If it is something that can be fast tracked, we immediately send the patient to where he or she needs to go, rather than having him or her sit down again and figure out where to go.

Their complaints, ages, and symptoms appear instantly on nurses' computer screens. Some answers trigger warning indicators, such as blinking red lights when patients acknowledge suicidal thoughts. At least two or three triage nurses are looking at their screens to see who is signing in, and three charge nurses are also checking them between patient care. Because of the intelligence and rules built into the technology, the nursing staff can immediately pull out the diabetic person with chest pains, or the forty-five-year-old woman with stroke-like symptoms.

The functionality of the system benefits everyone and has quantifiable patient care benefits. The technology has helped cut the waiting time for a person with chest pain to get an EKG in half. Some conditions are exacerbated by standing, so now, when patients are triaged, we get a better picture of their conditions, without them having the stress and aggravation of waiting on their feet for fifteen minutes. Another added benefit is that patient and visitor violence and frustration have decreased significantly. When the length of patient lines were so long that people were almost standing outside the door, quarrels regarding who was first or who cut occurred on occasion; now, the organized nature of the self-service technology has all but eliminated that.

Nurses benefit, too. They learn the system in approximately fifteen minutes and appreciate its efficiency. The staff in overcrowded emergency departments report that they are not as stressed, angry, frustrated, or disappointed, and they are happier when they leave because they have got patients through the ED process efficiently and safely.

Since every administrator has screen access, they and ED managers can monitor length of wait, acuity, and patient prioritization, and can determine where to redirect patients within ED areas. Administrators can call from their office, ask what is needed in the ED area, and deploy additional staff from less critical hospital areas. Patients are comfortable using the kiosks, and some are more apt to disclose symptoms, such as psychiatric problems. Improved registration speed, privacy, and service have measurably increased customer satisfaction and have lowered considerably the number of patients who leave without being seen.

Future Plans for NBI

Over the next two years, we hope to expand our self-service initiatives in multiple ways. We plan on implementing affinity card technology so that our "frequent flyers" will gain access within NBIMC utilizing a swipe card. We would also like to develop web portal access so that our patients and referring physicians can post critical information prior to a patient arriving at the medical center. A prime example illustrating this concept would be receiving all of the clinical documentation and lab results required for a patient before a transplant visit. Patients travel from all over the country to come to our hospital for lung, heart, and kidney transplants. They routinely arrive at the medical center with incomplete documentation, missing clinical results and other pertinent information that it would be helpful if they had prior to their arriving at the medical center. Utilizing the web and the self-service technology can help provide the infrastructure to not only ensure that patients have all the information uploaded onto the Internet before they arrive, but also verify when they check in for their patient visit.

In order to enhance our activity monitoring efforts, which has become a critical component of the day-to-day workflow in our twenty-seven outpatient areas and our emergency department, our medical center has invested in cellular and smart phone devices such as BlackBerrys for physicians and nurses. This provides them with a way to monitor their patients' status along the cycle of the visit regardless of whether they are in the medical center or somewhere off campus. We can provide real-time status updates on where the patient is in his or her check-in process. Additionally, we will be able to send text message reminders to a patient when it is his or her turn to be seen in the ER or when it is time to go to the exam room.

We are currently in discussions with our service vendor to include the ability to offer our patients the option of purchasing mail-order prescriptions to save them money at the point of service and to be able to monitor their adherence to medications and the progress they are making on the medications that have been prescribed to them. The kiosk will aggregate information about when they have filled the prescriptions, and how often, and report information such as how they are feeling, which then can be sent to the electronic medical record for physician review.

As part of our strong commitment to the community we serve, we are strategizing on developing a community self-service kiosk solution that will provide neighborhood churches and schools with technology that can provide a place to see available appointments, services rendered at the medical center, and valuable patient education. Our self-service initiatives provide us with the opportunity to empower our patients with technology and lead them along a journey connecting them to the NBIMC family and the Saint Barnabas Health Care System.

References

1. NCR. 2008. Survey information presented at the Self-Service Universe Conference, Orlando, FL.
2. UDC, 2008. Kiosks for self-service and interactive applications: Technical & Vertical Market Analysis, 2nd edition, January.

Chapter 8

The World of Health Analytics

Jason Burke

Contents

Introduction

Evidence-based medicine. Personal electronic health records. Disease management. Personalized medicine. These terms, among many others, reflect a rapidly growing change within the health sciences ecosystem—a transformative shift toward more information-based decision making related to patient care and healthcare cost management. For decades, the efficiencies and improvements attained in other industries through the adoption of information technology have largely been missing in healthcare, an ecosystem mired in paper records, administrative overhead, and labor-intensive business processes.

But that is all changing. The sustained rise in healthcare costs, consistent problems in patient safety, highly expensive prescription drugs, and inconsistent treatment outcomes have all contributed to a new drive toward making better use of the tremendous volumes of information flowing through the ecosystem. Whereas historically hospitals have looked to expansions in service lines and facilities to drive top-line revenue growth, analytics that provide business opportunities in utilization, cost containment, and quality control are now seen as critical enablers of bottom-line financial performance. Health plans that have relied on relatively simple business rules to determine the appropriateness of reimbursements are now looking to advanced analytical models to identify previously undetected fraudulent claims activities and patterns. Drug researchers, struggling to find ways to bring innovative and safe therapies to market faster and cheaper, are aggregating tremendous volumes of data covering many years of research to look for biomarkers that can accurately predict drug safety and efficacy in named patient populations. Across the board, electronic data, whether business based or science based, are now seen as the fuel to power the engines of business and clinical analytics driving the evolution of patient outcomes and wellness.

But those growing volumes of data contain a hidden burden: How can we efficiently and effectively manage such large and disparate volumes of information? How do we make it useful? With information flowing from every corner of the healthcare ecosystem, how do we prioritize which data are most important, and how can we simplify the inherent complexity down to something with which educated human beings can make rational decisions? Anyone seeking an easy answer to this dilemma will be disappointed.

Modern information technology, especially in the areas of data integration, data quality, data management, and advanced analytics, holds the key to unlocking the power of this information and the corresponding business and scientific transformation contained within. Advanced analytics and information management sit at the center of the new health enterprise—an information-driven business and science-informed medical practice that can dramatically reduce healthcare costs and improve health outcomes for all patients. But only if organizations embrace them.

Analysis Paralysis

The healthcare industry is no stranger to technology—hospitals have invested millions in medical devices for decades, for example. But capabilities with respect to information technology—electronic data collection, management, quality, analysis, and reporting—are reasonably new. Extensive paper-based forms, change-averse physicians, tightly controlled business processes, overtaxed nurses, and business demands on self-funding investments have conspired to inhibit the proliferation of information technology in much of the healthcare sector. But as the industry has sought to better understand its deep-rooted problems in cost, quality, safety, and outcomes, a growing recognition has emerged that information technology must be a priority for every health enterprise.

And yet, when we speak of advanced analytics in healthcare, it is not uncommon to hear a list of excuses why the industry is not ready for them:

- **More technology.** Many people argue that until the industry has had more time to implement more technology that collects information electronically, there is little use in investing in advanced analytics.
- **More integration and standards.** Some people argue that, because the industry has historically lacked data standards that facilitate information aggregation and sharing, any insights that might be derived from their existing data would be of questionable value.
- **Data privacy.** Inevitably, some people will question the appropriateness of using personal medical information outside the context of care for that particular patient; HIPAA is usually cited.

As organizations consider analytics-oriented projects and hear these concerns, it is quite easy to fall into "analysis paralysis"—continuously trying to find ways to overcome issues that cannot be overcome without doing the projects that elicited the issues in the first place. Organizations will always need more technology, but we have a lot today. We will always need better integration and deeper support in standards, but we have standards and integration models that are proven today. We should always be holding patient data privacy at the forefront of our minds, but we have many ways of protecting patient privacy while also allowing us to pursue improvements that will inevitably benefit those patients.

The question should not be whether to take on analytics as a corporate priority; the question should be how. And the answer is surprisingly simple, residing in the neonatal and pediatric units of every hospital in the world. Newborn babies, infants, and toddlers physiologically develop along a predefined biological path, one that serves to gradually bring new biological systems online and grow the systems already online until the person reaches adulthood. It is a long-term process, but one with clearly defined steps and associated personal abilities. Such is this case with analytics as they are born and grow inside companies.

Analytical Maturity and Objectives

The term *analytics* may be one of the most overused and misunderstood terms in the business community today, with the possible exception of *business intelligence.* Every software application that has the ability to run reports with numbers in them suddenly provides analytics. Any person who has taken a statistics course is suddenly capable of performing whatever analytics are needed for an organization. Even the definition of the term *analytics* is used in one context to describe web reporting, while in another context it describes the most obscure statistical methodology imaginable.

When we use the term *analytics* in healthcare, we are using it to mean something very specific:

> *Analytics* are the complete series of integrated capabilities needed to provide progressively deeper statistical insights into health-related information.

We are describing capabilities—a capacity that can be found or learned within organizations and individuals. Those capabilities should be complete, meaning they cover all of the needed areas of information access, integration, quality, storage, management, interpretation, and governance. Those capabilities are also progressive, meaning that the simpler capabilities need to be in place to enable the more sophisticated capabilities to operate. They are statistical in nature, not merely mathematical. And they are progressively deeper, meaning the insights derived from higher-order analytical capabilities offer greater value than those of lower-order capabilities.

The Eight Levels of Analytics

So what are these capabilities that organizations and individuals need to have? There are eight levels of analytical capabilities that any organization or person needs in order to fully address the challenges in healthcare (Figure 8.1):

1. **Standard reports.** Answer the questions: What happened? When did it happen?
2. **Ad hoc reports.** Answer the questions: How many? How often? Where?
3. **Query drilldown.** Answer the questions: Where exactly is the problem? How do I find the answers?
4. **Alerts.** Answer the questions: When should I react? What actions are needed now?
5. **Statistical analysis.** Answer the questions: Why is it happening? What opportunities am I missing?
6. **Forecasting.** Answer the questions: What if these trends continue? How much is needed? When will it be needed?
7. **Predictive modeling.** Answer the questions: What will happen next? How will it affect my business?
8. **Optimization.** Answer the questions: How do we do things better? What is the best decision for a complex problem?

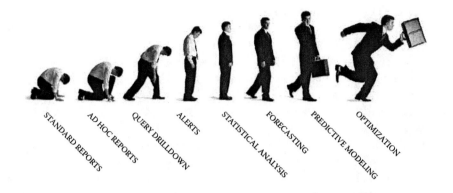

STANDARD REPORTS   AD HOC REPORTS   QUERY DRILLDOWN   ALERTS   STATISTICAL ANALYSIS   FORECASTING   PREDICTIVE MODELING   OPTIMIZATION

Figure 8.1

Let's use a hypothetical example to illustrate how these various capabilities are developed and used. Christopher Regional Hospital is struggling to understand why its operating margins are decreasing. In particular, the cardiac service line, typically associated with a good contribution margin, has seen a decline over the last six months. Hospital administrators decide to undertake an analytics initiative in order to understand what is causing the decline in contribution margin.

1. **Standard reports.** The problem was identified when the administrators consulted a series of standard reports that the hospital uses on a monthly basis. They realized the cardiac service line's contribution margin was down from the same period last year.
2. **Ad hoc reports.** These standard reports did not currently show all of the performance indicators the administrators needed to understand the issues, so they asked for a few specific reports related to the inpatient and outpatient volumes as well as statistics trending by fiscal period over the last year. These reports showed that patient visits were not down and the service line was fairly busy, and so the problems were not simply a matter of getting more patients. The administrators asked that these *ad hoc* reports become a part of the hospital's standard reporting environment.
3. **Query drilldown.** To explore the problem further, hospital administrators asked the head of the cardiac service line to investigate the problem and report back at the next service line committee meeting. He formed a series of hypotheses about potential causes, and then explored a number of other factors related to contribution margin, such as length of stay, payer, and service utilization. The reporting environment allowed him to use a web browser to dynamically divide, subset, and report on these business metrics. During his query drilldown work, the administrator noticed something peculiar—there were a lot of reimbursement denials for patients having a "rule out myocardial infarction" code. The director checked with the billing department and was

told that they are being denied because the hospital will not receive payment for "rule out MI" patients unless they are coded in an observation status and not as an inpatient.

4. **Alerting.** In order to understand what was happening with these patients, the director set up an alert that was sent each time a patient received the "rule out MI" code and had a status of an inpatient. Those alerts were sent to the case manager and the nurse manager of the cardiac unit so that they could monitor the care to understand what was happening.

5. **Statistical analysis.** The director then decided to analyze the data for this particular diagnostic code. Running a series of statistical analyses on this patient population, he found a correlation between inpatient status, longer lengths of stay, and days of the week the patient arrived in the emergency room. In particular, he noticed that patients who were admitted in an inpatient status, with lengths of stay between three and four days, who had come to the emergency room with chest pain on a Friday or a Saturday were most of the denials. This finding was reaffirmed when following up on the alerting procedure: the nurse manager of the cardiac unit knew that these patients required a stress test, and stress tests were not performed in the hospital on Saturdays or Sundays. Patients were admitted to stay through the weekend to receive their stress tests on Monday; standard procedure was to schedule the stress test within twenty-four hours, allowing the patients to be placed in a cardiac ICU bed and not be admitted. The director also realized when speaking with the nurse manager that more and more "rule out MIs" were taking up beds in the cardiac ICU.

6. **Forecasting.** After hearing the findings in the service line committee meeting, the administrators wanted to know what the impact of this trend would be over a longer time horizon. They constructed a forecast of patient admission, diagnosis, length of stay, and payments over the next twenty-four months based on the past four years of hospital data, census data for their region, and projections from several medical institutions. The forecast showed that their hospital's patient admissions around this condition were expected to grow 56% each year for the next two years due to the recent closing of area hospitals. It also showed that their relatively small drop in contribution margin today could easily grow into a bigger problem in the next eighteen months unless they found a way to address both the availability of stress testing on weekends and the problem this condition presents on utilization of beds in the cardiac ICU. This analysis highlighted the patient throughput issues that were just starting to develop, affecting the quality of care for the cardiac patients.

7. **Predictive modeling.** The hospital leaders now wanted to understand the value of more timely treatments and care focused on acuity. The administrators wanted to know whether receiving stress tests within twenty-four hours and removing cardiac rule-outs from the emergency room to an observation unit were beneficial from a quality, safety, and financial perspective. They

had staff construct a statistical model that could predict patient outcomes. By using historical patient information, the statistical model could predict the likelihood of death, readmission, disease progression, and long-term costs based on the timing and the treatment that was administered. This model showed opening an observation unit and staffing stress testing on weekends could decrease this condition's returns to the emergency room visits; reduce medical errors and negative outcomes, including death; and create more cardiac ICU beds, increasing throughput for critical cardiac patients and reducing expenses by staffing by acuity. They also found out something else.

8. **Optimization.** During the predictive modeling exercise, the hospital analysts used data mining software to look for trends in the electronic medical records that might have an impact on outcomes. They uncovered a previously unknown trend: patients under the care of one physician in the hospital were 32% less likely to be readmitted after a cardiac catherization. The administrators contacted the clinical chief of cardiology and informed him of the analysis. When the clinical chief questioned the physician about her treatment strategies, she indicated that she required her patients to follow up with a cardiovascular exercise and diet program. She had her staff follow up on her patients to make sure they completed program. Predictive modeling showed that patients that participated in that program, as well as received timely treatment, had 61% fewer admissions in the following two-year period.

The preceding example illustrates how health insights are derived through a successive series of steps. Each step provides vital information needed to make the next step feasible and effective. It would have been quite difficult, for example, to know what statistical analyses needed to be run if the organization did not already have some direction from the query drilldown. Each step is also more complex than the former, requiring deeper analytical skills, better data, and more coordinated engagement within the organization.

Business vs. Clinical Analytics

The numbers and types of analytics that can be applied to healthcare are practically endless, constrained only by the creativity of the human mind to ask intelligent questions and define mathematical inferences. When comparing health and life sciences to other industries' use of analytics, one characteristic stands out as somewhat unique: the questions, data, and decisions involved include traditional types of business information—sales, operations, etc.—but also include scientific information and interpretation. This distinction brings an additional level of complexity to looking at analytics as a transformative engine for healthcare. Whereas many software tools and people skills applicable to other businesses can be applied equally to health and life sciences, there are a variety of science-oriented capabilities

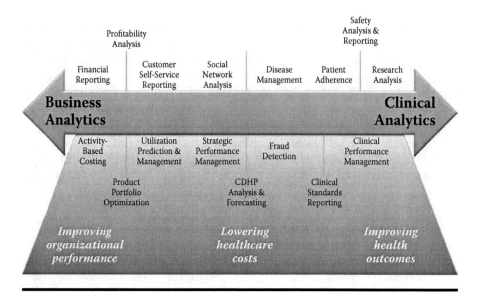

Figure 8.2

that are not as broadly available. And for many business insights in healthcare, it is the combined view of both business and scientific information that enables more educated decisions.

Any analytical solution in health and life sciences exists on a continuum of business-focused to clinically focused analytics (Figure 8.2). Some types of insights—assessing profitability of a business unit or providing a standardized financial reporting environment—mainly involve the use of information from business units, systems, and knowledge workers. Other insights, such as the safety dimensions of a drug therapy or the outcomes of a clinical research study, reside more clearly in the realm of patient information and scientific interpretation. Between these two extremes lies an entire continuum of analytical applications that provide a unique view into the operations of a health enterprise, the management of patient populations and diseases, and the primary determinants of costs, quality, and outcomes.

With such diversity and breadth of scope, it is difficult to develop any taxonomy of analytical capabilities that adequately conveys all of the various analytical dimensions of the ecosystem. However, at the highest level, any healthcare-related analytical application can be said to target at least one of three main business imperatives:

1. **Improving organizational performance.** These analytics focus on the financial and commercial performance of the organization. Profitability and performance management are commonly cited issues in this area.
2. **Lowering healthcare costs.** These analytics focus on cost avoidance, active cost management, cost reduction through improvements in efficiency, and other aspects of operational improvement. Detection and prevention of

healthcare fraud, as well as activity-based costing initiatives, often fall into this area.

3. **Improving health outcomes.** These analytics focus on improved patient outcomes, including areas of patient safety and treatment efficacy. Clinical research of novel drugs and therapies can be considered a component of this area.

Obviously, there is a close interdependency between these three business imperatives, and it is not uncommon for improvements in one area to impact the other areas. But for an organization considering a new analytics project, these imperatives represent a critical aspect of project scoping. For an analytics program to be successful, absolute clarity needs to exist in the program's intended objectives. Programs with scopes intending to cover all three imperatives are unlikely to be successful; the data, objective measures, people, and impacted business processes are dramatically different. But for targeted analytical programs, the impact to each of these imperatives can be equally dramatic.

With these imperatives and the business-clinical continuum as context, let us look more deeply into some representative programs.

Improving Organizational Performance

At its core, healthcare is a business just like any other industry. Profitability is linked to efficiency and competitive differentiation. Innovation breeds opportunity. Quality can command premium pricing. Customer relationships determine long-term revenue potential. These and many other business principles serve as the underpinning for a portfolio of analytical capabilities that can have a tremendous impact on the quality, safety, and cost of healthcare delivery.

Aside from issues related to clinical outcomes (considered separately in a subsequent section), there are three general categories of organizational performance analytics:

- Financial: Analytical capabilities related to revenue, operating costs, and investments. Typical topics include financial management, revenue cycle optimization, and profitability analysis.
- Operational: Analytical capabilities related to the way an organization operates internally. Typical topics include utilization management, human resources, and other enterprise-wide competencies.
- Commercial: Analytical capabilities related to the way an organization sells, markets, and interacts with its customer and partner base. Typical topics include customer targeting, retention, and sales and marketing effectiveness.

The following table highlights some of the more common performance-oriented analytical scenarios found across the healthcare ecosystem today.

Financial	• Financial management • Revenue management and cycle optimization	• Expense management • Contribution margin analysis • Provider profitability analysis
Operational	• Human resource performance management and optimization • Reporting standards and requirements • Utilization prediction, management, and analysis	• Strategic performance management • Operational performance management and monitoring • Inventory management
Commercial	• Cross-selling • Member/customer campaign management • Multichannel relationship marketing • Physician targeting • Provider/customer selection, retention, and acquisition • Sales force and territory optimization • Sales force effectiveness	• Customer satisfaction • Health plan reporting • Customer/group defection • Customer experience analytics • Provider/customer self-service reporting and explanation of benefits • Risk stratification

Let us look at one real-world example of an organization using analytics in this way. A large, nonprofit teaching hospital cares for over forty thousand inpatients and seven hundred and fifty thousand outpatients every year. Like any large hospital, its databases and reports are incredibly diverse, covering financial, quality, and patient satisfaction information. But it was quite difficult for executives to see the information in a way that would facilitate better decision making. For example, what was the relationship between patient-related services and productivity in the different care units?

The hospital developed a performance management system utilizing balanced scorecard concepts to draw correlations between measurements from the different areas of their organization. By combining data relating to fifty thousand patient encounters a year from twenty-nine different sources, the system analyzes and distributes operational metrics to executive management, physicians, and front-line employees throughout the hospital. Whether in a patient care setting or in the business office, about nine hundred employees at all levels can see how their actions, individually and as a whole, affect the organization and its patients. Over thirty metrics detail key financial information, length of stay, and patient satisfaction measures. Select physicians and nurses even have their own scorecards, enabling them to share information relating to finance, productivity, workload, and quality indicators with their colleagues.

Some department heads now routinely use the system to gauge hospital performance and spot anomalies relating to length of stay, spikes in certain diagnosis-related groups, and procedural delays. As an example, operating room efficiency and productivity are impacted significantly by start times. If more cases start on time in the morning, then efficiency and productivity increase. So by identifying patterns relating to delays in operating room start times, physicians can have a better understanding of the impact of specific test orders and procedures. Using this approach, the hospital can also identify best practices.

The key to unlocking the value of performance solutions is in the identification and measurement of key performance indicators (KPIs). In this area, healthcare actually has a fair amount of information already available from which to draw. Organizations such as the Joint Commission (http://www.jointcommission.org), the Agency for Healthcare Research and Quality (http://www.ahrq.gov), and the National Quality Forum (http://www.qualityforum.org) have completed extensive work in identifying critical healthcare KPIs that every healthcare enterprise should monitor. These measures cover the gamut of business and clinical analytics, and are themselves the subjects of entire books. The following table gives a small sample of these types of KPIs:

Financial	Operational
• Net revenue, profit/loss, and contribution margin per health system, facility, service line, condition, and physician	• Nurse-to-bed ratio overall and per nursing unit
• Actual and overtime expenses to budgeted per health system, facility, service line, and department	• Attrition overall, per role, and per department
	• Throughput red alerts per health system and facility
• Cost per service line, condition, physician	• Length of stay per health system, facility, service line, condition, and physician
• Nursing travelers' expense per health system, facility, service line, and department	• Percentage of 11 a.m. discharges per health system, facility, service line, nursing unit, and physician
• Ambulatory surgeries per health system, facility, and surgeon	• Number of tests performed by test, health system, facility, service line, condition, and physician
	• Door to bed time
• Clinic and ER visits per health system, facility, and clinic	• Registration to triage time
	• Days to appointment

continued

Financial	Operational
	• Physician order entry compliance
	• Registration to triage time
	• Days to appointment
	• Physician order entry compliance

Quality and Safety	Nursing Care
• Percent of patients who received recommended care, and percent of process measures met for specific conditions by health system, facility, service line, nursing unit, physician, etc.	• Percent of inpatients with a hospital-acquired pressure ulcer
	• Rate of urinary tract infections with catheters
	• Rate of bloodstream infections with catheters
• Percent of patients who received recommended surgical infection prevention, and percent of process measures met by health system, facility, service line, nursing unit, physician, etc.	• Ventilator-associated pneumonia
	• Smoking cessation counseling for acute myocardial infarction, heart failure, and pneumonia
• Infection rates for specific conditions by health system, facility, service line, nursing unit, physician, etc.	• Number of registered nurses per patient day and number of nursing staff hours (registered nurse, licensed vocational/practical nurse, and unlicensed assistive personnel) per patient day
• Medication errors per 1,000 orders	• Nursing work life scores related to participation in hospital affairs, foundations for quality of care, manager ability, staffing and resource adequacy, and collegiality of nurse–physician relations
• Pediatric IV infiltration rates	
• Psychiatric patient assault rate	
• Percent of major surgical inpatients with a hospital-acquired complication and death	
• Inpatient falls per inpatient days with and without injuries	

When considering a performance management program and its associated KPIs, it is important to keep several things in mind:

1. KPIs should be empirically measurable. The idea in performance management is to make better decisions based on real data.

2. KPIs should be linked directly to a business objective. Simply measuring performance with no intended action based on the measurement is a waste of effort.
3. KPIs are the indicator, not the problem or the solution. The goal in performance management is to use KPIs as a detection tool for the business; the root cause analysis of a failing indicator is a separate process often involving different analytical techniques.
4. Measuring and reporting are not the end goal. The reason to use analytics in performance management is not to create easy-to-read dashboards (though good reporting is required). Rather, the end goal is to be able to *predict* and *optimize* performance along those specific performance dimensions.

As you might imagine, one of the more significant areas to predict and optimize is costs.

Lowering Healthcare Costs

Many people would argue that the concept of lowering healthcare costs is a measure and benefit as opposed to a business imperative. In some sense, this is probably true. Many analytics initiatives related to organizational performance or healthcare outcomes are justified by illustrating the impact on health-related expenditures in R&D, marketing, reimbursements, and other sources. But considering the central role that rising costs are playing in healthcare market dynamics, it is also useful to consider cost reduction programs as a separate topic in its own right. In fact, many organizations place a greater emphasis on cost management initiatives than performance or outcomes, as the organizational "pain" is so acute.

One example of analytics applied in this way pertains to healthcare fraud. Historically, an organization's ability to detect abusive or fraudulent activity has been limited to solutions that are called rules engines. Rules engines—a simplification of the "alerting" tier in our taxonomy—maintain an inventory of known fraud and abuse schemes, and can draw a sample from the collection of all healthcare transactions to look for situations that violate the rules. There are problems here, though:

1. The rules engine is usually only collecting a sample of records; it is not looking at every transaction. So low-volume fraud transactions are likely to slip through undetected.
2. When a rules engine detects a deviation, it is only detecting a violation of a rule. There are countless reasons why that rule violation might occur that are perfectly legitimate. There is little ability to understand the actual likelihood a given incident is indeed fraudulent, or what the real financial impact of that violation might mean for the organization. As such, fraud investigators spend time investigating a large number of incidents that waste time and money.

3. The volume of false positives (transactions that are identified as fraudulent but actually are not) creates a situation where investigators have very limited bandwidth to investigate fraudulent activities. As such, they tend to focus their efforts on high-dollar transactions. Fraud and abuse schemes consisting of low-dollar transactions are unlikely to trigger an investigation.

4. In order for a rules engine to know about a fraudulent activity, the activity must have been previously detected and codified into a rule. So rules engines always suffer from a delay between someone finding a fraud scheme, someone else coding into a rules system, and then organizations implementing the updated rules. These delays can span from months to years. And even a slight modification to an existing fraud scheme can render its existing rule useless.

5. Generally speaking, there is a complexity ceiling for rules engines. Abuse patterns that do not easily lend themselves to the relatively simple structure of a codified rule—for example, a complex matrix of collusion—are not easily detectable by rules engines.

So the smart fraudster is one that generates low-dollar transactions at a relatively low and distributed volume so as to not show up in the rules engine sampling. Of course, there will always be a pattern to the activity, but as long as the volume doesn't look suspicious and the dollar value is low, the likelihood of detection remains small. Even if the fraudulent scheme is detected, by the time it becomes a rule deployed within healthcare institutions, the fraudster can be already working the next scheme.

The use of analytics for fraud detection is not encumbered by these short-comings. An analytical model looks for patterns, not rule deviations. As opposed to sampling a small group of transactions, an analytical model can be applied to every single transaction flowing through a healthcare system, even in real time. It is less likely to produce false positives because the detection is not based on somewhat arbitrary comparison criteria, but rather on a model. Indeed, an analytical model can even be applied to the targets identified by rules engines to help separate the real signals from the noise. Note also that the delay between fraud identification and deployment of a detection process is much lower because the analytical model can be "tuned" in real time based on real-world experience.

Analytical fraud models also offer the ability to detect fraudulent or abusive patterns whose complexity is larger than what can easily be understood by the human mind. For example, a collusion scheme might actually involve three people working in four different organizations and generating six different types of claims. It is quite difficult for an investigator to ascertain a pattern across so many variables and permutations. But by applying data mining algorithms that examine each of the variables, relationships, and interdependencies, a pattern of social "connectedness" between these three people can emerge that is markedly different from those of their cohorts.

Fraud is only one example of the potential contribution of analytics to cost management and reduction. Other examples include:

- Portfolio optimization—Ensuring that high-value products and services are progressed, and stopping investments in products and services predicted to be unviable or unprofitable.
- Product development and pricing—Balancing market opportunity to pricing strategy in order to maximize profit (not necessarily price), minimize leakage, and ensure competitiveness.
- Case management/readmission prediction—Identifying and targeting patient cost factors and proactively introducing interventions to avoid the costs.
- Activity-based costing and management—Understanding where an enterprise is actually incurring costs in specific activities, as well as identifying and predicting the outcome of potential changes.

Regardless of the specific focus area, all of these analytical opportunities revolve around a common concept of using prediction to maximize investments in the right areas of the business, and minimize exposure to areas that extend costs without sufficient upside.

Let's look at another real-world example. One of the Blue Cross and Blue Shield insurance providers in the United States sought to gain a better understanding of costs and cost overruns within its organization. Traditional accounting systems provide departmental budgets, but beyond budget line items, those systems typically lack the analytical sophistication needed to look at financial information along different cost dimensions: corporate vs. departmental processes, predicted vs. accrued costs, etc. In this particular case, the company's finance managers could perform basic budget variance at the corporate and department levels, but they could not break out costs by product or individual lines of business, or even scrutinize contributions to activity costs at the program level.

The lack of process-oriented insights, which is far from unique to this particular insurer, has several ramifications. First, there is no way of ensuring that a given customer contract would be profitable. In one case, executives believed the company was losing money on a particular contract, but had no comprehensive way to evaluate all of the costs that supported this agreement. Profitability calculations can be very complex, as the way that costs are accrued (i.e., by individuals) differs significantly from the way that pricing is structured (e.g., by family, employee, child, etc.). Second, this lack of visibility at the contract level is further complicated by the fact that the administrative costs of plans differ between large group plans, small group plans, individual products, and government plans. And third, even if a single contract is unprofitable, unless there is a mechanism to ensure cost management on an ongoing basis, future contracts will suffer similar problems.

To address these concerns, the insurer adopted a particular analytical framework focused on activity-based costing and management. This solution pulls data from its corporate and departmental account systems, enabling planners to explore and predict cost data at all different levels of the business. For many programs, budgets need to actually be set at the individual business activity level. As opposed to simply watching budget reports for cost deviations, the analytical solution allows them to actively monitor projected costs and compare actual costs with the allowable rates for each activity. It becomes much easier to recognize potential cost overruns and institute changes to the company's activities to fall within acceptable cost parameters.

Moving from reactive to proactive, this same approach is also used to help managers decide when to modify the pricing plans for contracts, or when to restructure expenses by outsourcing or consolidating tasks. This concept provides real value when considered at the enterprise level. Departmental budgets often mask the costs associated with cross-functional business activities such as corporate sustaining activities, sales and marketing, and product service and support. Using this approach, an organization can even establish and measure corporate benchmarks as part of a broader transformational strategy.

Ultimately, the solution allows the company to evaluate costs for every business process and to identify areas for implementing cost-saving measures and companywide process improvements. Marketing and underwriting can see how product costs vary depending on the size and type of the group plan; department managers can see what activities performed truly at cost; and executives can look at administrative costs for specific lines of business as a ratio to revenue, claims paid, or other financial metrics.

In this scenario, notice the many different levels of costs being impacted:

- Budget management—Ensuring programs and business units stay to budget.
- Activity management—Ensuring efficiency and consistency in execution.
- Work reduction—Spending less time manipulating data, improving decision speed.
- Profitability—Ensuring that contracts and pricing are actually profitable.
- Cost arbitrage—Facilitating outsourcing to lower-cost fulfillment options.

The breadth of scope and impact is one reason why reducing healthcare costs can stand on its own as a business imperative, and not simply reflect the outcome of other improvement programs.

Improving Healthcare Outcomes

Beyond any of the organizational productivity or cost issues presented so far, the Holy Grail in healthcare analytics is all about improving the health of patients. Though providers, payers, researchers, manufacturers, and policy makers can disagree on most other aspects of the healthcare ecosystem, everyone can agree that we need more health in healthcare. Analytics provide the means of finding that health, and bringing it to scale.

Health-oriented analytics are not new. Every prescription drug discovered and marketed in the past two decades was required to demonstrate safety and efficacy via statistical models before being approved for use. Epidemiologists rely on computational methods in studying the progression of diseases in populations. Analytical models and methods are used to explore the estimated 3 billion chemical base pairs and twenty thousand genes in the human genome. In truth, advanced analytics have been a long-standing tool in understanding the scientific bases of biology and medicine.

Despite this analytical heritage, the hardest health-related questions—the ones that will likely have the biggest impact toward the lives of patients—are just now rising to the surface. Why? There are several reasons:

1. Scientific advancement. Our understanding of the fundamental nature of human physiology, genetics, and disease is reaching a point where we can more directly apply the learnings toward making patients better.
2. Convergence. The health-related improvements needed in any one health market—providers, payers, researchers—require access to information in the other markets. As greater transparency and openness to collaboration unfold, new opportunities to apply advanced analytics arise as well.
3. Cost. The dramatically rising costs of healthcare around the world have brought a new level of discrimination in treatment efficiency and effectiveness. Rather than continuing to fund expensive treatments with unclear outcomes, a better fiscal policy would focus on funding the best treatments with the best cost structures.

So what types of opportunities exist now? The following table highlights some of the main categories of outcomes-oriented analytics. It is important to note that this list is just a sampling. The ability to positively impact the treatment programs and corresponding patient outcomes is limited only by the creativity of the human mind to develop novel ideas and test them. As you will see in the examples that follow, there are many different ways to look at health outcomes.

Prospective Performance and Intervention	Optimized and Targeted Treatments	Adverse Event Avoidance
• Disease and population management • Expedited research • Member and patient programs • Pay for performance • Provider performance • Provider/physician profiling	• Biomedical informatics • Clinical and patient decision support • Clinical program compliance • Clinical research analysis • Evidence-based clinical decision support • Clinical performance management • Patient adherence	• Adverse event detection and prediction • Biosurveillance • Clinical alerting • Clinical quality performance analysis and reporting

Consider the following real-world example. A professor of epidemiology at a large Canadian university is studying the risk factors and relationships between cardiovascular disease and cholesterol levels, lifestyle, diet, childhood experiences, and environmental factors. The research includes studying the incidence and distribution of diseases by combining massive amounts of data from many disparate sources: nutrition databases, healthcare delivery data, community demographic information, national patient surveys, and information supplied by Health Canada and the U.S. Centers for Disease Control and Prevention. By bringing these large, disparate information resources together, the professor has been able to develop statistical models that establish the relationship between high cholesterol intake at an early age and chronic diseases later in life. For example, the evidence indicates that cardiovascular disease has a long latency time, and that problems begin in early childhood. By looking at a variety of factors such as cholesterol intake, height, weight, and level of physical activity, the professor can predict childhood risks of adult cardiovascular illness and death.

So how can analytics like that be put into action? In one case, a large U.S. health services company uses data mining to help identify people who would benefit from preventive care services. The data mining software predicts hidden relationships in millions of member records to (1) determine patient risk levels and (2) develop more targeted intervention and prevention plans. Large volumes of clinical and operational data are applied in statistical models that can predict the members in greatest need of support programs. In addition, by identifying high-risk patients and implementing preventative actions against future conditions, health problems and treatments can actually be avoided.

In another case, a western European health research institute sought a way for doctors and patients to predict the effects of drugs, other treatments, and life-style factors on patients with rheumatoid arthritis. To do this, they developed two analytics-based solutions: one enables rheumatism patients to examine the factors that affect their health, and the other helps rheumatologists select the best treatment for each patient. A statistical methodology called factor analysis is used to test various treatment hypotheses with the support of randomized trials. The goal is to find the scientifically best combination of various lifestyle factors for each individual case. Patients choose what they would prefer to improve, such as pain, and up to four independent lifestyle factors, such as exercise, diet, and sleeping habits, which might conceivably reduce pain. The system then generates a test plan that the patient prints out as a diary of what should be tested each day. At the end of the period, the program calculates which combination of factors provided the best lifestyle impact.

Over fifty clinics have been involved in the collection of these data from patients and physicians: more than 26,500 patients and 144,000 consultations have been collected and analyzed. The predictive model uses patient data as the basis for predicting the results of various treatments such as different drugs and drug combinations. In other words, instead of a physician relying on a generic treatment plan that may or may not be the best option for a particular patient, the system assists doctors in choosing the best treatment for each patient based on that patient's profile. This approach has the added benefit of avoiding the costs associated with expensive treatments or drugs that are unlikely to be a good fit for a given patient.

Unfortunately, in many cases, humankind has yet to find cures or even strong treatments for diseases. It is in these areas where analytics can have a dramatic impact. For pharmaceutical and biotechnology companies, the development of a new medicine can take more than a decade—a decade of great expense for the developer and of prolonged anxiety for patients in need of new treatments. Meanwhile, the escalating cost of research and development, accompanied by the increasing complexity and expense of human clinical trials, threatens pharmaceutical innovation and drives up healthcare costs.

Using analytics, it is possible to develop simulations of human clinical research (clinical trials simulations) that can considerably expedite the development of novel therapies and save millions of development dollars. Simulated clinical trials are virtual replicas of actual clinical trials. The simulations take data models developed from actual clinical trials and develop clinical scenarios and putative trial results that take into account variability caused by treatment effects, survival times, adverse events such as the occurrence of headaches or nausea, and other events that occur during trials. Researchers might perform ten thousand simulations of a single scenario, which means an entire trial can generate millions of observations. Using this approach, a U.S. biotechnology company is actively exploring new treatments for HIV infection, hepatitis, various forms of cancer, inflammatory diseases such as rheumatoid arthritis, and many others. Its solution, which also takes advantage of grid computing technology, can produce as many as 1 million patients for 2 terabytes of data in a single simulation. The company has the ability to do over ten thousand replicates in an hour, and that rate is growing.

Summary

With all of the different dimensions of analytics covered so far, it is logical to ask where an organization begins in its journey toward deeper insights. As you might expect, there is no single correct answer—the journey depends on the traveler and the desired destination. In watching many organizations move through their analytical maturity process, one key theme emerges among successful companies: start where you are. As mentioned earlier, it is easy to fall prey to analysis paralysis, constantly evaluating abilities instead of instituting programs to change those abilities. You will never have enough electronic data, it will never be clean enough, there will always be conflicting priorities, and you will never have enough of the right resources to focus on the project. But in all likelihood, you have enough of all of the above to get started.

Another trap some organizations fall into is "boiling the ocean." It is impossible to take on all of these analytical challenges and opportunities at the same time.

And even if you could, it would not be advisable. Organizations and their knowledge workers need time to learn, determine what makes sense for their company, find the pitfalls and build bridges over them, and institutionalize those learnings for future projects. The intelligent enterprise identifies a significant, clearly defined business challenge and puts an agile team together to demonstrate success. With a successful project completed, the ability to launch the next initiative is much easier, and the people involved in the first project are now tour guides on the journey.

Using this approach, leading organizations often create an analytical center of excellence (ACE) within their enterprise. An ACE consists of a small, cross-functional group of people who help the many different parts of the company successfully leverage analytics. ACEs provide several benefits:

- Provide internal consulting and training on how to apply analytics to business problems
- Serve as business sponsors in the identification and management of data integration, quality, and management activities that support analytics
- Establish clear accountability for the advancement of analytical competencies within the enterprise
- Ensure consistency in the selection and use of enterprise architecture, analytical tools, and solutions to support analytics across the enterprise

Whether you are starting your first analytics initiative or finishing your hundredth project, you hopefully are getting a sense of the curiosity and excitement many people feel about analytics: there is always another question to ask with hidden gems in the answers. In healthcare, we are just at the beginning of seeing how analytics—whether biased toward the business or clinical sides of the spectrum—can transform our ecosystem. Analytics will give us better guidance on how to control costs—not just line items, but the hidden and true costs of healthcare. Analytics will help us identify and dismantle old assumptions about the way healthcare is delivered—not relying on gut instincts and hearsay, but real evidence. Analytics will allow us to determine not only the treatments that produce the best outcomes, but the real factors that determine optimum treatment efficacy and cost. The hidden gems in healthcare will surface, and with them will come better lives for patients everywhere.

Acknowledgment

I am grateful for the contributions of Cindy Berry and Rick Pro, both from SAS's Health and Life Sciences organization, to the content and review of this chapter.

Chapter 9

Enhancing Data Resources and Business Intelligence in Healthcare

Stephan Kudyba and Mark Rader

Contents

The healthcare industry has been a focal point in the pursuit of enhancing operational efficiency. The complex nature of the industry and its diverse technologies, procedures, medicines, and facilities to diagnose and treat individuals of all demographic and physical make-ups in a setting of ever-rising costs add up to a formidable and complex task. Management at Saint Clare's Health System was not dissuaded as they sought to improve their business of providing patients with high-quality treatment and care more efficiently.

Saint Clare's Health System is comprised of four hospitals and more than three thousand personnel who provide care across a spectrum of patient needs such as behavioral health, cardiovascular, diabetes, and dialysis. Management identified procedures in selected operations, the efficiency of which could be enhanced through the utilization of information technologies. More specifically, Saint Clare's sought to generate more robust information resources from digitizing activities in certain treatment and care procedures. The organization realized that there was a source of valuable information in existing paper documents, charts, and general treatment activities that could provide enhanced intelligence about the effectiveness of treatment procedures for patients. By transforming paper and procedural activity inputs into data resources, Saint Clare's could enhance efficiency by mitigating lost information, increase productivity of care-providing personnel, better identify areas for improvement of care procedures, and ultimately, enhance the quality of care for patients. Areas involving data assets include medical reports, nursing documentation, medical administrative records, radiology information, and pharmacy information.

Secrets to Success

The best technological platform and the most ingenious data-based strategy cannot yield positive results without proper implementation guidelines and organizational buy-in by stakeholders of the system. Essential implementation guidelines on the technology side in this case included an invited request for proposal (RFP) process to system vendors and an open forum of internal hospital users and stakeholders to gain a feel of the corresponding technology's functionality. Once the right platform was selected, formal and extensive training was conducted to ease the system into real-time usage. A true measure of success in increasing efficiency from system implementation does not revolve around technology functionality alone; it arises from continued usage by all hospital stakeholders and adoption of the system as an integral tool supporting everyday treatment activities. To achieve this, the organization launched a cultural change strategy that promoted use of the system to work smarter and more efficiently by leveraging its resources. So far, the results have been a success and the organization has experienced positive outcomes on a number of fronts.

Sources of Efficiency Gains

The IT platform enabled Saint Clare's to enhance efficiency in the short run by mitigating the potential risk of lost information (e.g., paper documents, charts, reports), which often plagues paper-based environments. By storing existing documents and initiating the ongoing input of procedural data, Saint Clare's created a more reliable method to organize, archive, and access information. Other gains include reducing the time for nursing staff to complete required paperwork, document vital treatment information for patients, and access past treatment information. The information download process has been enhanced by a user-friendly input interface, which also promotes a coherent, standardized database of treatment-related activities. Reduction in data access and downloading time from the previous paper report environment has increased the time available for nurses to concentrate on patient care. That is a classic case of increased productivity—accomplishing the same task in less time and increasing available employee time to address other tasks where the level of quality of each is increased.

"Patient Treatment" Intelligence

One of the most promising gains to efficiency lies in the ability to analyze the data that describe the treatment and care processes supported by the system. By transforming existing paper information into digital form and systematizing current and future procedure (treatment) information, Saint Clare's is creating building blocks to perform more advanced analytics of patient care activities. Systematizing data enables users to more effectively analyze data elements in a logical, coherent manner. When compared to reading hundreds of paper reports and charts in order to formulate trends in patient response to treatments, the system effect provides the capability to identify and view trends over time. This applies to patient treatment outcomes and also to the effectiveness of treatment types across a variety of patients. The accessibility of more descriptive, coherent, and timely reports and graphics gives doctors, nurses, and hospital staff enhanced treatment intelligence.

Positive returns from business intelligence are generally achieved over time as data resources grow and develop and as new software applications augment data analysis. Increased usage of business intelligence enabled by higher-quality information can assist treatment providers in better understanding treatment procedures, outcomes, and care for patients. With the establishment of an effective information management system and through the use of digital infrastructure, the implications for long-term efficiency gains through enhanced analytics and business (treatment) intelligence are far reaching.[1]

Introduction to Business Intelligence

In the purest form, business intelligence can be summed up to be the methodologies and technologies utilized for collecting, manipulating, analyzing, and presenting information that enables business leaders to both make informed decisions for the actions that will need to be taken and evaluate the effectiveness of actions that have already been executed. The information corresponding to processes that have been created and are continuously utilized by companies represents their current and primary business intelligence. Business intelligence actually originates with the employees of organizations. Workers utilize workflows, policies, and procedures based on best practices that evolve over years of experience, education, and training. There is no limit to the amount of actual business intelligence that is consciously maintained on any given day; however, the truly valuable information may actually lie in the areas that are not analyzed as deeply as they should be. This concept refers to the constant refinement of business intelligence applications, where today's environment calls for data to be recorded and utilized across processes of an organization that are pulled together and taken through evaluative methodologies that produce quick-hitting measures of company operations. In healthcare, facilities put their knowledge in the policies and procedures that they have found to be most effective for treating and managing their patients. Medical staff recognize and utilize these same methods, but refer to them as evidence-based medicine. In evidence-based medicine practice is based on what has been proven to be safe and effective in the treatment of any particular condition. Medical publications publish the findings, and standards and practice committees determine if and how the findings should be followed. In much the same way, business intelligence creates actionable items from available data in any environment and can provide the feedback required to determine what is the best methodology, practice, or steps to apply to a given situation.

In the following example we show how data being collected in healthcare can be rapidly evaluated using business intelligence with readily available tools. Figure 9.1 shows a series of diagnosis-related groupings, or DRG codes of medical diagnosis, for patients admitted to a hospital within a one-month period, who were readmitted to the facility within fourteen days of their initial discharge. The new diagnosis at the readmission is deep vein thrombosis (DVT). Immediately, there is a visual

**Number of Patients by DRG Readmitted
Within 14 Days of Discharge**

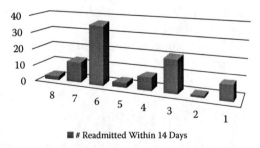

Figure 9.1   Histogram chart to evaluate readmissions.

understanding that the patients with a DRG code of 6 on their initial admission to the hospital are the most at risk for developing DVT during or after their stay at the facility. This assumption was immediately available because of the application of business intelligence methods to existing data across time periods within an electronic system. Now this report can be generated on demand and with very little effort. Previously, chart reviews would have been needed, which could introduce potential inaccurate numbers. Now it can be seen easily where the problem areas are and what patients need to be targeted for specific evaluations while admitted to the facility.

Herein lies the power of business intelligence that was not previously seen by the healthcare industry as a whole. Previously reviews were completed and case studies performed that targeted specific areas of demographics and conditions to produce a final result, but now we can create assumptions and gain direction from a system based on an even larger case mix. However, it must be kept in mind that these numbers are generated from a system that is simply collecting data in the manner in which it was designed. So the results may be indicators but not absolute definitive outcomes. The results of business intelligence are best when utilized as guiding points of information that will bring forward areas of review with a high acuity. This guiding light principle will bring forth new ideas and understanding of just how patients and outcomes are affected by the decisions made during their treatment. Business intelligence is not just a tool or a method, but a way of effectively evaluating the facts that are already known, and by applying knowledge of the business practice, or in this case of healthcare treatments, it is possible to identify areas of improvement and key indicators of best practices.

Business Intelligence in Electronic Medical Records

The intelligence side of business intelligence is by far the most astounding concept to emphasize when considering that what can be produced from a system is not only intellectual property that may not have been previously thought to be possessed by a healthcare organization, but the information needed to make business or healthcare decisions that may have been previously overlooked. In a typical paper-based medical records system, analysis is performed on an as needed basis, and with only a small subset of the full patient population, which may inadvertently miss many of the key cases that could drive change in a facility. Looking at a scenario in which a healthcare facility reviews ten patient charts of every unit once a month for regulatory compliance on treatment and handling of a particular condition, it is quite possible that much of the valuable information available to that facility may be overlooked. In one instance a hospital may have 9 nursing units, and each unit has approximately 150 admissions per month, totaling 1,350 patient charts that have the potential of being included in the reporting and providing evidence-based information. When a review of these charts is performed each month, ten are pulled for evaluation, and a time-consuming process is undertaken to determine if the charts meet the criteria to be included in the regulatory review, which may result in only five charts meeting the conditions needed to be included in the report. That equates to only 2.96% of the total available data being utilized in this healthcare facility to make a regulatory declaration of compliance. Not only is there a large set of data missing from the evaluation, but anywhere from 40 to 120 hours a month can be dedicated to doing a manual review of paper documentation per internal auditor, and a majority of the charts are never reviewed for inclusion in performance indicators. With the use of business intelligence tools and process evaluation and improvement methodologies of business management strategies such as Six Sigma, a healthcare facility or system can effectively reduce hours of manual analysis of patient data to immediate and easily digested indicators that represent every chart available in the EMR system, not just a small subsection, which can lead to misrepresented indicators of process, treatments, and business.

Evaluation

When an electronic medical record system is implemented in an organization a process begins with a simple set of facts and over time, a minimum of six months, a repository of workflow, treatment, and response information is established that, when put through a discriminating analysis, can be used to create a reliable and actionable set of information. This collection of facts will remain part of the database and be used to review charts on an as needed basis for historical purposes. Data or the collection of facts provides the basis of creating information describing a multitude of activities in healthcare facilities. To accomplish this, a deep understanding of the processes, workflows, data capture, and regulatory requirements must be established. This is where a business strategy or process and performance evaluation methodologies such as Six Sigma come into play. Six Sigma can be viewed as either a business strategy tool that is effective at identifying the areas that require change, or a performance evaluation methodology examining the effectiveness of process modification for a company. For an EMR, it is important to understand how the data that underpin business intelligence and strategic methods such as Six Sigma are collected.

Data Collection

What is required for consistent data is a system that collects and stores facts and records of events that involve minimal variances in the way they are input. Variance in data causes outliers that produce information that cannot be considered accurate, reliable, and actionable. Given a basic example of data collection in a system where free-text entry is utilized to collect records of medical history on patients as they arrive at the facility, what may occur is a previous diagnosis entered into the field three different ways by personnel who are performing the data entry. The first person entering data may enter a previous acute myocardial infarction as a "heart attack" since he or she is in a rush during the triage and needs to get the patient in quickly for immediate treatment. The next individual gathering the updated full history may enter it in as "AMI" to save time while collecting the rest of a lengthy history, and another may update this again with the full "acute myocrdial infarction" on a separate form to indicate a previous procedure was performed. The result is three different entries in two locations, with one of those entries having a spelling mistake. To simplify and correct these data issues from occurring, fields must be created that handle discrete information. A discrete field gives the individuals entering data the ability to select data elements that are prepopulated with all potential entries for a given entity. In the area of medical history it would not be prudent to list every potential diagnosis that exists in a single field, but a field for cardiac history would need to be created, and then only the most utilized potential entries listed. This gives fast access to the needed entry and allows little room for data variance. When using accurate discrete information, an analysis can be performed quickly on the fields to determine what patients came to the facility with a medical history of AMI and were treated at that facility for conditions that may have resulted from the diagnosis.

Data Integrity

When applying standard analytic concepts to an EMR, the initial set of data acquired from the first six months to one year of utilization could potentially show large variances and a significant number of outliers. This can be attributed to workflows and documentation being adapted from paper-based processes to the electronic system. Healthcare facilities may be tempted during the implementation of an EMR to take existing documentation and directly recreate the forms and layouts on the screen, which can lead to persistence of slow processes and create a harsh phenomenon known as duplicate data entry. The result of duplicate data entry on a business intelligence system is an unreliable and varying set of data that will be discredited immediately by anyone reviewing them who is familiar with the data being entered into the system. It must be emphasized again that it is imperative that from the inception of the system it is communicated to users that the information being presented in the reports is only as good as the level of quality and consistency of the data being entered into the system. Standard procedures for discrete data input will allow for consistency in data resources. Once this is established, an understanding of where to look for data becomes a major concern when conducting process evaluations. A major initiative to promote data integrity is through education.

Education is a key factor in determining that the methods by which electronic documentation is created and utilized are consistently reinforced with the users of the system. Not only is education imperative, but the design of the forms to guide personnel entering the same type of data into the same forms is critical to the reporting capabilities. When data are inconsistently entered into varying areas, there are no true indicators to target, and discrediting of the business intelligence platform quickly ensues given anomalies in output generated. Designing forms that reduce duplication of data entry develops a consistent means of data storage and discovery. Review of detailed data will indicate that reported aggregate numbers are accurate to what is being documented. Once the integrity of the system is established and it is accurate in its reporting capabilities, the questioning of system results is mitigated and emphasis is given to utilization of system output to improve processes to enhance patient care and outcomes throughout the facility.

Reviewing a Workflow

One of the driving forces of customer or patient satisfaction is the effectiveness of a process or workflow in a healthcare organization. Any facility can claim it has policies and procedures that address those factors that lead to a positive patient experience; reality, however, indicates that what is dictated on paper may or may not be consistent with applications. Patients who visit facilities where they are able to smoothly navigate from one point in the process of registration to the next step generally have more positive feedback than those experiencing difficulty finding their way from one end of the building where they register to the other end, where radiology and the laboratory are located. A lack of clear workflow design (e.g., user-friendly directions for patients undergoing a process of events) can no doubt result in a negative patient experience. The application of business intelligence reporting coupled with a Six Sigma DMAIC project methodology review can identify how to improve the existing workflow. Clear directions on moving the patient from one area to the next that incorporate the activities of both patients and healthcare providers are critical to enhancing workflow efficiency and ultimately the patient experience.

The Six Sigma DMAIC project methodology is used for projects aimed at improving an existing business process. Each of the letters in the acronym identifies a phase of the project and was inspired by Deming's plan-do-check-act cycle. The DMAIC project methodology is laid out as follows:

- *Define* high-level project goals and the current process.
- *Measure* key aspects of the current process and collect relevant data.
- *Analyze* the data to verify cause-and-effect relationships. Determine what the relationships are, and attempt to ensure that all factors have been considered.
- *Improve* or optimize the process based upon data analysis using techniques like design of experiments.

- *Control* to ensure that any deviations from the target are corrected before they result in defects. Set up pilot runs to establish process capability, move on to production, set up control mechanisms, and continuously monitor the process.

Given the preestablished processes that exist in the healthcare environment, business intelligence begins at the M phase of the project and continues through the final C phase. Each phase has distinct requirements that need to be accomplished before the process can move to the next phase. With the implementation of business intelligence, those taking part in the project can establish the goal, measure what currently exists, conduct analysis to identify key indicators, and produce information that can be acted upon. Improving the process in the I phase is supported by visual representation to those responsible for executing the process, where the final stage of continually monitoring the process is accomplished by the timely updating of data resources and analysis of reports and graphics

To illustrate the Six Sigma business intelligence approach, let us turn to a hypothetical healthcare application. In this case, an emergency room was honored with a national award for having the highest customer satisfaction rating of all the facilities participating in the survey. While this is a very prestigious award, this kind of recognition means further scrutiny by those visiting that see the award prominently displayed on the wall of the waiting area. In order to maintain these performance achievements, analysis of what is currently in place, including time frames from each point in the process, is required, where considering the time it takes to move the patient between each point in the process is essential. A brief review by the project initiators identifies that the average wait time for a patient is over forty-five minutes before he or she has a medical service exam (MSE) by a physician. This identifies the area of workflow improvement that must be addressed. In parallel to the workflow, policy, and procedure evaluation, all current workflow points need to be identified in the system. The ability to extract these points should be available since a typical EMR would have the ability to add tasks, markers, or events in the system to identify when you have reached a point in the workflow or process. Event elements of the workflow process can be analyzed since informatics applications have the ability to time-stamp these events that indicate start and completion times. In an ideal situation the identified points in the workflow would be created and completed automatically by the software as personnel move the patient through the emergency department and complete the tasks or events previously defined. This prevents missing data from personnel overlooking the need to enter any time stamp information. The ultimate result is a data resource that enables decision makers to identify bottlenecks in the workflow, investigate causes of delays, and if feasible, introduce guidelines to address the issues at hand.

Initial review of data includes a column for every step in the process that contains the time to complete that task. In this facility the patient arrives, which is the starting time stamp of the process, and then moves into triage with a nurse, and is assigned and moved into a bed in the emergency department. Nurse evaluation and a medical history review are then conducted and completed. Next, a medical service exam is performed by the physician, which may be followed by testing, procedures, medication administration, and treatment. Disposition of the patient is performed to indicate if the patient is going home after treatment or being admitted. These are just some of the initial steps that can be identified for tracking purposes, and the time frame between each step indicates where potential bottlenecks exist in the process. Identification of the areas between the arrival and the MSE become visible as extended time frames from arrival to the triage occur, and the time from the MSE being requested to when it was completed by the physician may become elevated. The next step is to look at what personnel are involved with moving the patient through the process, or perhaps personnel staffing levels at those times versus the number of patients coming to the facility for treatment. By doing this we complete the M and A phases of the project through measurement and analysis of what is currently in place by business intelligence tools available within the EMR. Further detail and alternate representation of the data would be needed to drive the changes in the I phase of the project. The timing of workflows is imperative to the successful treatment of a patient since the feeling of adequate care can generally be linked to the timeliness of movement of the patient through the emergency room, or any other department in a facility. However, one step that makes the largest impact is that of the physician coming in to see the patient. Of the data that have been collected to this point, the arrival time of the patient is available and it is known when the physician starts the MSE, or first visits the patient in the room, since there is a time stamp associated with the event and the physicians have agreed to log in to the computer and start the event prior to visiting with the patient. This agreement can be easily acquired from the physician since he or she will typically log in to the computer to gather the data that have been collected during triage and initial nurse evaluation. Upon the completion of the shift the system is left with time stamps and events from every patient and every physician, and the business intelligence system can now run automatically to produce the chart seen in Figure 9.2. What is immediately seen is that some physicians are adequate at arriving to see the patient and begin their exam in under thirty minutes, and typically those physicians have a lighter load than others. The physician that stands out is physician 6, since he had one of the lightest loads for the shift, but was unable to meet the required thirty-minute time frame. Now the administration can delve deeper into why this was occurring and sit down with the physician after reviewing the data to see if there was an outlier that caused the physician to fall outside the acceptable range. Whatever the reason, by simply having the data in place and available for them to see how well they are performing, the physicians will typically strive to meet the goal since they do not want to be the outlier in meeting the needs of both the patients and the facilities. Any administrator would love to be able to create an environment where personnel strive to increase performance and patient satisfaction without any monetary output to the physicians themselves.

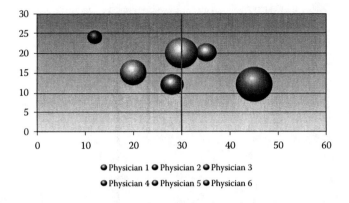

Figure 9.2 Bubble chart to identify physicians with average door to MSE times greater than thirty minutes.

Improvement may be needed in the specific areas that have been identified as a source of process delays. This can be accomplished through the analysis of process-related information via reports and graphics that depict excessive lag times for certain procedures beyond normal and acceptable levels. Initiatives such as increasing labor resources (e.g., specific healthcare personnel) to areas where bottlenecks occur, or systematizing procedures that cause undue delays in patient care activity (e.g., administrative) can be implemented. Applications of charts and graphics that report on daily performance metrics involve the C phase, which enables decision makers to quickly view on a daily basis, at a high level, reports indicating trends in process performance rates. Robust business intelligence technology enables users to drill into the low-level reports to see where incidents are causing delays and inhibiting process performance. This allows personnel to address problems as they are occurring to alleviate negative patient experiences in the pipeline. As an example of how you can identify causes in disruption of workflow, a Pareto chart was utilized to determine the main cause of patients being delayed in movement from the emergency department to the nursing units (see Figure 9.3). Again, we can rapidly identify the areas that need improvement, where it is understood that to make the largest improvement in process, you need to identify the causes of delay that happen 80% of the time. With a review of the chart the three main problems are the areas of the emergency department physician and the admitting physician exchanging their reports with each other, and the delay in the nursing staff giving a report to the admitting nurse on the unit. The directors of the organization now have a clear path to alleviate patients waiting excessive time before being taken to their bed. A new methodology for handling patient needs to be evaluated is required. Once that methodology is put in place, the same evaluation of data can be run again to see the results of time frames and the causes for delay. With enough data collected over time, trending can then be added to identify points in time and the changes that were put in place at that time to produce the effect on the statistical measures.

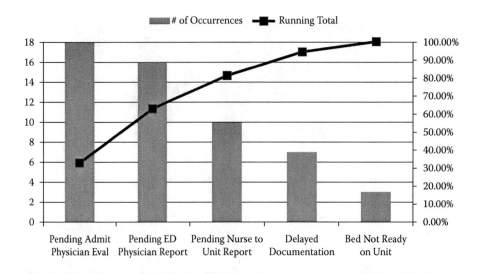

Figure 9.3

Data Mining

The advantage of leveraging data resources with business intelligence is extended through the utilization of data mining applications. These sophisticated analytic applications grounded in quantitative methodologies enable decision makers to identify actionable information in the form of recurring patterns and trends among data variables that describe various healthcare-related processes. These techniques have been utilized to determine likelihoods of patients to be classified as high risk for particular ailments, identify effective clinical and treatment procedures that lead to positive outcomes, uncover fraudulent financial activities, and help better describe performance of general operational processes that underpin various healthcare activities, such as identifying variables that account for excessive lengths of stay and throughput metrics (time for physicians to receive lab results). Data mining models enhance the ability to determine not just what has happened in healthcare performance, but why things are happening and what is likely to happen in the future.

Closing Comments

In order to accomplish an effective business intelligence platform, stakeholders that are involved in the processes and treatment activities that are incorporated in data, reports, and graphics; stored; and analyzed by the technology should have input into the design of system output. The result of including accurate and relevant data (e.g., those variables that appropriately underpin process activities) in a business intelligence platform that can quickly provide actionable analytic information describing processes and activities is a more efficient organization that better manages costs, produces an enhanced customer experience, and achieves high standards in patient care and outcomes.

Reference

1. Kudyba S. 2008, Productivity gains at St. Clare's health system, *Information Management Magazine*, March 11, 2008.

Chapter 10

Application of Healthcare Informatics to Improving Patient Safety and Outcomes

Learning from the Experiences of Trinity Health

Rajiv Kohli, Frank Piontek, Larry Sellers,
Tom Miner, and Paul Conlon

Contents

Overview

Most healthcare information technology efficacy publications emerge from academic institutions that often develop their own proprietary information systems (IS). However, most patients in the United States are discharged from community hospitals. Community hospitals often implement advanced technology with a focus on global safety or quality, yet are faced with cost issues pertaining to large implementations and generally lack resources to measure the impact of such systems. This explains, in part, the limited research conducted among community hospitals to measure the economic and performance outcomes of healthcare information technology. Therefore, it is important that experiences of community hospitals are documented and shared with hospital decision makers.

This chapter overviews the experiences of Trinity Health, a large multihospital community-based health system that initiated a systemwide information technology strategy to improve patient safety and clinical outcomes. Termed Project Genesis, the implementation of Trinity Health's strategy is represented through three case studies. Case study 1 makes the argument that hospitals must involve physicians and effectively communicate with them to implement safety and cost containment initiatives. Case study 2 presents Trinity Health's approach to developing an information systems tool, how physicians' access to information helped them identify changes to be made, and the resulting impact on patient safety and hospital outcomes. Finally, case study 3 presents an example of an IT-supported initiative that led to the reduction in adverse drug events (ADEs) among the hospitals of Trinity Health.

Introduction

Trinity Health is the fourth largest Catholic health system in the United States and employs 44,500 full-time equivalent employees with over 8,000 active staff physicians. Its facilities include 44 hospitals, 379 outpatient clinics/facilities, numerous long-term care facilities, home health and hospice programs, and senior housing communities across seven U.S. states. For FY 2008, Trinity Health revenues were $6.3 billion, including $376 million that were returned to the communities in the form of healthcare for the poor and underserved.

Trinity Health gained nationwide exposure when it received the 2004 National Committee for Quality Health Care's annual award. The effective creation and implementation of the intranet-based information system called Integrated Information Shared Services (I2S2) played an important role in gathering, processing, and delivery of information. I2S2 delivered safety and quality outcome indicators for decision makers across the organization. The implementation of information technology (IT) in Project Genesis employed an incremental step-by-step development approach in which the organizational and managerial issues were aligned with the IT.

Case Study 1: Physician-Led Informatics

This case study focuses on a continued initiative involving the tenets of customer relationship management (CRM) with the physicians.[1] Trinity Health learned from the CRM literature to build a service-oriented mechanism that consisted of delivering information and soliciting physician involvement. Trinity Health had previously deployed a web-based information system to deliver physician profiles of quality and costs. The Physician Profiling System (PPS) contained three fundamental hospital-based CRM characteristics: (1) administrative data-driven decision-making processes for healthcare problem identification, variation reduction, statistical process control, and other physician-driven performance pattern analyses; (2) identification of areas for improvement by benchmarking (either internal, external, or both) physician practices to desired patterns of quality and cost outcomes; and (3) involving the physicians as customers in improving operations using (1) and (2) by establishing critical success norms or other related evidence-based initiatives, particularly by using technology for rapid deployment, prompt feedback, and support for replication of best practices. The PPS deployment incurred an approximate cost of US$163,000 for the development and implementation in a single hospital. The return on investment (ROI) for that endeavor exhibited a mean decrease of 0.24 days of hospitalization, with an aggregate decrease of 845 total inpatient days along with multiple hospital department cost savings of US$1.42 million. For details of this initiative, please see Kohli et al.[1]

Approach

While the one-off PPS was successful and provided the proof of concept, Trinity Health could not afford a multihospital implementation, one hospital at a time. So it extracted the learning from the PPS, enhanced the existing decision support system's (DSS) reporting capabilities, and delivered it through a web-based system for the entire organization (see case study 2). The defining requirements emerging from the physician-led informatics initiative were as follows:

1. User-friendly design with common data structures for each ministry organization and a metadata level to speed query processing times
2. Enforced reconciliation of data with operational systems to ensure that all information systems provide consistent data
3. Seeking of value-added information such as cost accounting, expected reimbursement, and severity adjustment and assignment; such processes inform physicians about the impact of their decisions
4. Continuous improvement through cross-learning among ministry organizations and application development for quick deployment of best practices

Trinity Health created baseline assessments for disease categories (Figure 10.1) to achieve the objectives of the physician-led informatics and to enhance ongoing physician alignment. These objectives were to share an innovative model for depicting individual physician resource utilization, the ability to identify physician variation in the clinical management, and to demonstrate the use of comparative benchmarking.

Results

The results from physicians' involvement were manifested as lower average length of stay (ALOS) and reduced patient charges. By contrast, among the hospitals where data were yet to be shared with physicians, the ALOS and charges began to increase. Trinity Health continued to monitor outcomes through the utilization collaborative team (UCT). Hospital- and physician-specific scorecards were developed by the UCT and distributed. Figure 10.2 presents a sample physician utilization report.

The utilization-based scorecards compared each physician's actual vs. expected outcomes for ALOS, mortality, and patient charges for services. Comparable metrics for physicians within the specialty as well as other specialties are also reported. Finally, the scorecard presents a breakdown of charges by major categories such as lab, surgical, and pharmacy. Supported by the informatics, the physician and clinical staff practice changes resulted in lower than expected mortality rates as well as patient charges. With 2,932 patients, a drop in 0.32 days per patient in LOS equated to 938 fewer patient days, and a reduction of $661.27 per patient in charges resulted in savings of nearly US$1.939 million.

The deployment of physician-led informatics prompted various feedback comments. Some admitted that they didn't realize the procedure costs that much, while others found the scorecards helpful and expressed eagerness for the next report. The outcomes in the report card prompted some physicians to review previous patients' charts and examine why they were in the hospital for that long, resulting in a retrospective learning and ideas about patient safety, improvement in ALOS, and how to contain costs.

Benchmarking for Cerebrovascular Accidents or TIA				
	N	*Mean*	*Median*	*Sum*
Quality	449			
Mortality	449	0.093	0	42
Expected mortality	449	0.114	0	51.186
Complications	449	0.167	0	74.983
Readmissions	449	0.081	0	36.369
Expected readmissions	449	0.109	0.106	48.941
LOS	449	4.55	4	2,042.95
Expected LOS	449	4.67	4.84	2,096.83
Costs	449			
ER	449	$247.40	$233.50	$111,082.60
ICU	449	$659.70	$0.00	$296,205.30
Lab	449	$217.50	$110.80	$97,657.50
Misc.	449	$574.60	$538.70	$257,995.40
Pharmacy	449	$370.40	$143.30	$166,309.60
Radiology	449	$404.60	$260.10	$181,665.40
Room	449	$1,290.70	$1,052.20	$579,524.30
Supply	449	$54.45	$8.41	$24,448.05
Surgery	449	$19.62	$0.00	$8,809.38
Therapies	449	$256.20	$179.10	$115,033.80
Total cost	449	$4,095.60	$3,209.40	$1,838,924.40
Expected cost	449	$4,307.60	$4,342.50	$1,934,112.40

Figure 10.1   Benchmarking data to support physician informatics.

<table>
<tr><td>Trinity St. Elsewhere
Regional Medical Center</td><td colspan="2">**Physician Utilization Report**
by Physician Specialty and
Attending Physician Number for Select MS DRGs

Selected MS DRGs: 234,236</td></tr>
</table>

Physician Specialty Code: **0004 CARDIOTHORACIC SURGERY**

Physician Number and Name: **666 Piontek, Frank**

MS DRG Code	MS DRG Description		MS DRG Geometric Mean LOS	Patient Count
236	CORONARY BYPASS WO CARD CATH WO MCC		6.08	16

(National - 2005 V24)	Your Numbers	Ratio: observed/expected	Same Spec (excl. you)	Ratio: observed/expected	All Others (excl. spec)	Ratio: observed/expected
Actual ALOS	6.00	1.00	5.13	0.85	9.50	1.11
Expected ALOS	6.03		6.03		8.54	
Actual Mortalities	0	0.00	0	0.00	0	0.00
Expected Mortalities	0.05		0.05		0.01	
Actual Average Charges	52,402.80	0.76	49,983.28	0.72	63,206.97	0.69
Expected Avg Charge	69,373.76		69,653.75		91,124.72	
Number of Patients	16		23		2	

Revenue Code Group	# of Pts	Avg Charge	# of Pts	Avg Charge	# of Pts	Avg Charge
EMERGENCY	1	45.00	0	0.00	1	989.00
ICU	16	11,091.44	23	9,332.26	2	14,189.50
LAB	16	6,561.32	23	6,445.91	2	10,568.13
OTHER	16	1,509.63	23	1,588.04	2	2,138.50
PHARMACY	16	6,583.16	23	7,183.32	2	8,498.34
PROSTH	16	267.38	23	70.13	2	70.50
RADIOLOGY	16	1,132.75	23	1,043.22	2	969.00
ROOM	0	0.00	1	57.00	0	0.00
SUPPLY	16	12,123.00	23	11,936.71	2	12,567.00
SURGICAL	16	11,010.38	23	10,371.74	2	11,916.00
THERAPY	16	2,120.94	23	2,008.48	2	1,795.50

Figure 10.2 A sample physician scorecard.

Case Study 2: Integrated Information Shared Services (I2S2) Intranet

In the clinical arena, there is an expectation that quality must be measured on an ongoing basis. Healthcare organizations are monitored for quality and patient safety by the accrediting agencies and the U.S. government. Various agencies, public and private, publish hospital and physician comparisons (see http://www.hospitalcompare.hhs.gov, http://www.qualitynet.org/, and http://www.healthgrades.com/). Prior to many of the public sources of comparisons, Trinity Health desired transparency, so it published the quality performance for each MO on an intranet website called Integrated Information Shared Services (I2S2). The transparency of quality indicator performance enabled each hospital to identify another hospital with better performance. Conversations about higher performance led to performance improvement strategies and action plans.

Approach

I2S2 was originally planned as an intranet web-based site. The development and maintainance was to be outsourced. However, due to the projected high costs of development, in-house resources completed the project. The I2S2 design uses content management software. Content management software is most often used for storing, controlling, and publishing industry-specific documentation such as articles, manuals, and guides. The content may include files, graphs, images, databases, and documents with links to other websites (for more information, see http://www.contentmanager.eu.com/history.htm). Content management software integrated the interdependent layers of data for managing Trinity Health's content as well as for publishing the results to *any* individuals across the organization.

I2S2 recycles automatically every two hours. Costs include the server hardware, the content management software, and the incremental labor from IT and clinical operations staff needed to input content. The benefits clearly outweigh the costs. I2S2 is now a web content management (WCM) system. This simplfies the publication of the web content and allows the domain experts to focus upon creating content. The advantage of the WCM-based architecture is the ease of use. Since the majority of contributions are from clinicians, content submission does not require technical knowledge of HTML or file uploads. As a result of the WCM, I2S2 is fully transparent to the over fifty thousand Trinity Health employees who simply have to sign on to the Trinity Health web page for the vast information resources available to them.

The spectrum of I2S2 content, shown in Figure 10.3, can be logically organized in three primary areas: governance, data requirements, and guidelines and education. Below are descriptions of the salient topics for which I2S2 delivers support for decision makers. For each of the three areas, we discuss topics for which information is available.

1. Governance
   - Excellence in care experience. Patient satisfaction data, employee engagement, and physician satisfaction data are at the core and should be used to improve the overall experience of the patients and their families.
   - The Advance Practice Institute provides data to promote evidence-based best practices through advanced skills of nursing leaders, development of leadership skills to facilitate and complete projects, and the fostering of networks for creative thinking and issue resolution in the practice of evidence-based care.
   - Care improvement provides evidence-based tools, strategies, and resources to assist in providing excellence in care for specific clinical conditions such as AMI (Acute Myocardial Infarction), pneumonia, diabetes, heart failure, newborn and neonatal, obstetrics, orthopedics, and vaccine information.

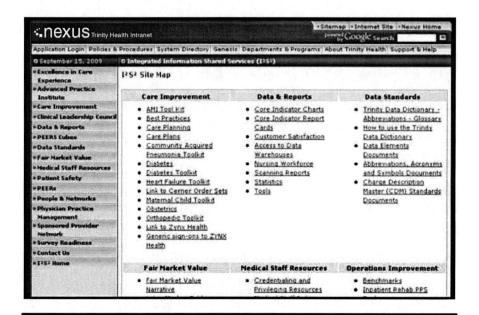

Figure 10.3   I2S2 user interface listing a site map with various categories of information and reports available.

- – The Clinical Leadership Council provides documentation for value and strategies of Trinity Health clinical services in accordance with the Trinity Health strategic plan. The goal is to develop high-quality and world-class service and to optimize value for the entire health system while maintaining organizational integrity and regulatory compliance. Minutes of monthly meetings and links to evidence-based practices and core clinical indicators are also provided.

2. Data requirements
   - – Data standards connect decision makers to tools and resources related to Trinity Health's data standardization activities and include the data dictionary, approved abbreviations, dangerous abbreviations, supply chain links, glossary, data elements documents, and charge description master with standards. Additionally, the charge description master file contains standardized detailed information on all services provided by the institution, including description, department codes, service code, etc.
   - – The Data and Reports section provides views of clinical data, such as core indicator charts, report cards, customer and physician satisfaction data, medication/pharmacy scorecards, and scanning reports. For FY 2009, twenty-eight core indicators are also available for each Trinity Health hospital, as well as other indicators for emergency room care, home care. and long-term care. Decision makers can also access data warehouses and download data for further analysis.

- Patient Safety and Potential Error and Event Reporting (PEERs). This site links to best practices and related websites, patient safety tool kits, and numerous quality and safety reports for clinicians, as well as Trinity Health historical safety data. PEERs was designed by Trinity Health physicians, nurses, attorneys, and quality and risk management professionals to capture near-miss and errors/events data. Modeled after NASA's voluntary reporting system, PEERs is rated very high in the ease of use and insuring anonymity.

3. Guidelines and education
   - Medical Staff Resources delivers policies, procedures, links, articles, and more on current issues affecting medical staffs. Links and related topics include credentialing and privileging resources, medical staff by-laws, rules and regulations, medical staff development plans, hospital–physician partnerships, peer review, and physician recruitment and satisfaction development forums.
   - Fair Market Value. This site provides information to find competitive national survey data and the fair market value narrative that provides a methodology on how to complete a fair market value assessment. The links are in compliance with the Stark II regulations that established a new safe harbor for determining the fair market value of physician compensation.
   - People and Networks is a resource to find a person who has the information decision makers need to move forward with an idea or project. The clinical operations department provides additional assistance in connecting people. Other items include information pertaining to the Pharmacy Council, the Health Information Management Council, the Educator Network, and related links.
   - The Physician Practice Management site provides a variety of practice management tools to assist the physician networks in best practice management from a broad spectrum of business disciplines, including finance, operations improvement, compliance, legal, human resource management, planning and marketing, clinical quality, insurance and risk management, and payer contract negotiations.
   - Sponsored Provider Network provides networking opportunities for executives, controllers, and physician leaders to share best practices in revenue management and expense reduction to drive improved financial and operational performance of the employed primary care physician networks. The meetings are rooted in the application of correct business principles and sharing of management philosophy to develop and achieve performance targets.
   - The Survey Readiness link connects administrators and clinicians to resources and useful tools for The Joint Commission preparation and continual readiness. It also contains Trinity Health hospitals' Joint Commission survey highlights, news flashes, and hot topics.

Results

I2S2 has emerged as the go-to online resource for decision makers at Trinity Health. The users span the spectrum of functions across the hospitals. Usage statistics for August 2009 tracked 2,972 average daily hits. Over 901 pages were viewed by Trinity Health users, who viewed an average of 12.69 pages per visit. These metrics indicate that I2S2 had indeed been helpful in delivering pertinent information to decision makers. It can be hypothesized that availablity of data and the expanse of use contributed to an informed decision maker and resulted in improved performance outcomes.

Trinity Health received the 2004 National Committee for Quality Health Care's Annual Award. At that time it was only the twelfth healthcare system in the United States to be so designated. In 2009, Trinity Health was named as one of the top ten health systems in the *Thomson Reuters 100 Top Hospitals®: Health System Quality/ Efficiency Study*, which identifies the top U.S. health systems by objectively measuring the clinical quality and efficiency of member hospitals.* Therefore, it is reasonable to assume that I2S2 contributed to Trinity Health hospitals' above national average performance and top decile ranking on many critical measures. This information delivery tool is dynamic and must be updated regularly. To ensure that the information in I2S2 remains current, relevant, and appeals to a wider user base, Trinity Health has instituted a process for reviewing the topical areas and the content available to decision makers, as well as a forum where innovative uses of data are shared.

Each year Trinity Health reviews its quality indicators and targets areas for improvement. Changes in the scientific evidence, data definitions, and public awareness are a few of the several reasons for the periodic review of the I2S2 clinical indicators. Other reasons include improvements in performance and the board's oversight. Trinity Health has established the following internal criteria for choosing indicators to monitor and disseminate through I2S2:

1. Applicable to multiple reporting organizations (e.g. JCAHO/CMS)
2. Sufficient patient volume to demonstrate change in performance
3. Emerging opportunities for improvement (includes variation in performance)
4. Evidence of improved process that influences the indicator
5. National norms for indicator are available
6. Alignment of metrics with the Trinity Health strategic plan
7. Burden of data capture does not exceed the value of the indicator

---

* http://www.reuters.com/article/pressRelease/idUS87944+10-Aug-2009+PRN20090810. The study evaluated 252 health systems—with a total of 1,720 hospitals—on measures of clinical quality and efficiency. The top ten represent the top 2.5% of the systems studied. Five measures of performance were used to evaluate systems: mortality, complications, patient safety, length of stay, and use of evidence-based practices. All of these are available in I2S2. I2S2 allows decision makers in all Trinity Health hospitals to leverage the collective clinical knowledge and best care practices and for rapid replication and improving the quality, safety, and satisfaction of patients throughout the course of their delivery of care.

The process of selecting quality indicators involves representatives from each of the ministry organizations (MOs), and is subsequently approved by senior management and the board.

In order to assist in this sharing of ideas, the I2S2 People and Networks section enables individuals to identify who to call for assistance. I2S2 has become a virtual library resource for standardized content. Any employee or physician can access the website and view a current or historical document that shows a six-month rolling average performance. A link for each indicator for a particular MO allows the user to drill down and view a twenty-four-month trend graph.

Case Study 3: Clinical Adverse Drug Event (ADE) Alert System

Background

In the 1990s the pressure of managed care challenged U.S. hospitals to ask the following questions: How does a healthcare organization link patient care quality with investment in clinical IT? What part of healthcare is in need for urgent technological support? At about the same time, the issue of adverse drug events or medical errors had gained attention through various publications.[2,3] Subsequent studies examined hospitals' responses and established that ADEs could be prevented.[4]

Previous research indicates that implementation of computerized ADE systems involves at least three steps: (1) capturing patient data electronically, (2) applying algorithms, rules, and queries to find cases that might be consistent with ADEs, and (3) determining the accuracy of the systems.[5] Many hospitals have information systems that contain integrated patient encounter data that include demographics, pharmacy orders, and laboratory results.[6] Some hospitals create their own systems, while others integrate off-the-shelf commercial products. There are two forms of ADE systems. *Basic systems* perform functions such as drug-allergy checking, dosage guidance, formulary decision support, duplicate therapy checking, and drug-to-drug interaction evaluations. *Advanced systems* perform more complex functions, including dose adjustment, guidance for medication-related laboratory testing, and drug-disease contraindication flags.[7]

Approach

Trinity Health led the effort to build an advanced ADE alert system with support from a commercial provider, Discern Expert, Cerner Corp., as part of Project Genesis. A rules engine with seventeen ADE alert rules was installed. These alerts were triggered using a computerized algorithm after examining demographics, clinical lab values, and medications.

A key assumption to construct an ADE model is that as much as possible, all data about the events and actions taken must be derived and analyzed to develop the model. For instance, the ADE information must include the drugs administered, mode of administering the drug, patient demographics, actions taken, and the result. For an ADE system to be successful, it is imperative that data standards must be developed and followed. The scope of data standardization for the first phase included general laboratory results, pharmacy descriptions/CDM (Charge Description Master), and a partial list of ADT (Patient admitting/discharge/transfer systems)/registration data elements required to support the ADE functionality and patient chart capabilities. However, achieving data standardization is also a political exercise in building consensus. Trinity Health entrusted its Functional and Clinical Councils and Standards Leadership Team with approval from the COO/CFO and Clinical Leadership Council (CLC) oversight groups. The Standards Leadership Council directed the implementation of policies and procedures for change management, audit and reporting mechanisms, and outcome measurement. Data standards have met the requirements and are adjusted to meet the changing business environment.

After literature reviews for medication safety and quality from the pharmacoepi-demiological and pharmacoecomonical literature, rules were generated using computerized algorithms to examine demographics with clinical lab values and medications. An example of a rule is presented below.

Trinity Health ADE Alerts

An alert is triggered based on a number of grouped events. A rules engine with seventeen of these alerts is generated by computerized algorithms examining patient demographics, clinical lab values, and medications. The ADE alerts are triggered in real time so that any change in medication or lab result will be evaluated as soon as reported. This allows pharmacy intervention immediately and eliminates the possible twelve- to twenty-four-hour delay seen before implementation of the system. The pharmacists rely on the system to screen new lab results as they are reported, and this allows the pharmacists to prioritize their workflow to address the most critical issues and patients in a timely manner. The following is an example of this alert process. A pharmacist inputs a physician order for a potassium-containing or potassium-sparing drug. Yet the patient has a lab result for serum potassium > 6.0 mEq/L. Consequently, the potassium medication dose or medication itself needs to be adjusted for these patients since the alert is evoked when a high potassium level is evidenced. Current orders are checked for any of the specified drugs that may cause hyperkalemia.

Trinity Health's experience suggests that in order to successfully implement an ADE system, the following conditions must be met:

1. This project must have executive support for the adoption of defined data standards.
2. The data standards must be approved by the senior leadership and implemented organization-wide.

3. All hospitals and entities must actively participate in the Functional and Clinical Councils.
4. Project participants must provide a timely response to data requests and data review to ensure timely implementation.
5. Following the implementation of data standards, the organization must provide ongoing support of the change management process and commitment to the standards developed.
6. The implementation should be stratified and should be deployed in areas where quick results can be achieved. Learning from such projects can be applied to more complex applications.
7. The recommended model must be accurate, consistent, user-friendly, and compliant with existing computer applications and all governing bodies.
8. Although data standards do not cause any operational changes, redesign efforts must be accommodated in the clinical and patient administration projects.
9. A change management process will be defined and followed to add to the standards. Conformance to standardization will be monitored and reported.

Results

Once buy-in from the stakeholders was achieved, work planning and milestone schedules for the laboratory and pharmacy were established. Trinity Health's philosophy is to design once, implement many times. The ADE application followed this guiding principle to implement the ADE system across several hospitals. For ease of maintenance and updates, the computing hardware was standardized and the ADE application software was centrally developed. In using the ADE system, Trinity Health focused on evaluating the effects and derived benefits from usage and expected to achieve cost savings and reductions in patient mortality in line with the published literature that decreases in the harmful events save both human lives and money.

The ADE project implementation assigned a project manager, a data manager, a systems technical analyst, a systems business analyst, and an administrative support staff. There were 4.5 FTEs (Full-time equivalent employees) at start-up and implementation, and now 2.5 FTEs are assigned for maintenance and reporting. Below are additional activities required by the hospitals to support the ADE project:

Lab kickoff meeting	2 hours/site	Laboratory Council
Lab phone interview	1–2 hours/site	Med Tech
Lab Standards Review	8 hours/site	Med Tech x 3 sites
Lab standards approval	3 hours	Laboratory Council
Pharmacy kickoff meeting	2 hours	Pharmacy Council

Pharmacy phone interview	1–2 hours/site	Pharmacists
Pharmacy standards review	24 hours	Pharmacy subgroup
Pharmacy approval	3 hours	Pharmacy Council
Pharmacy mapping review	8 hours/site	Pharmacist
Reg./HIM/pt. acct. kickoff meeting	2 hours/site	Directors
UB92 review	8 hours	Pt. admin./reg./HIM managers
UB92 mapping review	8 hours	Pt. admin./reg./HIM managers

In deploying the ADE system among the hospitals, the senior leadership declared that a financial impact analysis was not required. The urgency and the impact on patient mortality outweighed the need for economic justification. As seen above, labor was the cost driver for implementing the ADE system. The question then is: How much cost has to be absorbed when the financial benefits are not assessed? For ADEs there are significant financial costs affixed to each event. Yet there are clinical "costs" as well in human pain and suffering, not to mention litigation. Previous literature has cited that each ADE costs about $6,685,[8] and that computer systems play a decisive role in preventing ADEs.[9] Thus, there is significant evidence in the literature to support that preventing ADEs can reduce hospital costs in addition to increasing patient care quality.

At Trinity Health the impact of implementing the ADE system was principally evident in the reduction in pharmacy costs, a savings of 5%. These pharmacy cost savings in the targeted hospitals exceeded US$3.5 million. Internal and external control groups demonstrated no such cost savings. There was also evidence of decreases in severity adjusted LOS and mortality rates.[10]

Conclusion

This chapter chronicled three case studies as milestones in the journey of Trinity Health to gather, process, and disseminate data to improve patient safety and outcomes. We established that in order for hospitals to be effective in using information for improved decision making, physicians' leadership and involvement is necessary. Once metrics are agreed upon, an effective data delivery mechanism must be put in place. Through rich descriptions and examples we presented Trinity Health's intranet-based information system, I2S2. Descriptions of categories of information content provide an overview of range of data available to the decision makers. Finally, we presented an example of a value-added application that emerged from the leadership by physicians and the development effort of the information systems professionals to implement an ADE alert system. Lessons learned from building the ADE system will assist readers in avoiding pitfalls and preparing for their own value-added applications.

References

1. Kohli R, Piontek F, Ellington T, VanOsdol T, Shepard M, Brazel G. 2001. Managing customer relationships through an e-business decision support application: A case of hospital physician collaboration. *Decis. Support Syst.* 32:171–87.
2. Bates DW, Leape LL, Petrycki S. 1993. Incidence and preventability of adverse drug events in hospitalized adults. *J. Gen. Intern. Med.* 8:289–94.
3. Grasela TH, Walawander CA, Kennedy DL, Jolson HM. 1993. Capability of hospital computer-systems in performing drug-use evaluations and adverse drug event monitoring. *Am. J. Hosp. Pharm.* 50:1889–95.
4. Bates DW, Leape LL, Cullen DJ, et al. 1998. Effect of computerized physician order entry and a team intervention on prevention of serious medication errors. *JAMA* 280:1311–16.
5. Evans RS, Pestotnik SL, Classen DC, Horn SD, Bass SB, Burke JP. 1994. Preventing adverse drug events in hospitalized patients. *Ann. Pharmacother.* 28:523–27.
6. Raschke RA, Gollihare B, Wunderlich TA, et al. 1998. A computer alert system to prevent injury from adverse drug events—Development and evaluation in a community teaching hospital. *JAMA* 280:1317–20.
7. Wolfstadt JI, Gurwitz JH, Field TS, et al. 2008. The effect of computerized physician order entry with clinical decision support on the rates of adverse drug events: A systematic review. *J. Gen. Intern. Med.* 23:451–58.
8. Senst BL, Achusim LE, Genest RP, et al. 2001. Practical approach to determining costs and frequency of adverse drug events in a health care network. *Am. J. Health Syst. Pharmacy* 58:1126–32.
9. Yan Q, Hunt CA. 2000. Preventing adverse drug events (ADEs): The role of computer information systems. *Drug Inf. J.* 34:1247–60.
10. Piontek F, Kohli R, Conlon P, Ellis J, Jablonski J, Kini N. Forthcoming. Impact of adverse drug event alert system on cost and quality outcomes in community hospitals. *Am. J. Health Syst. Pharmacy.*

Chapter 11

Data Mining in Healthcare

Wullianallur Raghupathi

Contents

Overview

With the development and maintenance of large health data repositories of structured and unstructured data, health organizations are increasingly using data analytics, including data mining, to analyze and utilize the patterns and relationships found in the data to make improved clinical and other health-related decisions. This chapter discusses the potential of data mining in healthcare and describes the various applications of data mining methods and techniques. A brief review of examples of data mining in healthcare is also offered. An ongoing project in the mining of the unstructured information in cancer blogs is also described. Conclusions are then offered.

Introduction

Health data, including general patient profiles, clinical data, insurance data, and other medical data, are being created for various purposes, including regulatory compliance, public health policy analysis and research, and diagnosis and treatment.[17] The data include both structured data (e.g., patient histories as records in a database) and unstructured data[25] (e.g., audio/video clips, textual information such as in blogs or physician's notes). Data mining methods can be applied to search and analyze these large repositories to shed light on a wide range of health issues, including drug reactions, side effects, and other issues. For example, data mining techniques revealed the association between Vioxx, the arthritis drug, and increased risk of heart attack and stroke. The drug was withdrawn from the market (http://www.informationweek.com/news/business_intelligence/mining/showArticle.jhtml?articleID=207300005).

In another example, IBM has been working with the Mayo Clinic for mining the data of millions of patient records to "analyze the information, look for similarities from one patient and another, and identify patterns" (http://www.healthcareitnews.com/news/data-mining-key-phase-2-ibm-mayo-partnership).

Healthcare organizations, including hospitals, HMOs, and government entities such as the Centers for Disease Control (CDC), are establishing numerous health data repositories. These are typically large, relational databases that store different types of clinical and administrative data from primary electronic health sources such as hospital admission records. These repositories collect comprehensive data on large patient groups in longitudinal fashion, thereby permitting the examination and analysis of patterns and trends over time.[17] Tasks include utilization statistics and outcomes. The data can be used for quality assurance and clinical management queries.[5,23] Although the breadth and depth of the repositories include a variety of health and medical data, including genetic data, biomedical data, and data for general health issues such as quality control (e.g., medical error patterns), data mining applications are relatively new.[3,4,10,21] Additionally, challenges are also foreseen. For example, large repositories may lead to a combinatorial explosion of alternatives. On the other hand, the multiple dimensions of the data for very complex relationships are typically rarely available because the relationships are spread thinly across the several dimensions.[17] Fortunately, the developing large medical and health repositories can alleviate these challenges to an extent. These are providing integrated views of the patient encounters. Data mining of these quantitative and qualitative data has great potential for improving the quality of healthcare and reducing the costs of healthcare delivery.

In this chapter we discuss the potential of data mining in healthcare. An outline and discussion of the steps involved is also provided. Our ongoing research in the data mining of health-related blogs using the Unstructured Information Management Architecture is then described. Finally, conclusions are offered.

Data Mining in Healthcare

The Value of Data Mining

Data mining is defined as "the nontrivial extraction of implicit previously unknown and potentially useful information from data."[8] The value for healthcare delivery is enhanced when the data mining has specific purposes and health/medical questions to answer. Typically, the healthcare process being data rich, many potential patterns can be discovered by the use of different types of algorithms. However, the patterns have value for enhancing the quality of the healthcare delivery process only when specifically addressing a particular issue or question. For example, using a data mining method involving clustering, a user can automatically discover distinct patient sets classified by one or more variables. It is not necessary to hypothesize a solution or delve into the details of the clustering. An application with a well-defined user interface has the potential to make the mining process transparent and seamless.[1] The application with the underlying algorithm works on the data repository to enable the user to find solutions (e.g., categorizing patients, grouping patients by drug reactions, profile of emergency visit patients) in the most promising way. The data themselves become an active part of the solution. To this end, data mining is data driven. As Mullins et al. suggest, it is pertinent as a strategy to "discover" patterns already known to be true in the preliminary stages of the health data mining task. It is important to confirm the tool, build confidence in the approach, and often, serendipitously, revelations may occur.[17]

In healthcare, therefore, pattern-discovering algorithms in the data mining process can transform raw data into useful decision-making information with minimal intervention by the user, be it a physician or a hospital administrator. The data repositories created by health delivery organizations and health insurance companies are not in vain as the role of the data is enhanced. These organizations can tap into the discovery role of data mining, just as the financial services industry has done, and provide higher-quality healthcare as participants in the healthcare delivery process are empowered with useful information.

In the healthcare domain encompassing bio informatics, medical informatics, and health informatics, data mining offers many new opportunities for practitioners and researchers. Some of the more significant ones include:[1]

- Discovery of previously unknown facts (e.g., correlation between a drug and side effect). In this situation the application learns associations and flags the user, or the application facilitates the health data to identify value (e.g., potential drug discovery).
- Organization of large repositories of health and medical data for very complex problems (e.g., pandemic patterns and clusters). In this regard, the application can provide real-time alerts as to particular situations that require immediate attention, as well as provide insight into what might occur next.
- Prediction of the future in various situations and scenarios (e.g., what-if analysis in clinical trials, consequences of certain actions on public health policy). Data mining can help forecast trends (as in epidemics) and threats as well as opportunities, thereby enabling the organization, be it for profit or nonprofit, to deal with the future effectively with knowledge.[1]

Data Mining as a Process in Healthcare

The typical types of healthcare questions that are solvable by data mining techniques can be divided into two main categories: those that are solved by discovery techniques and those solved by predictive techniques.[1] If the healthcare problem requires the researcher to find useful patterns and relationships in the data (e.g., relationship between a particular diet and blood pressure), that problem will lead the researcher to a discovery method. On the other hand, if the healthcare problem requires the researcher to predict some type of value (e.g., the radiation dosage for a particular profile of cancer patients), that problem would obviously lead the researcher to a predictive method. In the pharmaceutical industry, for example, a range of methods, including associations, sequences, and predictive methods for clinical disease management, associations and prediction for cost/quality management, and segmentation and clustering for patient groupings in clinical trials, have tremendous potential.

Typical questions include:

- What do my patients look like?
- What is the drug dosage–patient profile association?
- With which other drugs does the new drug interact negatively?
- What effect does use of a particular drug for a disease have on other conditions?
- Does the drug cause side effects, and if so, what?

Many of the typical problems and questions can be resolved by one of a few data mining techniques.[1] They include three discovery techniques (clustering, associations, and sequences) and two predictive techniques (classification and regression).[1]

Discovery Techniques

The data mining techniques based on this method find health or medical patterns that preexist in the data, but with no *a priori* knowledge of what those patterns may be. One could think of these patterns as serendipitously discovered, although the goals are inherently present in the data themselves. Three of the popular discovery techniques include:

1. The *clustering technique* groups health/medical records into segments by how similar they are based on the characteristics under study. Clustering could be used, for example, to find distinct symptoms of diseases with similar characteristics to create a disease/patient segmentation model.
2. *Association* is a type of relationship analysis that finds relationships or associations among the health/medical records of single transactions. A potential use of the association method is for health group analysis, that is, to find out what diseases tend together to form a group, such as viral or bacterial (or patient groups), which is quite useful in epidemic/pandemic surveillance and identifying cause-treatment protocols for particular diseases.
3. The *sequential* pattern discovers associations among health/medical records, but across sequential transactions. A hospital could use sequential patterns (longitudinal studies) to analyze admissions over time, and to provide customized patient care.[1]

Predictive Techniques

The predictive techniques of classification and regression are data mining techniques that can help forecast some type of categorical or numerical value (e.g., optimal dosage of a drug, drug pricing, etc.).

1. The technique of *classification* can be used to forecast the value that would fall into predefined grouping or categories. For example, it can predict whether a particular treatment will cure, harm, or have no effect on a particular patient.
2. On the other hand, the technique of *regression* is used to predict a numerical value on a continuous scale, for example, predicting the expected number of admissions each hospital will make in a year. In contrast, if the range of values is between 0 and 1, then this becomes a probability of an event occurring, such as the likelihood of a patient dying (repeat visits) or getting well, for example.[1]

In many instances a combination of data mining techniques is necessary (e.g., first perform patient segmentation using the clustering technique to identify a target group of patients); this is followed by a grouping analysis using the associations technique with the transactions (data) only for the target group to find drug affinities on which to base treatments.[1]

Mining and Scoring

The five mining techniques outlined above are used against current health/medical data to create a data mining model. The process of applying an existing mining model against new data is called scoring.[1] Each of the five techniques has an associated scoring method that is used to apply against new data. Cluster scoring can be used, for example, to assign a new patient to the appropriate clinical trial based on the existing cluster model (or a drug for treatment).

In order to select the initial mining technique, one may develop a short list of typical health questions that the most common mining method or combination of methods may help answer. For example:

1. What do my patients look like? Clustering
2. Which patients should be targeted for drug (treatment) promotion (trial)? Clustering
3. Which drugs should I use for the trial (treatment)? Association or sequential patterns
4. Which drugs should I replenish in anticipation of an epidemic? Associations
5. Which of my patients are most likely to get well (based on a protocol)? Classification or regression
6. How can I identify high-risk patients? Clustering
7. When one drug fails, which others are most likely to fail too? Sequential patterns
8. Who is most likely to have another heart attack? Classification or Regression
9. How can I improve quality of care (or patient satisfaction)? Clustering plus associations

Build and Deploy Data Mining Application

The process of building and deploying a data mining application is highly iterative.[1] This process may include three specific steps:

1. Health/medical data preparation
2. Creation and verification of the particular mining model
3. Deployment of the model in some way

The process of data preparation involves finding and organizing the health/medical data for the chosen mining technique. Once the data are ready for use, the mining technique can be involved in the development of the mining model, which is then confirmed by the developer. It is possible that the process goes through several iterations until one obtains a refined data model. After confirmation, the model is ready to be deployed for use. Generally speaking, the data preparation step comprises the identification of the specific data requirements, the appropriate location of the data, and the extraction and transformation of the data into the appropriate format for the chosen mining technique.[1]

The data mining model is created once the data are transformed and ready for use. The particular application/tool is used on the data set after choosing the technique and providing the parameters. Multiple algorithms may be used with the input parameters. In predictive techniques additional steps may be involved, including a training phase and a testing phase. The resulting model can be stored and possibly viewed using an appropriate visualization tool in the application.[1] The visualization process plays a critical role in presenting information about model quality, specific results such as associations, rules, or clusters, and other information about the data and results pertinent to the particular model. This information enables the data mining analyst to evaluate the model quality and determine whether the model fulfills its healthcare purpose. If need be, improvements to the input data, model parameters, and modeling technique can then be made to obtain a good model that reflects the healthcare objective.[1] In the final step, the data mining results are deployed in the healthcare organization as part of a business intelligence (data analytics) solution. Data mining results can be deployed by several means:

1. *Ad hoc* decision support: Use data mining on an *ad hoc* basis to address a specific nonrecurring question. For example, a pharmaceutical researcher may use data mining techniques to discover a relationship between gene counts and disease state for a cancer research project.
2. Interactive decision support: Incorporate data mining into a larger health intelligence application for ongoing interactive analysis.
3. Scoring: Apply a data mining model to generate some sort of prediction for each health/medical record, depending on model type. For example, for a clustering model, the score is the best-fit cluster for each patient. For the association model, the score is the highest-affinity item (variable), given other items (variables). For a sequence model, the score is the most likely action to occur next. For a typical predictive model, the score is the predicted value or response.[1]

Examples

Mullins et al.[17] report on the application of Health Miner to a large group of 667,000 inpatient and outpatient digital records from an academic medical system. They used three unsupervised methods: Clici mines, predictive analysis, and pattern discovery. The initial results from their study suggested that these approaches had the potential to expand research capabilities through identification of potentially novel clinical disease associations. In other examples, the prior analyses using large clinical data sets have typically focused on specific treatment or disease objects.[17] Most have examined specific treatment procedures, for example, cesarean delivery rate,[15] coronary artery bypass graft (CABG) surgery volume,[19] routine chemistry panel testing,[2] patient care, cancer risk for nonaspirin NSAID (nonsteroidal/anti-inflammatory drugs) users,[24] preoperative beta-blocker use and mortality and morbidity following CABG surgery,[6] and incidence and mortality rate of acute (adult) respiratory distress syndrome (ARDS),[22] to name a few. These studies have several factors in common: large sample size, clinical information source, and they support or build upon pre-established hypotheses or defined research paradigms that use specific procedures or disease data. Clinical outcome algorithms have also been applied to harness large health information databases in order to generate models directly applicable to clinical treatment. These models have been used successfully to create mortality risk assessments for adults[12-14] and pediatric intensive care units.[20]

In other studies, Uramoto et al. describe the application of IBM TAKMI (Text Analysis and Knowledge Mining) for biomedical documents to facilitate knowledge discovery from the very large text databases characteristic of life science and healthcare applications. MedTAKMI dynamically and interactively mines a collection of documents to obtain characteristic features within them.[26] By using multifaceted mining of these documents together with biomedically motivated categories for term extraction and a series of drill-down queries, users can obtain knowledge about a specific topic after seeing only a few key documents.

Inokuchi et al. describe MedTAKMI-CDI, an online analytical processing system that enables the interactive discovery of knowledge for clinical decision intelligence (CDI). CDI supports decision making by providing in-depth analysis of clinical data from multiple sources.[11,27] These and other examples indicate the potential and promise of data mining in healthcare.

Mining of Cancer Blogs with the UIMA

In this section we describe our ongoing research project in the use of the Unstructured Information Management Architecture (UIMA) in mining textual information in cancer blogs. Health organizations and individuals such as patients are using information in blogs for various purposes. Medical blogs are rich in information for decision making. Current software such as web crawlers and blog analysis are good at generating statistics about the number of blogs, top ten, etc., but they are not advanced/useful computationally to help with analysis and understanding of the social networks that form in healthcare and medical blogs, the process of diffusion of ideas (e.g., the commonality of symptoms and disease management), and the sharing of ideas and feelings (support and treatment options, what worked). Therefore, there is a critical need for sophisticated tools to fill this gap. Furthermore, there are hardly any studies or applications in the content analysis of blogs.

There has been an exponential increase in the number of blogs in the healthcare area, as patients find them useful in disease management and developing support groups. Alternatively, healthcare providers such as physicians have started to use blogs to communicate and discuss medical information. Examples of useful information include alternative medicine and treatment, health condition management, diagnosis-treatment information, and support group resources. This rapid proliferation in health- and medical-related blogs has resulted in huge amounts of unstructured yet potentially valuable information being available for analysis and use.[25] Statistics indicate health-related bloggers are very consistent at posting to blogs.

The analysis and interpretation of health-related blogs are not trivial tasks. Unlike many of the blogs in various corporate domains, health blogs are far more complex and unstructured. The postings reflect two important facets of the bloggers: the feeling and the mind of the patient (e.g., an individual suffering from breast cancer but managing it). How does one parse and extract the deep semantic meanings in this environment? Mere syntactic analysis would not do.

The Unstructured Information Management Architecture (UIMA) defines a framework for implementing systems for the analysis of unstructured data.[7,16,18,25] In contrast to structured information, whose meaning is expressed by the structure or the format of the data, the meaning of unstructured information cannot be so inferred.[25] Examples of data that carry unstructured information include natural language text and data from audio or video sources. More specifically, an audio stream has a well-defined syntax and semantics for rendering the stream on an audio device, but its music score is not directly represented.[9] The UIMA is sufficiently advanced and sophisticated computationally to aid in the analysis and understanding of the content of the health-related blogs. At the individual level (document-level analysis) one can perform analysis and gain insight into the patient in longitudinal studies. At the group level (collection-level analysis) one can gain insight into the patterns of the groups (network behavior, e.g., assessing the influence within the social group), for example, in a particular disease group, the community of participants in an HMO or hospital setting, or even in the global community of patients (ethnic stratification). The results of these analyses can be generalized. While the blogs enable the formation of social networks of patients and providers, the uniqueness of the health/medical terminology comingled with the subjective vocabulary of the patient compounds the challenge of interpretation. Taking the discussion to a more general level, while blogs have emerged as contemporary modes of communication within a social network context, hardly any research or insight exists in the content analysis of blogs. The blog world is characterized by a lack of particular rules on format, how to post, and the structure of the content itself. Questions arise: How do we make sense of the aggregate content? How does one interpret and generalize? In health blogs in particular, what patterns of diagnosis, treatment, management, and support might emerge from a meta-analysis of a large pool of blog postings? The overall goal, then, is to enhance the quality of health by reducing errors and assisting in clinical decision making.

Additionally, one can reduce the cost of healthcare delivery by the use of these types of advanced health information technology.

Therefore, the *objectives* of our project include:

1. To use UIMA to mine a set of cancer blog postings from http://www.thecancerblog.com
2. To develop a parsing algorithm and clustering technique for the analysis of cancer blogs
3. To develop a vocabulary and taxonomy of keywords (based on existing medical nomenclature)
4. To build a prototype interface with Eclipse (based on our existing work in the use of Eclipse in the development of an electronic health record system)
5. To contribute to social networks in the semantic web by generalizing the models from cancer blogs

The following levels of development are envisaged:

First level: Patterns of symptoms, management (diagnosis/treatment)
Second level: Glean insight into disease management at individual/group levels
Third level: Clinical decision support (e.g., generalization of patterns, syntactic to semantic)

Typically, the unstructured information in blogs comprises:

■ Blog topic (posting)—What issue or question does the blogger (and comments) discuss?
  – Disease and treatment (not limited to)—What cancer type and treatment (other issues) are identified and discussed?
■ Other information—What other related topics are discussed? What links are provided?

What Can We Learn from Blog Postings?

Unstructured information related to blog postings (bloggers), including responses/comments, can provide insight into "diseases" (cancer), "treatment" (e.g., alternative medicine, therapy), support links, etc.

1. What are the most common issues patients have (bloggers/responses)?
2. What are the cancer types (conditions) most discussed? Why?
3. What therapies and treatments are being discussed? What medical and non-medical information is provided?
4. Which blogs and bloggers are doing a good job of providing relevant and correct information?

5. What are the major motivations for the postings (comments)? Profession (e.g., doctor) or patient?
6. What are the emerging trends in disease (symptoms), treatment and therapy (e.g., alternative medicine), support systems, and information sources (links, clinical trials)?

What Are the Phases and Milestones?

This project envisions the use of UIMA and supporting plug-ins to develop an application tool to analyze health-related blogs. The project is scoped to content analysis of the domain of cancer blogs at http://www.thecancerblog.com. Additional open-source plug-ins and an Eclipse development environment with Java/XML plug-ins, limited AJAX capability, and a social network analysis tool such as Apache Agora would provide the desired capabilities. In a typical scenario, the cancer blogs can be stored in an open-source Derby database application.

Phase 1 involved the collection of blog postings from http://www.thecancerblog. com into a Derby application.
Phase 2 consisted of the development and configuration of the architecture—keywords, correlations, clustering, and taxonomy.
Phase 3 entailed the analysis and integration of extracted information in the cancer blogs; preliminary results of initial analysis (e.g., patterns that are identified).
Phase 4 involved the development of taxonomy.
Phase 5 proposes to test the mining model and develop the user interface for deployment.

We propose to develop a comprehensive text mining system that integrates several mining techniques, including association and clustering, to effectively organize the blog information and provide decision support in terms of search by keywords.

Conclusions

The development and application of large repositories of patient-specific clinical, medical, and health data generated during patient encounters in the routine delivery of healthcare was, until recently, limited to static uses of utilization management, quality assurance, and cost management.[17] However, with the focus on reducing medical errors through evidence-based health management, these repositories are being subjected to more sophisticated analyses using data mining techniques. These techniques offer numerous opportunities to perform in-depth analysis of the data to gain new insights into the healthcare process with the resultant decision support for a range of tasks. In the future, we will see not only an increased use of data mining techniques in healthcare but also their integration with health intelligence and health organization strategy. The overall goals include the delivery of quality care with a simultaneous decrease in costs.

References

1. Ballard, C., Rollins, J., Ramos, J., Perkins, A., Hale, R., Dorneich, A., Milner, E. C., and Chodagam, J. 2007. *Dynamic warehousing: Data mining made easy.* IBM Redbook (www.redbooks.ibm.com).
2. Bock, B. J., Dolan, C. T., Miller, G. C., Fitter, W. F., Hartsell, B. D., Crowson, A. N., Sheehan, W. W., and Williams, J. D. 2003. The datawarehouse as a foundation for population-based reference intervals. *American Journal of Clinical Pathology* 120:662–70.
3. Brosette, S. E., Sprague, A. P., Hardin, J. M., Jones, W. T., and Moser, S. A. 1998. Association rules and data mining in hospital infection control and public health surveillance. *Journal of the American Medical Informatics Association* 5:373–81.
4. Downs, S. M., and Wallace, M. Y. 2000. Mining association rules from a pediatric primary care decision support system. *Proceedings of the AMIA Symposium* 2000:200–4.
5. Einbinder, J. S., and Scully, K. 2002. Using a clinical data repository to estimate the frequency and costs of adverse drug events. *Journal of the American Medical Informatics Association* Suppl. S:S34–38.
6. Ferguson Jr., T. B., Coombs, L. P., and Peterson, E. D. 2002. Preoperative beta-blocker use and mortality and morbidity following CABG surgery in North America. *Journal of the American Medical Association* 287:2221–27.
7. Ferrucci, D., and Lally, A. 2004. Building an example application with the Unstructured Information Management Architecture. *IBM Systems Journal* 43:455–75.
8. Frawley, W., Piatetsky-Shapiro, G., and Mathews, C. 1992. Knowledge discovery in databases: An overview. *AI Magazine*, pp. 213–28.
9. Gotz, T., and Suhre, O. 2004. Design and implementation of the UIMA common analysis system. *IBM Systems Journal* 43:476–89.
10. Holmes, J. H., Durbin, D. R., and Winston, F. K. 2000. Discovery of predictive models in an injury surveillance database: An application of data mining in clinical research. *Proceedings of the AMIA Symposium* 2000:359–63.
11. Inokuchi, A., Takeda, K., Inaoka, N., and Wakao, F. 2007. MedTAKMI-CDI: Interactive knowledge discovery for clinical decision intelligence. *IBM Systems Journal* 46:115–33.
12. Knaus, W. A., Wagner, D. P., and Lynn, J. 1991. Short-term mortality predictions for critically ill hospitalized adults: Science and ethics. *Science* 18:389–94.
13. LeGall, J. R., Lemeshow, S., and Saulnier, F. 1993. A new Simplified Acute Physiology Score (SAPS II) based on a European/North American multicenter study. *JAMA* 270:2957–63.
14. Lemeshow, S., Teres, D., Klar, J. S., Avrunin, S. H., and Gehlbach, J. R. 1993. Mortality probability models based on an international cohort of intensive care unit patients. *JAMA* 270:2478–86.
15. Lin, H.-C., and Xirasagar, S. 2004. Institutional factors in cesarean delivery rates: Policy and research implications. *Obstetrics & Gynecology* 103:128–36.

16. Mack, R., Mukherjea, S., Soffer, A., Uramoto, N., Brown, E., Coden, A., Cooper, J., Inokuchi, A., Iyer, B., Mass, Y., Matsuzawa, H., and Subramaniam, L. V. 2004. Text analytics for life science using the Unstructured Information Management Architecture. *IBM Systems Journal* 43:490–515.

17. Mullins, I. M., Siadaty, M. S., Lyman, J., Scully, K., Garrett, C. T., Miller, W. G., Muller, R., Robson, B., Apte, C., Weiss, S., Rigoutsos, I., Platt, D., Cohen, S., and Knaus, W. A. 2006. Data mining and clinical data repositories: Insights from a 667,000 patient data set. *Computers in Biology and Medicine* 36:1351–77.

18. Nasukawa, T., and Nagano, T. 2001. Text analysis and knowledge system mining. *IBM Systems Journal* 40:967–84.

19. Peterson, E. D., Coombs, L. P., DeLong, E. R., Haan, C. K., and Ferguson, T. B. 2004. Procedural volume as a market of quality for CABG surgery. *JAMA* 291:195–201.

20. Pollack, M. M., Patel, K. M., and Ruttimann, U. E. 1996. PRISM III: An updated pediatric risk of mortality score. *Critical Care Medicine* 24:743–52.

21. Prather, J. C., Lobach, D. F., Goodwin, L. K., Hales, J. W., Hage, M. L., and Hammond, W. E. 1997. Medical data mining: Knowledge discovery in a clinical data warehouse. *Proceedings of the AMIA Symposium* 1997:101–5.

22. Reynolds, H. N., McCunn, M., Borg, U., Habashi, C., Cottingham, C., and Bar-Lavi, Y. 1998. Acute respiratory distress syndrome: Estimated incidence and mortality rate in a 5 million-person population base. *Critical Care* (London) 2:29–34.

23. Scully, K. W., Pates, R. D., Desper, G. S., Connors, A. F., Harrell, F. E., Pieper, K. S., Hannan, R. L., and Reynolds, R. E. 1997. Development of an enterprise-wide clinical repository: Merging multiple legacy databases. *Journal of the American Medical Informatics Association* Suppl. S:32–36.

24. Sorensen, H. T., Friis, S., Norgard, B., Mellemkjaer, W. J., Blot, J. K., McLaughlin, A., and Ekbom, J. A. B. 2003. Risk of cancer in a large cohort of nonaspirin NSAID users: A population-based study. *British Journal of Cancer* 88:1687–92.

25. Spangler, S., and Kreulen, J. 2008. *Mining the talk—Unlocking the business value in unstructured information*. IBM Press: Upper Saddle River, NJ.

26. Uramoto, N., Matsuzawa, H., Nagano, T., Murakami, A., Takeuchi, H., and Takeda, K. 2004. A text-mining system for knowledge discovery from biomedical documents. *IBM Systems Journal* 43:516–33.

27. Wang, X. S. Nayda, L., and Dettinger, R. 2007. Infrastructure for a clinical-decision-intelligence system. *IBM Systems Journal* 46:151–69.

Chapter 12

Using Data Mining to Build Alerting Systems for Decision Support in Healthcare

Billie Anderson, Cali M. Davis, and J. Michael Hardin

Contents

Introduction to Healthcare Alerting Systems

Alerting systems for healthcare have been in existence since the 1950s in the United States and focused initially on the development of diagnostic systems.[1] One of the earliest examples of a successfully implemented healthcare alerting system was in an emergency department in the United Kingdom between 1969 and 1974 that diagnosed the cause of abdominal pain.[2]

More recently, researchers have used advances in data mining to enhance healthcare alerting systems. Perhaps the most notable recent development in data mining alerting systems is the Washington-based company Veratect, which used data mining techniques to predict the swine flu eighteen days before the World Health Organization (WHO). Eighteen days before WHO issued the alert about the possible swine flu pandemic, Veratect reported a strange outbreak of respiratory disease in La Gloria, Mexico, noting that local residents thought the flu outbreak was related to contamination from pig breeding from nearby farms. Veratect uses a data mining technique to automatically search terms of thousands of websites daily for early signs of medical problems. When items of interest are found, the results are turned over to analysts who post the results on the company's website.[3]

Data mining alerting systems are algorithms that require training a set of solutions to a problem and can make decisions on new problems with incomplete facts. They are commonly used in biomedical pattern recognition. These types of alerting systems will be the main focus of this chapter. The three main algorithms that will be emphasized are logistic regression, decision trees, and artificial neural networks (ANNs). Before a description of these algorithms is described, an overview of data mining for healthcare alerting systems is discussed.

An Overview of Data Mining for Healthcare Alerting Systems

Over the last decade there has been widespread use of medical information systems and an explosive growth of medical databases. These stockpiles of data mainly contain patient data. But the data's hidden value, the power to predict certain trends, has largely gone untapped. Unless the data are used properly, it is a waste of resources to collect and store them. The data gathered in medical databases require specialized tools for storing and accessing data, data analysis, and effective use of the data. In particular, the increase in data causes great difficulties in extracting useful information for decision support.

To counter the difficulty of trying to analyze large amounts of data, the medical community has turned to data mining techniques. Data mining is the analysis of data sets to find unsuspected relationships and to summarize the data in novel ways that are both understandable and useful to the data owner.[4] Data mining, in general, can help extract regularities hidden in the data and formulate knowledge in the form of patterns and rules.

Published reviews of using data mining alerting systems in the healthcare industry have concluded that the most promising systems are for drug dosing and preventive care.[5,6] These studies serve to alert against adverse effects from prescription drugs, or to promote greater compliance with practice guidelines in health maintenance activities such as vaccinations and mammography. One review paper noted that computer-aided evaluation of mammograms already helps to cut the number of missed lesions by half without increasing the false positive rate.[7]

Data mining has been used to automatically identifying new, unexpected, and potentially interesting patterns in hospital infection control at the University of Alabama Hospital. A decision support system was implemented that used association rules to represent outcomes and monitor changes in the incidence of those outcomes over time. The hospital was able to demonstrate that the data mining decision support system developed proved to be effective and efficient in identifying potentially interesting and previously unknown patterns.

In terms of specific data mining algorithms such as decision trees and logistic regression, there are many published studies in which they have been used to develop alerting systems in healthcare. Chae et al. published a study in which a decision support system was developed to analyze and monitor trends of quality indicators.[9] The study discusses an analysis of healthcare quality indicators using data mining for developing quality improvement strategies. Specifically, important factors influencing inpatient mortality were identified using a decision tree method of data mining based on 8,405 patients who were discharged from the study hospital during the period of December 1, 2000, to January 31, 2001. Important factors for the inpatient mortality were length of stay, disease classes, discharge departments, and age groups.

Delen et al. reported a research study in which they developed several prediction models for breast cancer.[10] Specifically, they used three popular data mining methods: decision trees, ANNs, and logistic regression. They acquired a large database of breast cancer patient information: 433,272 patients with seventy-two predictor variables. The purpose of the models was to predict survival five years from the date of diagnosis. The results of the study indicated that the decision tree performed the best among the three models examined. The decision tree helped identify certain important predictor variables that clinicians could look for when examining new patients.

Recently, medical researchers have begun to examine the methodology of particular data mining algorithms such as ANNs to develop alerting systems. Gant et al. report that there are over five hundred academic publications featuring the use of ANNs in the medical community.[11] The published literature suggests that ANN models have been shown to be valuable tools in reducing the workload on clinicians by detecting patterns and providing decision support.[12,13]

One notable use of ANNs is within the realm of detecting cervical cancer. Cervical cancer detection has benefited from the PAPNET system, one of very few ANNs to gain the Food and Drug Administration's (FDA) approval for clinical use.[14] The system uses ANNs to extract abnormal cell appearance from vaginal smear slides and describe them in histological terms.[15] The alternative, more conventional way is to rescreen the slides under a microscope. It has been shown that the PAPNET system has uncovered a higher proportion of false negatives than conventional microscopic rescreening as confirmed by cytologists.[16]

Case Study of Decision Support Systems

The objective of this case study is to use SAS® Enterprise Miner™ 6.1 to build a decision tree, logistic regression, and ANN to predict five-year survival of colorectal cancer (CRC) patients. First, a description of the data set is given. Then, the three data mining models used will be summarized. Finally, we will show how to use SAS Enterprise Miner 6.1 to build a valid analytical process flow for these data mining methods. In the demonstration, it will be assumed that the user knows how to import data into Enterprise Miner and produce an analytical workflow. The results of the modeling nodes will not be shown or discussed. The purpose of this demonstration is to collect the appropriate diagnostic statistics from Enterprise Miner and do a comparison to see which predictive model performs the best.

Description of Data

The target variable for the predictive models is a binary variable indicating survival (or death) five years postsurgery for patients with CRC. The input variables used to build the predictive models consisted of age, race, and different types of variables that described tumor state, tumor differentiation, and the location of the tumor. Two CRC biomarker variables were also available. There were 500 observations and 107 input variables.

Using all the described variables, a logistic regression, decision tree, and ANN will be built using SAS Enterprise Miner 6.1. The following is a brief description of each model type.

Data Mining Models

Logistic Regression

A logistic regression model was built to model the probability of survival (or not) five years postsurgery for CRC. Logistic regression is used to model data when the target variable is binary (e.g., survive—yes/no; recurrence-yes/no). The probability of an outcome is related to a set of predictor variables by an equation of the form

$$\log[(p/(1-p)] = \beta_0 + \beta_2 X_1 + \ldots + \beta_k X_k$$

where p is the probability of survival five years postsurgery for CRC, β_0 is an intercept term, $\beta_1, \ldots, \beta_k$ are the coefficients associated with each variable, $X_1, \ldots, X_k$

are the values of the predictor variables, and k is a unique subscript denoting each variable. The standard assumption is that the predictor variables are related in a linear fashion to the log odds $\{\log[p/(1 - p)]\}$ of the outcome of interest.

Decision Trees

The type of decision tree used in this analysis was a classification and regression tree (CART).[17] The settings in SAS Enterprise Miner can be adjusted to create such a tree. CART is an algorithm that is used to split the data into smaller segments called nodes that are homogeneous with respect to the outcome variable. At each node, the algorithm examines all predictor variables and all values of the predictor variables with respect to determining the best predictor variable and a value of that predictor variable that will best separate the data into more homogenous subgroups with respect to the outcome variable. In other words, each node is a classification question, and the branches of the tree are partitions of the data set into different classes (those patients who will survive/not survive five years postsurgery). This process repeats itself in a recursive, iterative manner until no further separation of the data is feasible. Therefore, the terminal nodes at the end of the branches of the decision tree represent the different classes.

The second part of the algorithm is known as *pruning*. Pruning is applied to the decision tree to ensure that the algorithm does not overfit the training data. At each subsequent node, smaller amounts of observations are available. Toward the end of the splitting algorithm, idiosyncrasies of the training observations at a particular node can display a pattern that is specific only to those observations that can become meaningless and detrimental for prediction when applied to larger populations. Pruning removes smaller branches that failed to generalize using the validation data set.

Artificial Neural Networks

The original development of the neural network was inspired by the way the brain recognizes patterns.[18] The goal of an ANN is the same as in logistic regression, predicting an outcome based on the values of predictor variables. The approach used in developing the neural network model is quite different from logistic regression.

ANNs have the ability to "learn" mathematical relationships between a series of input (predictor) variables and the corresponding output (outcome) variables. This is achieved by "training" the network with a training data set that consists of the predictor variables and a known outcome variable. Once the ANN has been trained, the model can be used for classification on a validation data set.

Figure 12.1 is a diagram illustrating an ANN that has been trained to predict the probability of a patient dying of CRC five years postsurgery based on only two predictor variables, age and race. ANNs are often represented in diagrams such as the one presented in Figure 12.1. The circles in the diagram are known as *nodes*.

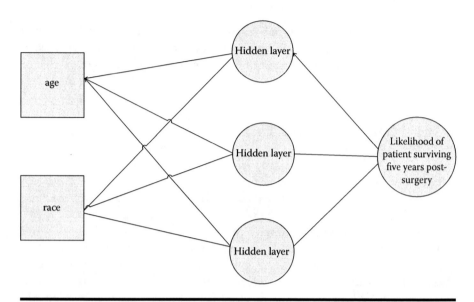

Figure 12.1   Diagram of neural network trained to predict the probability of a CRC patient's survival five years postsurgery on the basis of age (X_1) and race (X_2).

A typical neural network consists of three layers of nodes: input, hidden, and output nodes. The values of the predictor variables reside in the input node. The output node contains the predicted output of the network. The hidden nodes in the diagram contain a function known as the *activation function* that allows the network to model complex nonlinear associations between the predictor variables and the outcome.

Each input node is connected to each hidden node, and each hidden node is connected to the output node. In this example, there are two input nodes where the values of age (X_1) and race (X_2) are input into the network along with a bias weight, which is the equivalent to an intercept term found in a regression model.

The input nodes are connected to the hidden nodes by a *connection weight* (the connection weights are the lines in Figure 12.1 connecting the input and hidden nodes). The connection weights can be thought of as the neural network equivalent of the β coefficients in a logistic regression model. At each hidden node the connection weights are passed to an activation function, most commonly the sigmoid function. The activation function uses the connection weights to model any nonlinear relationships among the predictor variables and the outcome variable. Another set of connection weights are then passed from the hidden node to the output node to obtain the output of the network. This output of the network corresponds to the predicted probability of the outcome variable.

In the ANN analysis performed there were as many input nodes as predictor variables: three hidden nodes (the default setting in SAS Enterprise Miner) and one output node (probability of survival five years postsurgery for patients with CRC).

Each box represents an input node in which the predictor variables are input into the network. Each line represents a connection weight. Each circle in the middle of the diagram represents the hidden layers where the relationship between the predictor variables and the outcome is modeled. The last circle at the end of the diagram is where the probability of survival is output from the network.

Assessment of Data Mining Models

Kolmogorov–Smirnov Statistic

The Kolmogorov–Smirnov (KS) statistic was used as the measure to evaluate model performance. The KS statistic measures the difference between two different distributions. The actual KS statistic is the maximum difference between two different distributions. In this case, the two distributions of interest are the estimated probabilities of belonging to the survival or nonsurvival groups produced by the models. If the two distributions are the same, this implies the model did not effectively separate between survivors and nonsurvivors (implying a small KS statistic). On the other hand, significantly different distributions suggest good separation between the two groups (implying a larger KS statistic). The KS statistic has a known theoretical probability distribution, so a p-value was computed to determine if the two distributions are significantly different.

The predictive models were built on the training data set, and the validation data set was used to obtain the KS statistics and the corresponding p-value.

Area under the Receiver Operating Characteristic Curve

Another common predictive model diagnostic is the area under the receiver operating characteristic curve (AUC). For every given probability cutoff, the confusion matrix in Table 12.1 is computed.

The receiver operating characteristic (ROC) curve is a plot of the false positive rate (x-axis) and true positive rate (y-axis) for every single probability cutoff. The ROC curve gives an indication of how well the models are separating between those patients who died and those that survived. A good predictive model will go up fairly steep and then start to level off. There is a 45° diagonal reference line on the ROC plot, as shown in Figure 12.2. The diagonal line represents where the false positive and true

Table 12.1   Example of a Confusion Matrix

	Truth	
Predicted	*Good*	*Bad*
Good	True positive	False positive
Bad	False negative	True negative

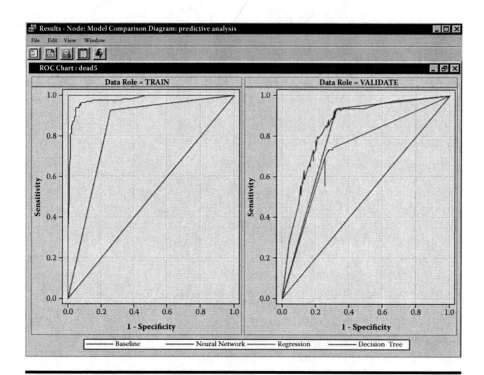

Figure 12.2   ROC plots for the three predictive models.

positive rates are the same. If the ROC curve falls below this diagonal line, the model is no better than randomly assigning patients as dead or alive five years postsurgery. A model that has an ROC curve above this line is considered to be a good predictive model. Hence, the higher the AUC value, the better the predictive model.

ROC curves have been shown to be valuable tests in evaluating the detection of certain types of cancer.[19] With the appropriate use of ROC curves, investigators of cancer detection tests can improve their research. In many cases, ROC curves help the medical community focus on classification rules with low false positive rates, which are most important for the detection of cancer. However, these ROC curves should always be put in perspective, because a good classification rule for the detection of cancer does not guarantee that cancer screening will reduce cancer mortality.

Three Data Mining Models for Colorectal Cancer

Figure 12.3 displays the analytical process flow used in SAS Enterprise Miner 6.1.

Once the data are brought into Enterprise Miner, the first issue that needs to be addressed is to split the modeling data set into training and validation data sets.

A critical step in prediction is choosing among competing models. Given a set of training data, you can easily generate models that very accurately predict a target

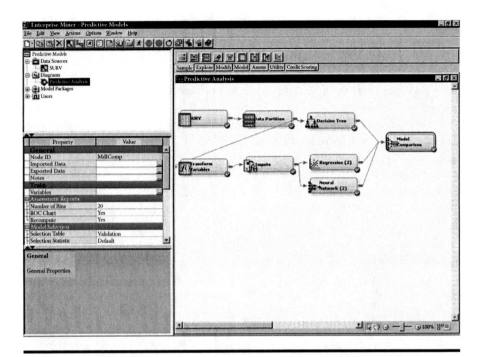

Figure 12.3   Analysis flow for the three predictive models in SAS Enterprise Miner 6.1.

value from a set of input predictor variables. Unfortunately, these predictions might be accurate only for the training data themselves. Attempts to generalize the predictions from the training data to an independent, but similarly distributed sample can result in substantial reductions in accuracy.

To avoid this pitfall, SAS Enterprise Miner is designed to use a validation data set as a means of independently gauging model performance. Typically, the validation data set is created by partitioning the raw analysis data. Observations selected for training are used to build the model, and observations selected for validation are used to tune and compare models. For this modeling exercise 60% of the data were allocated to the training data set and 40% were allocated to the validation data set.

The first analysis built was the decision tree. Decision tree models are advantageous because they are conceptually easy to understand, yet they readily accommodate nonlinear associations between input variables and one or more target variables. They also handle missing values without the need for imputation. CART was the specific decision tree used in this study. Enterprise Miner help files discuss how to set up the decision tree node as a CART.

The next node used in the analysis was the transform node. Sometimes, input data are more informative on a scale other than that on which they were originally collected. For example, variable transformations can be used to stabilize variance, remove nonlinearity, improve additivity, and counter nonnormality. Therefore, for many models, transformations of the input data (either dependent or independent variables) can lead to a better model fit. These transformations can be functions of either a single variable or more than one variable. For this analysis, many of the input variables were highly skewed. Several different transformations were examined. The best transformation, in terms of making the input variables more symmetric, was the log.

After the transform node was used, the imputation node was used for the logistic and ANN models. In SAS Enterprise Miner, however, models such as regressions and neural networks ignore observations altogether that contain missing values, which reduces the size of the training data set. Less training data can substantially weaken the predictive power of these models. To overcome this obstacle of missing data, imputation of the missing values can be performed before the models are fit. For this analysis, the imputation technique chosen was the mean.

After the models are run, the model comparison node allows the user to obtain diagnostic statistics such as KS and AUC.

Figure 12.3 displays the ROC curves for each of the three models. Based on the AUC values in Table 12.2, the ANN is outperforming the other two models. In terms of which model is best at separating those patients who will and will not die five years postsurgery, the ANN is also superior based on the KS statistics displayed in Table 12.3. Also note the p-value reported for each of the KS statistics; all

Table 12.2   AUC for ANN, CART, and Logistic Regression Models

Model	AUC
ANN	0.85
CART	0.80
Logistic regression	0.73

Table 12.3   KS Statistic for ANN, CART, and Logistic Regression Models

Model	KS (p-value)
ANN	1.42
	(<0.0001)
CART	0.98
	(<0.0001)
Logistic regression	0.72
	(<0.0001)

indicate that there is a significant difference between the distribution of the survival and nonsurvival populations. This result indicates that all the models are doing a good job separating these two populations. Overall, the ANN is the champion model for this particular data set.

Conclusion

In conclusion, we demonstrate that using predictive models and their ability to separate between survival and nonsurvival for CRC patients five years postsurgery is a promising approach for developing a diagnostic evaluation for CRC. This initial case study reveals the strong potential for data mining methods for CRC. Particularly, this study has shown the promise of using ANNs for decision support among researchers and clinicians in the CRC community.

In this case study, the ANN outperformed the more well-known and understood models, such as the decision tree and logistic regression. In particular, ANNs have been shown to be very powerful and superior over decision trees and logistic regression in predicting a clinical outcome in patients with CRC.[20–22]

As described above, a series of recent reports in the literature have shown that data mining techniques such as ANN provide higher predictive accuracy than familiar, traditional models such as logistic regression.[23–26] ANNs and other data mining tools are often called "black box" techniques since the logic used to determine the final model is not transparent. This lack of transparency is the greatest disadvantage that medical researchers find when they use ANNs for decision support. Yet, for this one disadvantage, there are many advantages for the medical community to use ANNs for clinical decision support. Claimed advantages of ANNs include:

1. Ease of optimization with the advancement of easy-to-use software such as SAS Enterprise Miner
2. Accuracy for predictive inference, with potential support for clinical decision making

As shown in this chapter, data mining models, especially ANNs, can be developed that accurately predict the outcome of a medical condition. These predictive models can be valuable tools in medicine. They can be used to assist in determining successful treatments, prognosis, or interventions. However, there are areas of concern in the development of ANNs as data mining models for use as alerting systems in the medical community. The FDA in the United States has issued a guidance document for software for medical support.[12] The document has a section on using ANNs. Some of the points highlighted by this document are that ANNs can behave in a nondeterministic way. The medical researchers must be able to justify and explain the choices made for the ANN model and the topology. The researchers must also be able to describe how overfitting is avoided (for example, using training and validation data sets). The document specifies additional data sets to be processed through the ANN to ensure that performance remains as expected.

While data mining can provide useful information and support to the medical community by identifying patterns that may not be readily apparent, there are limitations to what data mining can do. Not all patterns found are interesting. For a pattern to be interesting, it should be logical and actionable. Data mining requires human intervention to exploit the extracted knowledge. For example, data mining can provide assistance in making the diagnosis or prescribing the treatment, but it still cannot replace the physician's intuition and interpretive skills.[6]

Data mining methods used as alerting systems in healthcare are capable of identifying patterns and discovering relationships in large medical databases, but without cooperation and feedback from the medical community, the results are useless. The patterns found via data mining methods should be evaluated by medical professionals with many years of experience in the problem domain to decide whether the patterns are logical, actionable, and novel enough to be directed in new clinical research directions. Data mining should not aim to replace medical professionals and researchers, but to complement their invaluable efforts to save more human lives by appropriate intervention using some of the healthcare alerting systems described in this chapter. Intervention and decision support can be found more quickly with data mining techniques.

References

1. Miller, R. A. 1994. Medical diagnostic decision support systems—past, present, and future: A threaded bibliography and brief commentary. *J. Am. Med. Inform. Assoc.* 1:8–27.
2. Beaver, K. 2003. *Healthcare information systems*, Chap. 17. 2nd ed. Auerbach Publications: New York.
3. Linder, B. Data mining predicted swine flu 18 days before WHO. http:\\infopackets.com\news\technology\it.
4. Cios, K. J., and Moore, G. W. 2002. Uniqueness of medical data mining. *Artif. Intell. Med.* 26:1–24.
5. Hunt, D. L., Haynes, R. B., Hanna, S. E., and Smith, K. 1998. Effects of computer-based clinical decision support systems on physician performance and patient outcomes. *JAMA* 280:1339–46.
6. Richards, G., Rayward-Smith, V. J., Sonksen, P. H., Carey, S., and Weng, C. 2001. Data mining for indicators of early mortality in a database of clinical records. *Artif. Intell. Med.* 22:215–31.
7. Weiner, M. G., and Pifer, E. 2000. Computerized decision support and the quality of care. *Managed Care* 9:41–51.
8. Brossette, S. E., Sprague, A. P., Hardin, J. M., Waites, K. B., Jones, W. T., and Moser, S. A. 1998. Association rules and data mining in hospital infection control and public health surveillance. *J. Am. Med. Inform. Assoc.* 5:373–81.

9. Chae, Y. M., Kim, K. S., Tark, K. C., Park, H. J., and Ho, S. H. 2003. Analysis of healthcare quality indicators using data mining and decision support systems. *Expert Syst. Appl.* 24:167–72.

10. Delen, D., Walker, G., and Kadam, A. 2005. Predicting breast cancer survivability: A comparison of three data mining methods. *Artif. Intell. Med.* 34:113–27.

11. Gant, V., Rodway, S., and Wyatt, J. 2001. *Clinical applications of artificial neural networks,* 329–56. 1st ed. Cambridge: Cambridge University Press.

12. Lisboa, P. J., and Taktak, A. F. G. 2006. The use of artificial neural networks in decision support in cancer: A systematic review. *Neural Networks* 19:408–15.

13. Lundin, M., Lundin, J., Burke, H. B., Toikkanen, S., Pylkkanen, L., and Joensuu, H. 1999. Artificial neural networks applied to survival prediction in breast cancer. *Oncology* 57:281–86.

14. Nieminen, P., Hakama, M., Viikki, M., Tarkkanen, J., and Anttila, A. 2003. Prospective and randomized public-health trial on neural network-assisted screening for cervical cancer in Finland: Results of the first year. *Int. J. Cancer* 103:422–26.

15. Boon, M. E., and Kok, L. P. 2001. *Clinical applications of artificial neural networks,* 81–89. 1st ed. Cambridge: Cambridge University Press.

16. Mango, L. J., and Valente, P. T. 1998. Neural-network-assisted analysis and microscopic rescreening in presumed negative cervical cytological smears: A comparision. *Acta Cytologica* 42:227–32.

17. Brieman, F. J., Olson, R. A., and Stone, C. J. 1984. *Classification and regression trees.* Montery: Wadsworth & Brooks & Cole.

18. White, H. 1989. Learning in artificial neural networks. *Neural Computing* 1:425–26.

19. Baker, S. G. 2003. The central role of receiver operating characteristic (ROC) curves in evaluating tests for the early detection of cancer. *J. Natl. Cancer Instit.* 95:511–15.

20. Snow, P., Kerr, K., Brandt, J., and Rodvold, D. 2001. Neural network and regression predictions of 5-year survival after colon carcinoma treatment. *Cancer* (Suppl.) 91:1673–78.

21. Grumett, S., Snow, P., and Kerr, D. 2003. Neural network and regression predictions of 5-year survival after colon carcinoma treatment. *Clin. Colorectal Cancer* 4:239–44.

22. Anand, S. S., Smith, A. E., Hamilton, P. W., Anand, J. S., Hughes, J. G., and Bartels, P. H. 1999. An evaluation of intelligent prognostic systems for colorectal cancer. *Artif. Intell. Med.* 15:193–214.

23. Finne, P., Finne, R., Auvinen, A., Juusela, H., Aro, J., and Maattanen, L. 2000. Predicting the outcome of prostate biopsy in screen-positive men by a multilayer perceptron network. *Urology* 56:418–22.

24. Matsui, Y., Egawa, S., Tsukayama, C., Terai, A., Kuwao, S., and Bab, S. 2002. Artificial neural network analysis for predicting pathological state of clinically localized prostate cancer in the Japanese population. *Jpn. J. Clin. Oncol.* 32:530–535.

25. Remzi, M., Anagnostou, T., Ravery, V., Zlotta, A., Stephan, C., and Marberger, M. 2003. An artificial neural network to predict the outcome of repeat prostate biopsies. *Urology* 62:456–60.

26. Song, J. H., Venkatesh, S. S., Conant, E. A., Arger, P. H., and Sehgal, C. H. 2005. Comparative analysis of logistic regression and artificial neural network for computer-aided diagnosis of breast masses. *Acad. Radiol.* 12:487–95.

Chapter 13

Data Mining Techniques to Enhance Healthcare Cost Savings through the Identification of Abusive Billing Practices and the Optimization of Care Enhancement Services

Theodore L. Perry, Johnny E. Gore,
Jeffrey W. Erdley, and Jeremy D. Lowery

Contents

Introduction

The healthcare industry in the United States is faced with a number of difficult issues that amplify the complexity of managing available medical resources while enhancing cost and delivery efficiencies. Some of these issues include (1) growing population immigration potentially introducing new or formally eradicated health conditions, (2) increasing age of the overall population, (3) escalating costs for defensive medicines (e.g., CT, MRI, and other imaging services), (4) rising fraudulent or abusive medical billing practices, (5) optimizing existing healthcare facility usage (e.g., staffing doctors and nurses along with designated bed utilization rates), and (6) requiring groups to use health maintenance organizations (HMOs) or preferred provider organizations (PPOs).[1]

One way healthcare organizations are attempting to improve their efficiencies in providing services and treating illnesses is through the development and management of robust data resources and the utilization of analytic techniques to identify patterns and trends in provider billing behaviors as well as patient populations. With this type of information, efficiency is enhanced by more accurately identifying the sources of resource demand by focusing on the needs of specific patient segments and initiating strategic healthcare management to better allocate available resources in meeting those demands.[2,3]

The utilization of analytic techniques in strategic healthcare management is also increasing.[4] More formal analytic techniques such as stochastic trees are used to help increase operational efficiencies by enhancing the decision-making process in medical treatment procedures.[5] Other analytic methodologies involving data mining techniques enable decision makers to identify patterns in clinical, claims, and activity-based historical data, to better understand explanatory relationships in data and create models to more accurately predict future resource healthcare demand.[6] For example, artificial neural networks show great potential in identifying relationships in historical medical claims data that can be used for disease classification and prediction.[7–9] Ultimately, reducing—through enhanced predictive capabilities—the uncertainties in medical delivery resource requirements increases efficiencies across the healthcare industry sectors.[10]

Research addressing the use of quantitative-based decision support systems to enhance efficiency in the healthcare sector is on the rise given the development of data resources and availability of sophisticated analytic methods.[11] There is great interest today in the application of population segmentation and predictive modeling to enhance care management programs by correctly focusing resources and interventions on the segment of a population who would benefit the most from interventions.[11–13] Additionally, similar analytic techniques allow researchers to identify healthcare billing errors, which often result from fraud, waste, or abuse of medical services and procedures.

Technical Requirements and IT Framework

There are numerous technical hurdles in performing analyses of healthcare claims data. Some of these challenges include the fact that these data sets are usually very large (e.g., one year of medical claims for one state Medicaid program is usually well over 100 Gigabytes), contain numerous fields of various data types (e.g., most healthcare claims data sets have at least eighty unique fields), are aggregated from various, disparate systems (e.g., outpatient claims, inpatient claims, and pharmacy claims are usually processed on completely different systems), and require an extensive ETL (i.e., extract, transform, and load) process before any analyses can begin. Consequently, the availability of an adequate IT framework is essential.

Figure 13.1 illustrates an optimal IT framework for healthcare claims data analysis. Obviously, there are various technical configurations that would accomplish the same end state. Nevertheless, as illustrated in the figure, at a minimum an appropriate IT framework should have the following elements: (1) Health Insurance Portability and Accountability Act (HIPAA)–compliant security measures, (2) adequate disk space and memory for data or application servers, (3) data management and analytic software, and (4) backup and storage devices.

Identification of Abusive Billing Practices

The adoption of standard procedural and diagnosis coding systems by government and commercial health insurance payers changed the face of our healthcare payment and delivery system. One result of these billing and payment system changes was the development of data-driven approaches to detect claims processing errors.

Early efforts focused entirely on the claims adjudication processes. Errors were defined as exceptions to payment rules such as eligibility on the date of service (e.g., patient was not covered by plan benefits during the service period), duplicate billings (e.g., receiving payment for the same service more than once), gender-mismatched procedures (e.g., performing a service on a male that can only be performed on a female), and provider-procedure misalignment (e.g., performing a service outside the scope of a provider's licensure).

The next step in the evolution of claims processing technology allowed for the development of system edits based on healthcare plan benefit rules. For example, a particular service might only be allowed a certain number of times per year (e.g., ten physical therapy services per year), or a service might be excluded from payment coverage (e.g., denying an emergency room visit based on final diagnosis code).

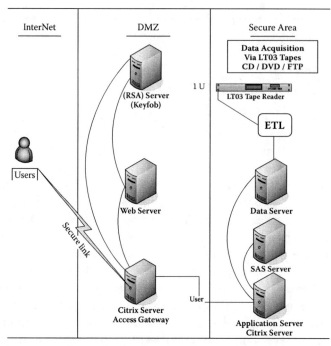

InterNet   **DMZ**   **Secure Area**

Data Acquisition
Via LT03 Tapes
CD / DVD / FTP

1 U   LT03 Tape Reader

(RSA) Server
(Keyfob)

ETL

Users

Web Server   Data Server

Secure link

SAS Server

User

Citrix Server
Access Gateway

Application Server
Citrix Server

Software License Requirements

1. SAS 9.1
2. SQL Server 2000
3. Citrix Client
4. Remote Secure Access (RSA) Client
5. MS Professional
6. Encryption Software
7. Backup Recovery

Additional Requirements

Backup Tapes
LT03 : 50 800 meg
Offsite Storage for disaster recovery

Backup Tapes
LT03 : 50 800 meg
Offsite Storage for
disaster recovery

Figure 13.1   Optimal IT framework for healthcare claims analysis.

With the advent of managed care and quality of care initiatives, the focus changed from improving claims payment systems to developing procedures that reduce over-utilization and abuse. Our current healthcare payment systems are a consequence of this approach, which integrated claims payment processing with medical record review. The problem with this system is twofold: (1) claims processing systems are designed to pay claims, not investigate claims, and (2) medical record review focuses on discrete services and events, not overall practice patterns or trends.

Health and Human Services understood both the shortcomings of these systems and the magnitude and prevalence of fraud and abuse in the healthcare system. As a response to the Balanced Budget Act of 1997, Congress began pressuring Medicare and Medicaid contractors to stop/slow actual fraud and abuse in these programs. This resulted in initiatives such as the Medicare E&M Project (medical review of samples of evaluation and management service documentation) and Prepayment

Edit Validation Project (manual review of processing edit accuracy). Though both of these initiatives further illustrated the enormity of fraud and abuse, this approach was not able to significantly affect outcomes, due to the large numbers of human resources needed. Consequently, leading experts began suggesting a data-driven approach as an alternative to these initiatives.[14,15]

Over the last decade, there have been countless fraud and abuse initiatives from health plans and IT vendors attempting to consolidate multiple sources of information into a system that will allow for easier data mining and analytic activities—some relatively successful, others not. The main problem faced by today's healthcare fraud and abuse programs is they are based almost entirely on human intelligence (i.e., whistle-blowers). Data are used to support a case, not identify it. Enhancements in system processing activities have reduced adjudication (or processing) errors to relatively small rates (3 to 5%). These error rates are most commonly cited by payers as evidence of an overall decrease in healthcare claims overpayments. Nonetheless, claims processing systems depend on this assumption: *if the service is documented and submitted correctly on the claim form, then it was actually performed.* Unfortunately, this assumption is incorrect. For example, a recent report illustrates how this false assumption has created an environment in which over $104 billion in healthcare payment errors exists and continues to grow in both government and commercial arenas.[16]

Despite a climate of increased scrutiny, most improper healthcare payments associated with federal programs continue to go unidentified as they drain taxpayer resources away from the missions and goals of our government. They occur for many reasons, including insufficient oversight or monitoring, inadequate eligibility controls, and automated system deficiencies.[17] At present, most attempts to stem fraud and abuse focus on (1) whistle-blowers, (2) accidental recognition of an irregularity by a claims processor, (3) attempts to identify "target" providers by total dollars paid, (4) attempts to identify target providers or members by total number of prescriptions or pills dispensed or received, and (5) attempts to identify target providers or members by drug class dispensed or received (e.g., narcotic analgesics).

Although there is a place in the detection of fraud, waste, and abuse for each of these categories, the science of data mining, provider and member profiling, and statistical analysis has revolutionized the investigative precision available through computerized review.

In order to better understand the impact of payment errors in the private arena, HHS, Inc. conducted an industry research project and presented the findings at the 2005 National Managed Health Care Congress's Annual Conference in Washington, D.C.[18] Perhaps the most important element of this report was the quantification of the negative impact overpayments have on employers and their employees, thereby creating a dangerous fiscal environment for most companies. As more and more overpayments are made, it becomes increasingly problematic for companies to withstand this unreasonable and unnecessary depletion to their bottom line.

Table 13.1 Comparison of Healthcare Claims Payment Error Rates

Healthcare Sector CY 2005 Estimates	Personal Health Expenditures	Assumed 6% Payment Error Rate	Assumed 9% Payment Error Rate
Private	$787.0B	$39.3B	$62.8B
Medicare	$387.1B	$33.1B	$33.1B
Medicaid	$297.8B	$15.3B	$24.2B
Totals	$1,471.9B	$87.7B	$120.1B

HHS, Inc.'s estimates of CY 2005 industry-wide estimates are shown in Table 13.1. The payment error lower- and upper-end rates were based on HHS, Inc.'s modeling assumptions for Medicare, Medicaid, and private insurance sensitivity to documentation and coding errors.

As illustrated, even under the most conservative payment error assumption (i.e., 6%), there were at least $39.3 billion in healthcare claims errors during CY 2005. Clearly, consequences of these errors are far reaching, such as higher insurance premiums, higher deductibles, lower employment benefits, and lower take-home pay.[19]

Relationship between Clinical Severity and Cost

Comparing and profiling healthcare providers in order to identify billing irregularities is performed using various means, such as grouping by provider specialty (e.g., internal medicine, rehabilitation center, orthotic device vendor), comparing utilization measures (e.g., inpatient services per thousand), or evaluation of dollars paid to the provider. All of these attempts have been met with a standard objection by the provider community: "My patients are sicker than yours." In other words, since the clinical severity level varies from patient to patient, simple comparative analyses across providers often lack face validity (i.e., it does not measure what it is *supposed* to measure), resulting in inappropriate benchmarks and poor payment error identification rates.

In order to provide valid comparisons, it is necessary to account for each patient's primary and comorbid health conditions, while adjusting his or her provider's profile by specialty, place or service, geographic area, and any other factor that might account for practice or billing variability. Additionally, comparisons between providers and their peer groups (e.g., radiologist to radiologist or cardiac care facility to cardiac care facility) accounting for the average severity of the provider's patients, region of practice, and practice environment (e.g., commercial, Medicare, or Medicaid) often reveal abnormal billing patterns or trends, which may result in the identification of fraudulent or abusive healthcare claims.

To further illustrate the importance of ensuring the validity of these types of comparisons for billing error detection, Figure 13.2 represents the relationship between a patient's clinical severity and medical cost. Obviously, the more adverse the medical

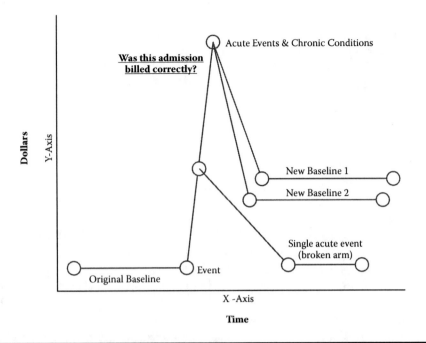

Figure 13.2   Relationship between clinical severity and medical cost.

event, the more it usually costs. Likewise, patients suffering from chronic conditions cost more than healthy patients. As shown in the figure, in the case of a single acute event (e.g., a broken arm), cost will rise and then drop to its previous baseline. Following a chronic event, costs quickly rise and then drop to a new baseline that is higher than the original baseline. This is true because there is now a new chronic condition or a change in an existing chronic condition that results in increased cost.

If, as shown in this figure, two clinically alike patients were admitted to comparable facilities for identical reasons (e.g., both patients were billed using the same diagnosis-related group (DRG)), then one might expect their postevent costs to be similar. However, if their postevent costs were significantly different, then one might question the validity of the inpatient billing code (i.e., DRG), which is oftentimes based on the actual clinical severity of the patient. In other words, as illustrated below, if the observed postevent cost (i.e., new baseline 2) is significantly lower than the expected postevent cost (i.e., new baseline 1), then it is possible that the patient represented by new baseline 2 was not actually as clinically severe as the inpatient billing code indicated, thereby raising the probability of an incorrect and overbilled inpatient stay.

Prediction of Billing Errors

To demonstrate the effectiveness of implementing an analytic modeling approach similar to that described in the previous section, Health Research Insights, Inc.

(HRI) evaluated its inpatient claims error detection model by comparing the predictive value of its error identification model with the predictive value of two different comparison (i.e., null) models using a sensitivity curve. HRI's inpatient claims error detection model used raw healthcare claims data to develop statistically valid comparisons between providers, patients, and healthcare procedures and services. These comparisons allowed for the evaluation and ranking of inpatient claims from highest to lowest risk for billing errors.

For this analysis, the first null model was defined by the common industry heuristic, *the highest cost inpatient claims have the highest probability of error*, which was referred to as the *highest cost model*. The second null model was defined by chance selection, *the 50% probability of error*, which was referred to as the *coin toss model*.

The sensitivity table (Table 13.2) compares the true positive capture (i.e., sensitivity) of the three models at various screening thresholds. The healthcare claims data used for this study were provided during the 2006 Centers for Medicare and Medicaid Services Predictive Modeling and Data Display Special Study. The sensitivity table shows that the *inpatient claims risk ranking model* consistently performed better than both the highest cost model and the coin toss model across the entire screening threshold domain. At a screening threshold of 10% (i.e., the top 10% of the inpatient medical claims sorted from highest to lowest risk for error), the inpatient claims risk ranking model accurately identified 42% of inpatient claims with errors, while the highest cost model accurately identified 20% and the coin toss model accurately identified 10% of inpatient claims with errors. The inpatient

Table 13.2   Sensitivity Comparisons of Inpatient Claims Errors by Model

Screening Threshold	HRI Model True Positive Capture	Highest Cost Model True Positive Capture	HRI Improvement	Coin Toss Model True Positive Capture	HRI Improvement
3%	18%	12%	50%	3%	500%
5%	30%	15%	100%	5%	500%
10%	42%	20%	110%	10%	320%
15%	50%	22%	127%	15%	233%
20%	59%	25%	136%	20%	195%
25%	65%	32%	103%	25%	160%
30%	68%	36%	89%	30%	260%
50%	84%	62%	35%	50%	68%

claims risk ranking model represented a 110% improvement over the highest cost model and a 320% improvement over the coin toss model at the 10% screening threshold. A comparison of the true positive capture rate for all three models at various screening thresholds appears in Table 13.2, demonstrating the usefulness of developing and implementing similar analytic models for healthcare claims error detection. Data-driven models such as this would allow healthcare claims payers to efficiently and economically oversee their adjudication processes and significantly decrease their claims payment error rates.

Targeting At-Risk Individuals for Vaccination Programs

Though the incidence of hepatitis A virus (HAV) and hepatitis B virus (HBV) has declined since universal immunization strategies were implemented for children, vaccine-preventable hepatitis continues to be a major concern in the United States. Higher incidence among adults, recent immigrants, and those living at or below the poverty level continues to pose a significant public health challenge, with certain groups representing a disproportionately high risk for contracting one or both of these diseases.[19]

Identification of individuals at highest risk for vaccine-preventable hepatitis is problematic when developing risk-based immunization programs for large managed care populations, such as Medicaid members. This is primarily because traditional risk identification procedures involve face-to-face interactions, which cannot be accomplished across an entire population and are oftentimes inadequate to assess an individual's risk. Consequently, retrospective risk group identification and individual member targeting techniques are often used to predict the clinical and economic impact of these conditions and diseases.[20,21] Importantly, these techniques can be used to identify those individuals who fit known risk groups but in whom *the risk might not be apparent* to their providers.

HRI conducted a study to demonstrate the usefulness of data mining techniques in analyzing healthcare claims data to target *known* and *potential* risk groups for vaccine-preventable hepatitis and to evaluate the potential economic impact of a risk-based immunization approach. A retrospective matched group study was conducted using two years of Medicaid data purchased from Thomson Medstat (MarketScan Multi-state Medicaid Database). The hepatitis risk groups studied were patients with human immunodeficiency virus (HIV), sexually transmitted diseases (STDs), and chronic liver disease (CLD).

Study Data and Analytic Methods

Data were acquired from Thomson Medstat (MarketScan Multi-state Medicaid Database) for use in this study. These data represented two complete years (2004 and

2005) of healthcare claims from a sample of Medicaid claims comprised from eight Medicaid programs. Medicaid members who were identified as being eighteen years of age or older by December 31 of each study year (2004 and 2005) were eligible for inclusion, yielding 3.46 million members for 2004 and 3.71 million members for 2005 with unadjusted total claim paid dollars of $6.95 billion and $7.33 billion, respectively. Hepatitis risk groups were defined using International Classification of Disease codes (ICD-9). Members with two unique claims on different dates of service with HIV- STD-, or CLD-specific ICD-9 codes within the same calendar year (i.e., January through December 2004 or 2005) comprised the study population.

The risk condition (i.e., HIV, STD, or CLD) and comparison groups were based on preexisting factors, as determined through the analysis of each complete calendar year of study data. The factors were (1) age— exact match by year of birth; (b) gender—exact match; (c) race—exact match; and (d) clinical severity score—±0.10. The clinical severity score was derived using the Centers for Medicare and Medicaid Services (CMS) Hierarchical Condition Category (HCC) adjustment factors.[22] HCC severity adjustment factors were calculated for every member in order to minimize the threat to interval validity caused by assignment bias presented by this study design.[23] Individual subject's HCC values were used along with demographic factors (i.e., age, gender, and race) and hepatitis risk categories (i.e., HIV, STD, and CLD) to decrease study bias and strengthen the value of the reported relationships.

Analyses on the 2004 and 2005 Medicaid data set were conducted, including the following healthcare claim types: (1) inpatient, (2) outpatient, (3) professional, (4) skilled nursing facility, (5) home health, and (6) hospice. Algorithms based on the entire twenty-four months of continuous claims data were used to identify the study subjects with HAV and HBV. Additionally, algorithms were used to identify the hepatitis risk factors of HIV, STDs, and CLD.

These identification algorithms used combinations of diagnosis (ICD-9) and procedure codes (CPT [Current Procedural Technology] and HCPCS [Healthcare Common Procedure Coding System]). The precision and accuracy of each algorithm were validated by comparisons of established disease condition prevalence rates reported by the National Institute for Health (NIH) and the Centers for Disease Control (CDC).[24] Although some members had healthcare claims indicating more than one of the risk conditions of interest, only those members with claims indicating one of the risk conditions (i.e., HIV, STD, or CLD) were included in each risk condition group. Members selected for the comparison groups did not have any healthcare claims evidence of the risk conditions. Outcomes were represented as unadjusted rates for the risk condition and comparison groups by gender and race. The remaining outcomes were represented as averages for age, clinical severity (i.e., HCC score), and paid amounts (i.e., aggregate healthcare claims costs). T-tests were used to determine whether the averages between the risk condition and comparison groups were statistically different for clinical severity and paid amounts.

Study Results

The total numbers of members during 2004 who were identified with HIV, STD, and CLD were 16,285, 242,223, and 138,417, respectively. Similarly, the total numbers of members during 2005 who were identified with HIV, STD, and CLD were 17,302, 257,750, and 129,584, respectively. Since groups were selected based on the presence or absence of HAV or HBV, all matched groups had equal numbers of members. As summarized in Tables 13.3 and 13.4, on average members who had either HAV or HBV in addition to the risk conditions of HIV and STD experienced significantly higher costs than those members without HAV or HBV. Furthermore, differences between risk condition group and comparison group costs were significantly different, except for the CLD/HBV groups. These

Table 13.3   2004 Average Healthcare Claims Cost Differences by Study Group

2004 Risk Condition Group	Comparison Group	Matched Group Size (n)	Average Cost Difference per Recipient	p-Value[a]
HIV with HAV	HIV without HAV	1,877	$1,041.93	<0.001
HIV with HBV	HIV without HBV	3,031	$1,602.55	<0.001
STD with HAV	STD without HAV	25,755	$1,591.56	<0.001
STD with HBV	STD without HBV	42,379	$3,414.25	<0.001
CLD with HAV	CLD without HAV	16,771	$5,056.80	<0.001
CLD with HBV	CLD without HBV	17,567	($300.91)	= 0.17

[a] Student's t-test.

Table 13.4   2005 Average Healthcare Claims Cost Differences by Study Group

2005 Risk Condition Group	Comparison Group	Matched Group Size (n)	Mean Cost Difference per Recipient	p-Value[a]
HIV with HAV	HIV without HAV	1,607	$1,802.11	<0.001
HIV with HBV	HIV without HBV	3,193	$1,852.53	<0.001
STD with HAV	STD without HAV	36,163	$556.56	<0.01
STD with HBV	STD without HBV	40,154	$943.28	<0.01
CLD with HAV	CLD without HAV	15,749	$697.95	<0.05
CLD with HBV	CLD without HBV	18,026	($244.75)	= 0.11

[a] Student's t-test.

outcomes demonstrate how the appropriate application of data mining techniques with healthcare claims data can be used to reveal cost-savings opportunities for disease intervention programs.

Discussion and Conclusions

In this chapter, two examples were presented demonstrating the application of data mining techniques to create *actionable information* for healthcare policy and process. As the healthcare debate continues in our country, it is important to understand how to use available information to support healthcare delivery models, especially considering the current economic situation in the United States. There are more data sources today than ever before, which presents an unprecedented opportunity for research and development.

At the most basic level, data mining is simply the search for valuable information in large volumes of data. Because data mining of healthcare claims involves the analysis of very large data sets, it is a cooperative effort between human and computer. The human will design the databases, define research problems, and set research goals, while the computer is responsible for examining the data in every possible manner to reveal patterns of data that match these research goals. Given the scope and magnitude of medical care delivery, this process is necessitated by the need to extract business-critical information from data repositories to the degree necessary to be competitive in the healthcare business information arena.

As demonstrated in this chapter, the most important feature of data mining that distinguished it from all other forms of data sorting or data querying is its ability to *predict future behaviors*. Prediction is the heart of a true data mining approach, and an analyst who uses *real* data mining techniques is essentially applying the classical problem of prediction from prior samples. This means that, over time, data are collected and the correct answers (i.e., true interpretation of these data) are contained in the previous cases (i.e., historical data). The objective of data mining is to reveal the patterns in the historical data that ensure reliable predictive answers to new cases.

Data mining uses an ever-increasing number of techniques to analyze data. However, there are two major categories of data mining problems: (1) prediction problems and (2) knowledge discovery problems. As described above, prediction is the main goal of data mining. It takes the known answers related to past cases and projects these answers to new cases. Knowledge discovery is related to decision support and is often used when information is insufficient for prediction. As should be evident, knowledge discovery is complementary to predictive data mining, essentially forcing one to fully understand the data before attempting to predict future outcomes. As in most data mining efforts, it is important to focus initially on knowledge discovery problems. Otherwise, answers to prediction problems could be potentially suspect.

Table 13.5 Data Mining by Solution Type

Knowledge Discovery Problem Types	Prediction Problem Types
Outlier detection problems: Math or distance solutions	Classification/discrimination problems: Math or logic solutions
Clustering problems: Math or distance solutions	Regression problems: Math solutions
Association rule problems: Math or logic solutions	Time series problems: Math solutions
Descriptive and visualization problems: Math or logic solutions	Neural net problems: Math solutions
Segmentation problems: Math, distance, or logic solutions	Nearest-neighbor problems: Distance solutions
Correlational problems: Math or distance	Decision tree problems: Logic solutions

Table 13.5 lists several of the types of problems that fall within the two categories of data mining problems, broken down by solution type (e.g., math, distance, and logic solutions).

As illustrated in the table, there are many different predictive model types. Each model has relative strengths and weaknesses; however, they all can be used successfully to predict the outcomes of future events. It is important to remember that each model is based on the premise that patterns tend to repeat themselves. Consequently, if a representative model can be constructed, then reliable predictions can be made from it.

If, for example, one of our objectives is to decrease medical costs while increasing the quality of care for our health plan members, then in order to reach this objective, we have four goals: (1) identify members who have experienced a decrease in medical costs and an increase in quality of care, (2) identify members who have experienced a decrease in medical costs and a decrease in quality of care, (3) identify members who have experienced an increase in medical costs and an increase in quality of care, and (4) identify members who have experienced an increase in medical costs and a decrease in quality of care. To accomplish these goals, we must first identify those features that effectively measure medical cost and quality of care for these members. Then we uncover the underlying data patterns that match these goals. Ultimately, these underlying patterns will be used to build representative models and applied to new cases to reliably predict a member's medical cost/quality of care outcomes.

In summary, the first example used in this chapter illustrates how analytic techniques can assist in the identification of healthcare claims overpayments and billing errors. With healthcare claims payment error rates over 10% of the total healthcare spend, protection of government (e.g., Medicare and Medicaid) and commercial (e.g., self-insured companies) plan assets represents serious issues regarding the identification and recovery of these overpayments.[25] Additionally, concerns about the overall health and wellness of the population are motivating new and innovative ways to collect and analyze healthcare data. The second example in this chapter demonstrates how individuals can not only be treated for current healthcare conditions, but also be targeted for preventive care and vaccination programs. Prevention of the onset of chronic conditions may be the single most important economic issue facing us in the twenty-first century.[26] Application of healthcare claims data mining techniques will be central to meeting this challenge.

References

1. Smith-Daniels, V., Schweikhart, S., and Smith-Daniels, D. 1988. Capacity management in health care services: Review and future research directions. *Decision Sciences* 19(4):889–919.
2. McLaughlin, C., Yang, S., and Van Dierdonck, R. 1995. Professional service organizations and focus. *Management Science* 41(7):1185–1193.
3. Heskett, L. 1983. *Shouldice Hospital Ltd.* Boston: Publishing Division, Harvard Business School.
4. Hazen, G. B. 1992. Stochastic trees: A new technique for temporal medical decision modeling. *Medical Decision Making* 12(3):163–178.
5. Hazen, G. B. 2000. Preference factoring for stochastic trees. *Management Science* 46(3):389–403.
6. Xiaohaua, H. 2005. Temporal rule induction for clinical outcome analysis. *International Journal of Business Intelligence and Data Mining* 1(1):122–136.
7. Caudill, M. 1989. Using neural nets: Representing knowledge. *AI Expert* 4(12):34–41.
8. Perry, T., Kudyba, S., and Lawrence, K. 2007. Identification and prediction of chronic conditions for health plan members using data mining techniques. In *Data mining methods and applications.* New York: Taylor & Francis 175–182.
9. Swingler, K. 1996. *Applying neural networks: A practical guide.* New York: Academic Press.
10. Kudyba, S., and Hoptroff, R. 2001. *Data mining and business intelligence: A guide to productivity.* Hershey, PA: Idea Group.
11. Walczak, S., Brimhall, B., and Lefkowitz, J. 2006. Nonparametric decision support systems in medical diagnosis: Modeling pulmonary embolism. *International Journal of Healthcare Information Systems and Informatics* 1(2):65–82.
12. Cousins, M. S., Shickle, L. M., and Bander, J. A. 2002. An introduction to predictive modeling for disease management risk stratification. *Disease Management* 5:157–167.
13. Ash, A. S., Zhao, Y., Ellis, R. P., and Schlein-Kramer, M. 2001. Finding future high-cost cases: Comparing prior cost versus diagnosis-based methods. *Health Service Research* 36:194–206.
14. Ridinger, M. H., and Rice, J. J. 2000. Predictive modeling points way to future risk status. *Health Management Technology* 21(2):10–12.

15. Perry, T. L. 2004. Technology-driven outcomes. *Health Management Technology* 25(1):40–43.
16. Stegman, M. E. 2005. Coding and billing errors: Do they really add up to a $100 billion health care crisis? *Journal of Health Care Compliance* 7–8.
17. General Accounting Office (GAO). 2001. *Strategies to manage improper payments—Learning from public and private sector organizations.*
18. HHS, Inc. 2005. *$100 billion lost each year in "America's hidden healthcare crisis," payment errors are undermining the nation's economy and eroding the financial stability of the healthcare industry* 1–16.
19. Personal health expenditure (PHE) with out-of-pocket (OOP) expenditure estimates. 2009. www.CMS.HHS.Gov/NationalHealthExpendData.
20. Raghupathi, W. 2007. Designing clinical decision support systems in health care: A systemic approach. *International Journal of Healthcare Information Systems and Informatics* 2(1):44–53.
21. Perry, T. L., Tucker, T., et al. 2004. *The application of data mining techniques in health plan population management*, chap. VII. IT Solutions Series: Managing Data Mining. Idea Group, Inc.
22. Centers for Medicare and Medicaid Services. *Hierarchical condition categories risk adjustment program.* Centers for Medicare and Medicaid Services, Baltimore, MD.
23. Pope, G. C., Kautter, J., Ellis, R. P., et al. 2004. Risk adjustment of Medicare capitation payments using the CMS-HCC model. *Health Care Financing Review* 25.
24. www.NHLBI.NIH.gov and www.CDC.gov.
25. Blesch, G. 2009. Prone to error. ModernHealthcare.Com, February 2 39(5):32.
26. Committee on Quality of Health Care in America. 2001. *Crossing the quality chasm: A new health system for the 21st century.* Washington, DC: Institute of Medicine, National Academy Press.

Index